What's in a Surname?

David McKie formerly worked for the *Guardian* as a political reporter, deputy editor, chief leader writer and author of the 'Elsewhere' and 'Smallweed' columns. His much-praised account of a Victorian conman, *Jabez: The Rise and Fall of a Victorian Rogue*, was shortlisted for the Whitbread Biography Award. He has also written such widely acclaimed books as *Great British Bus Journeys* and *McKie's Gazetteer*.

Praise for *What's in a Surname?*

's a book of great zest and interest . . . there are wonderful uptions of bare lists of anecdotes and, interesting titbits . . . cKie has a whimsical cast of mind and a fine sense of umour.'

Sam Leith, *Guardian*

'he local case studies are certainly illuminating but *What's a Surname?* becomes altogether more engrossing when McKie urns to matters of general interest – names that have passed nto the language, names adopted by film stars and pop ingers and names that embarrass their holders.'

Literary Review

McKie is an excellent guide.'

Who Do You Think You Are? magazine

This book is a quirky and entertaining celebration of our shared heritage.'

Discover Your History magazine

ALSO BY DAVID McKIE

Jabez: The Rise and Fall of a Victorian Rogue
Great British Bus Journeys: Travels Through Unfamous Places
McKie's Gazetteer: A Local History of Britain
Bright Particular Stars: A Gallery of Glorious British Eccentrics

What's in a Surname?

A Journey from Abercrombie to Zwicker

DAVID McKIE

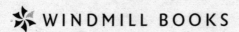 WINDMILL BOOKS

Published by Windmill Books 2014

2 4 6 8 10 9 7 5 3 1

First published in Great Britain in 2013 by Random House Books

Windmill Books
The Random House Group Limited
20 Vauxhall Bridge Road, London SW1V 2SA

Addresses for companies within The Random House Group Limited
can be found at: www.randomhouse.co.uk/offices.htm

The Random House Group Limited Reg. No. 954009

www.randomhouse.co.uk

A CIP catalogue record for this book
is available from the British Library

ISBN 9780099558941

The Random House Group Limited supports the Forest Stewardship
Council® (FSC®), the leading international forest-certification organisation.
Our books carrying the FSC label are printed on FSC®-certified paper. FSC is
the only forest-certification scheme supported by the leading environmental
organisations, including Greenpeace. Our paper procurement policy can be
found at: www.randomhouse.co.uk/environment

MIX
Paper from
responsible sources
FSC® C016897

Typeset in Dante MT by Palimpsest Book Production Ltd, Falkirk, Stirlingshire
Printed and bound by CPI Group (UK) Ltd, Croydon, CR0 4YY

To the memory of my brother Robert, and
Margaret, his wife, born Margaret Ling
who are buried in the churchyard of
St Nicholas, Elmdon, Essex

On an evening in the latter part of May a middle-aged man was walking homeward from Shaston to the village of Marlott, in the adjoining Vale of Blakemore, or Blackmoor . . . Presently he was met by an elderly parson astride on a gray mare, who, as he rode, hummed a wandering tune.

'Good night t'ee,' said the man with the basket.

'Good night, Sir John,' said the parson.

The pedestrian, after another pace or two, halted, and turned round.

'Now, sir, begging your pardon; we met last market-day on this road about this time, and I zaid "Good night," and you made reply "Good night, Sir John", as now.'

'I did,' said the parson.

'And once before that—near a month ago.'

'I may have.'

'Then what might your meaning be in calling me "Sir John" these different times, when I be plain Jack Durbeyfield, the haggler?'

The parson rode a step or two nearer.

'It was only my whim,' he said; and, after a moment's hesitation: 'It was on account of a discovery I made some little time ago, whilst I was hunting up pedigrees for the new county history. I am Parson Tringham, the antiquary, of Stagfoot Lane. Don't you really know, Durbeyfield, that you are the lineal representative of the ancient and knightly family of the d'Urbervilles, who derive their descent from Sir Pagan d'Urberville, that renowned knight who came from Normandy with William the Conqueror, as appears by Battle Abbey Roll?'

Thomas Hardy, *Tess of the D'Urbervilles*

Contents

Orientations

A Road Map for the Journey

'Who in the world am I? Ah, that's the great puzzle.'
Lewis Carroll, *Alice in Wonderland*

They order these things much more neatly in South Korea. There, almost half of a population of nearly fifty million share five surnames: Kim (which alone accounts for more than a fifth of them), Lee, Park, Choi and Chong. Much the same is probably true of North Korea – one cannot be sure because the North is so secretive – but certainly when the two nations held their historic meeting in 2000 to try to settle their differences, the leaders on either side of the table had the same surname: Kim.

And yet, how tedious it would be if British surnames had this same neatness – and terseness: Park is a longer than average name in Korea. Koreans don't have names which ramble away into the distance like Featherstonehaugh or Haythornthwaite or McGillicuddy (and even ours look pinched compared with some of those common in Sri Lanka). They don't have the rich profusion of names you find in any big city phone book here. We no longer possess some of the more extraordinary names of people you might have met in the streets of medieval England: Chaceporc, Crakpot, Drunkard, Gyldenbollockes (centuries before David Beckham), Halfenaked, Scrapetrough, Swetinbedde – though the London phone book still serves up many that can amuse and surprise. Here, within ten columns, you can find an array that, even when you discount those that do not sound home-grown, such as Slabberkoorn, Slagmuylders, Slobodzian, Sluzsky and Slysz, still leaves us with a fine crop of surnames, some enticing, some soothing, but others, names that their owners might not have chosen had they been given the choice. Here, for instance, are Slaby, Slankard, Slapp (and Slapper), Slark, Slatcher, Slay, Slaymaker, Sledge, Slee, Slingo and Slogan, not to mention Sloggem and Sloggett, Slomp, Slood, Slorance, Sluce, Sluggett, Slutter and Sly.

Their inevitability is part of the point about surnames. Your forename is one that was chosen: your parents picked it and blessed you (or saddled you) with it; but the surname involves no choice: they're the ones we were born with.

For centuries, those fascinated by surnames, anxious to dig into the antecedents not just of themselves and their families but of the world at large, could be numbered in dozens. Mr Tringham, that innocent, fatal meddler in Thomas Hardy, was a typical case: a parson with an inquisitive mind, time on his hands, and examples of the generous profusion of English surnames arrayed in the nave before him every Sunday morning. But through the twentieth century a taste for these interests developed until the pursuit of surnames, and of family histories generally, became a craze, an addiction, even in a sense a religion, with its own high priests – the species of academic now known as onomasticians (onomastics is the study of names) – and its own private language: non-paternal transmissions resulting from non-paternity events, charactonyms, isonomy, brick walls, daughtering out, lexeme retrieval, uxorilocality. There is even a name for this addiction: progonoplexia.

There are two main threads in the excavation of surnames: their geography and their history. People want to know: where did we Bostocks begin? And, why did we begin as Bostocks, rather than, say, Blenkinsops or Blanchards? Among the many devices available to help answer such questions today, there is a service, free on the internet, called Public Profiler, based at University College London, which will tell a Bostock in the space of a couple of minutes where Bostocks were most profuse at the time of the 1881 census and where they were most common at the close of the twentieth century. (The least common surnames are excluded. For the 1881 census, Steve Archer's *Surname Atlas* CD has the lot.) For the UK, the bluer the tint of an area on their maps, the more numerous your targets will be. In 1881, Bostocks materialise throughout the West Midlands, most of all around Crewe, but are also sturdily represented in Wales. By 1998 they're as strong in Nottingham as in Crewe, and are settled in significant numbers in new areas across north and mid-Wales, in East Anglia and in central London, areas where a century earlier you might easily have gone through life without meeting a Bostock.

Or take the names Gale and Judd, which will crop up quite frequently in this book. In 1881 they are bluest – that is, most numerous – in Dorset and Wiltshire, and to a lesser extent in Hampshire, and northwards and eastwards into Surrey and Berkshire. There are splashes of Gale in County Durham and around Peterborough, but nothing appears in Scotland and not much in Wales. By 1998 Hampshire is as Gale-rich as Wiltshire, and they now show up bravely in Leeds and its environs and in south-west London. Wales is filling up with them, but still there's no colour in Scotland. Likewise in both 1881 and 1998 Scotland and most of Wales appear to be Juddless. That does not mean there are no Judds at all. There will always have been the occasional Judd eager to marry a girl called – to pick out a surname at random – McKechnie, coming to find a home and a job in the stronghold of the McKechnies, which was, and is, south-west Scotland. But they must have been far too few to make any mark on the map.

That's the geography. But we also have much more reliable information than earlier explorers were able to draw on – how many of our surnames came to be formed. Though some of the experts subdivide them, adding in such elements as diminutives (usually names ending in -kin), names resulting from migration, and even names shown on the street signs under which people adopting these surnames were living, the core of British surnames can be loosely grouped into four classes: patronymics, names derived from a father, like Johnson and Jones, both of which indicate a forebear called John; then names that derive from places – either established settlements (Bolton, Bradford, Stepney) or local features (Bridge, Wood, Hill). If a man's name was Bradford, it is safe to assume that he came from somewhere other than Bradford. You would not have been called John of Bradford if you lived in Bradford, since all Johns there would have had a claim to that name as well. Next come occupational names, to which class is usually added names that derive from an office. Smith, Wright, Butcher, Baker (though not Candlestickmaker; the third occupant of the tub in the nursery rhyme has failed to generate a surname). Brewer and Thatcher are obvious occupational names, derived from still common employments. Others – Dempster (originally a judge: the term is still in use in the Isle of Man), Napier (in charge of the household linen), Mercer (a dealer in textiles), along with more recondite usages such as Pulver (one who earned his living by pulverising – grinding things into dust), Currier (perhaps a leather worker, perhaps one who groomed horses), and Tozer (a man employed to comb, card, or tease out wool) – come from jobs that have largely ceased, so far as I know, to exist. Sheriff, Marshall, and Stuart (from Steward) are characteristic names that derive from office.

Surnames deriving from nicknames are often the most entertaining, but also often make least sense today. These names, more than the rest, were what people called you, not how you described yourself. They announced that you were Short, Stout or Long; that you had a Brown or a Black appearance; that you usually went about in a Green coat. Like so many nicknames, some were applied maliciously. Some no doubt were ironic, like the nicknames often applied in sport, where a batsman famous for his slow rate of scoring can become known as Slasher Mackay (though another, equally famous for slowness, was nicknamed *Barnacle* Bailey). But many must have been quite wildly inappropriate within a few years of being bestowed. A man called Thynne might in middle age have better deserved the name Stout. A man called Young would once have been young, or at any rate younger than one who bore the same name in a household; but that would not be so for ever.

So already, uncertainty looms. It will continue to do so as long as one goes on exploring. As the first great student of surnames warned in 1603, 'to find the true original of Surnames is full of difficulty'. This was the wise antiquary William Camden, to whom I shall often return. A later expert liked to warn against the 'bogs and quagmires' into which some of his contemporary sleuths had fallen, though from time to time he can be found up to his waist in them too. And the more one studies these things, the more troublesome they become. What one generation thinks it is sure about, the next will begin to dispute.

The whole territory is landmined with ambiguities. Names derived from a forebear are usually least contentious. Few would dispute that the name Johnson began with a man whose father's name had been John, although Tyson, one of the names that crops up in this book, is disputed: once often classed as a name that derived from the shortened name of a forebear, it's now more often thought to have come from the French word *tison* meaning a firebrand – a highly excitable, easily angered, character. Nicknames too often look indisputable, but even then, where Brown began as a nickname, there is no way of knowing whether it denoted the colour of its owner's complexion or that of the coat he wore.

But names that derive from place names are worse. Bostock is identified as a name that comes from a place. There's a place called Bostock in Cheshire. Therefore, the surname Bostock derives from a place in Cheshire? The most one can safely say is 'maybe'. There could be some other long lost village or farmstead which was also a source for this name. Many hundreds of villages disappeared in the years of plague, or were lost because the land where they stood was unproductive.

Suppose your name is Newton. People originally called your forebears that because, perhaps alone in their new community, they came from a place called Newton. But which Newton? There are 148 places called Newton in the Ordnance Survey Gazetteer – and that excludes ones like Newton Abbot that come equipped with a suffix; and it's safe to assume there would once have been even more. There are thirty-seven Nortons and thirty Suttons – again excluding those with a prefix or suffix: the equivalent surnames might derive from almost any one of them. As with many of the questions that the study of surnames raises, there is little chance here of a definitive answer.

Occupational names are full of hazards too. Farmer? That sounds easy enough. A man who owns or runs a farm. But farmer used also to mean tax collector. Rymer? A peripatetic poet, possibly; but also a man who made rims for wheels. Reader is not just someone who reads (when many couldn't); it may well mean thatcher. Walker wasn't a name for someone who walked. Everyone walked. A Walker carried out the same work – treading or crushing cloth – as a Fuller elsewhere. Everywhere there are names where some earlier surname dictionaries offer a single answer but later ones accept that they're mired in ambiguity. Such is the pace and breadth and depth of modern research that definitions can be swathed in doubt within months of having been printed. The directors of an ambitious survey based at the University of the West of England – now under way – say their findings will undermine a great many more assumptions.

Through most of our history, few names were written down, mainly because to be able to write was a notable distinction. You needed a feudal lord, or rather his agents, a government official, or more often a cleric, to translate the name you thought was yours into writing. Sometimes such office-holders, baffled by what they heard, made up and wrote down a name that sounded quite like it. People who came before them might have no surname at all; so they smartly invented one for them. Such names were not always bestowed with a kindly intent.

*

We need also to look at migrations. The great majority of people in Britain settled and stayed until well through the nineteenth century close to the places where they were born; and more surprisingly, the patterns established then still prevail today. But sometimes there have been significant internal movements across the country, usually provoked by economic distress. It used to be said that a name beginning with Tre-, Pol- or Pen- denoted a Cornishman. Cornwall still has its contingents of Tres, Pols and Pens, but they occur in other places too, and the fact that they do tells us something important. They crop up in significant numbers in the Cleveland and Middlesbrough areas of the north-east, reflecting a substantial internal migration that came out of the collapse of the Cornish mining industry in the 1860s and 1870s. Many of those who were so displaced left to seek work in California and Southern Australia, but others chose Cleveland, Cumbria and the Furness peninsula. In the 1930s, numbers of Welshmen, almost as if they had been advised to 'Go east, young men', settled in prospering English towns like Swindon and Slough. Their surnames travelled with them and took root in fresh localities.

Such changes, however, brought few new names to the national mix – a less abundant mix, despite today's grossly multiplied population, than we had before the Black Death and lesser plagues destroyed so many thousands of lives and swept off so many established surnames with them. What has from time to time replenished the stock has been – and continues to be – fresh arrivals from all over the seven seas, bringing with them names unknown in this country before. In December 2012 there was published, to widespread astonishment, a set of findings from the 2011 census. These showed that immigration into England and Wales (Scotland and Northern Ireland are treated separately) had risen far faster through the previous decade than had previously been understood, exceeding even the forecasts put out by the pressure group MigrationWatch UK. The proportion of people in England and Wales assessed as white British had fallen by seven percentage points to 80 per cent. The changes, as is always the case in such contexts, were sharpest in London, where the proportion of citizens classed as white British had fallen to 60 per cent. And close to one in four Londoners had been born overseas – almost three times the figure for England and Wales.

This island has seen many waves of migration, and each since the Conquest has left its seeding of surnames behind – in London most of all. More recent changes are doing so too, affecting London first, but spreading. Already at the start of this century surnames like Patel and Ali and Khan were steadily climbing the charts. They continue to do so. But a further crop of previously unfamiliar names is now joining them. Poland has come to match India and Pakistan as one of the most numerous sources of new arrivals in Britain, reflecting the influx which followed Poland's accession to the European Union in 2004. The average Briton finds Polish names are more tongue-twisting than the now familiar Patel or Ali or Khan. To discuss the outstanding performance of the Polish team that drew with Russia in the opening stages of the 2012 European Cup required the pronunciation of names hardly attempted across much of the country before, such as Piszczek, Wasilewski, and the captain, goal scorer and commentator's nightmare, Jakub Błaszczykowski. Mercifully, Wojtkowiak,

Matuszczyk and Wawrzyniak were only substitutes. Such exotic imports will multiply as further newcomers arrive from European Union countries such as Romania and Bulgaria.

*

This book is not designed as a step-by-step handbook to the business of disentangling names – and it is certainly not a guide as to how to pronounce them. There are plenty of books, and internet sites (of very varying quality), to help you do that, the best of which I shall list at the end. I am more concerned with the wider implications of Juliet's question to Romeo: 'What's in a name?'; with the part that names play in forming a sense of identity and a sense of belonging, their effect on the psyches of those who carry them; with the manipulation of names to influence and to sell; and with the impact a name may have on friends and neighbours and casual acquaintances. But it also engages with fiction, because fiction can often illuminate what names mean to people better than any simple collection of facts can do, and because the choice and deployment of names in plays and novels is so often essential to how a book enters the mind of the reader.

One place where people begin to brood on names and those who possessed them is the kind of country churchyard whose simple dead were immortalised by the poet Thomas Gray in his 'Elegy written in a Country Churchyard'. The churchyard is taken to be that at Stoke Poges in Buckinghamshire where the mother whom he adored was buried, though the ivy-mantled tower may have been borrowed from the church of St Laurence, Upton, in nearby Slough. Why, many people have wondered in scenes like these – doing their best to decipher inscriptions worn away by the weather, or clustered over by ivy – were so many people in this village called Trevelyan or Tresilian, Fraser or Foster, Noakes or Noyes?

I have looked for answers to essentially local questions like these in six villages across the land called Broughton. Of the nineteen Broughtons in the gazetteer that I used (there are others with prefixes, like Brant Broughton, or suffixes like Broughton Poggs, which I discounted) I picked those which were still likely to be self-contained villages, discarding those that have now become suburbs of bigger places. I chose one from the south of England – Broughton in Hampshire, home to the Judds and the Gales – and one from the north – Broughton in Furness, a small town once teeming with Tysons; one from East Anglia; one from the East Midlands; one from Scotland; and one from Wales. The Scottish and Welsh Broughtons are closer to the border with England than I would have preferred, but the Scottish Highlands fail to provide a Broughton. There is certainly one on the Orkney island of Westray, whose records I also dipped into, but the patterns of names on Orkney, which until 1468 belonged to Denmark, are distinctively different from anywhere else in Scotland, except for Shetland.

I also looked at Broughton near Kettering in Northamptonshire, where the records display a ripe collection of unexpected names such as Hight and Sail, but this was not far enough distant from the Broughtons of Cambridgeshire and Lincolnshire to illustrate local contrasts. There are two Broughtons in Yorkshire, but both are too small for analysis. Yet, flawed though this spread may be, it clearly confirms that names which dominate some parts of the land are hardly known at all across much of the country. Other aspects of life may be losing it, but surnames retain their old local flavour. You expect to meet Tysons in Furness; were you to meet substantial numbers in Hampshire, that would be a surprise.

'Beneath those rugged elms, that yew-tree's shade,' wrote Gray in the most famous declaration ever made on this subject, 'Where heaves the turf in many a mould'ring heap, / Each in his narrow cell for ever laid, / The rude Forefathers of the hamlet sleep.'

Who were they, the rude Forefathers who lie in this and so many other country churchyards; where did they come from? And how did they come by the names we see on their gravestones? I began my quest for the answer at the gate of the church of St Mary in Broughton, a village only three miles short of the Wiltshire border, but, as it's been since the earliest days of this English county, wholly and happily Hampshire.

Constellations

Gales in the South. Sails in the Midlands. Pains in East Anglia

Alas, poor Yorick! I knew him, Horatio; a fellow
of infinite jest, of most excellent Fancy.
William Shakespeare, *Hamlet*

The testimony of the stones

At the gate of the church of St Mary in the Hampshire village
of Broughton, just across the road from the pub that his family
ran for most of the nineteenth century, there's a gravestone that
marks the spot where Tom Gale is buried. 'In loving memory',
it says, 'of Tom Gale, who died May 24th 1900 aged 36 years.'
And then, with what might just be a hint of remorse:

We never fathomed half his worth
Till now dear loved one thou art gone.

Close by is a cluster of Morgans, and another of Doswells,
surrounded by stones that have long since lost their inscriptions
to the winds and rains of these downlands. Happily their names
were charted and are still to be found in a register in the church.
A succession of Gales is among them, from Sarah, daughter of
Joseph and Mary, who died in 1774 at twenty-seven, to Eliza,
interred here in 1938 having lived to be ninety-three. Further

into the churchyard it is easy to find Amos Gale, and Ann, his late-married wife, whom he outlived by six years, dying in 1899 at seventy-six. But also under this earth are Sabina, widow of John Slaiden Gale, who died, like Sarah, at twenty-seven, in 1831; here, from the mid nineteenth century, are Miriam and her widower Henry, the widow Jane Gale and Joseph, the son who died, at twenty, five months before her. There's another Gale on the village war memorial: one of twenty-seven Broughton men killed in the First World War. Gale, the standard reference books tell us, is a name that can mean one of two things: the light – as derived from an Old English word that means pleasant, merry, joyful, even licentious – but also the dark, hinting at gaols and gaolers. In this context, a mixture of light and dark seems appropriate. It is also a name that proliferates in Hampshire, in Wiltshire, and in neighbouring counties, as do others like Doswell and Offer and Futcher and Marsh that congregate in this churchyard, interspersed with names that are rarer in this part of England, such as Morgan.

Many such surnames had been in this village for centuries. People called Cooper, Dawkins, Doxell (probably the predecessor of Doswell), Gale, Kelsey, Mersh (which would later transmute to Marsh), Morgan, Pragnell, Steele – all very familiar names in nineteenth-century Broughton – had been assessed for the hearth tax of 1665, some being rich enough to pay and others too poor and therefore exempt. The names of others on the taxmen's list did not survive into later centuries: Fabin, Maphew and Undee, for instance; along with a poor widow whose surname is given as Hated. The names that persist derive from disparate sources. Cooper is occupational. Dawkins derives from Daw, which in turn comes from David: the 'kins' at the end is diminutive – little Daw. Doswell is thought to derive from a lost medieval village. The original Marsh probably lived by a marsh, though this name may also come from a place name in Buckinghamshire or Lincolnshire; Kelsey is traced to a place name in Lincolnshire as well, while Pragnell may come from another lost community, this time in Hampshire. Morgan is a very old Celtic name that has been translated variously as 'sea bright' or 'great defender'. Steele looks to be a nickname, meaning hard and resolute, though it might also come from an ancestor who worked with hard metals.

All these are very much local people. Some of the more exceptional graves in a rural churchyard belong to people whom professional or business interests brought into a place where their surnames were until then unfamiliar, and this one is no exception. The brilliant young Dr Edward Fox, Fellow, as his gravestone records, of University College, Doctor of medicine and Doctor of surgery, dead at thirty in 1897, was one of the eleven children of Dr Luther Fox, who came to Broughton to practise from the neighbouring village of Mottisfont, and whose long service to the village is commemorated in a window in the church. Here too are the Reverend Mr Stanlake Lee, born in Cookham in what used to be Berkshire, who was priest here for over fifty years (his mother was rumoured in the village, romantically but no doubt wrongly, to have been the Mrs Fitzherbert who had gone through an illegal marriage ceremony with George IV), together with his notably less popular successor Alfred Woodin, from Petersham, Surrey, remembered for the snootiness of his wife (who came from Camden Town). One of the people whose grave is close to the church was a Whicher – Martha Lucretia, relict of George Joseph Whicher – which led me to hope that the celebrated Victorian detective might be a Broughton man. But no, he was born in Camberwell.

Incomers like the rectors are the exception. In the 1851 census, the first which asks for birthplaces, nearly six in ten of the people of Broughton were found to have been born there. A further 17 per cent were born elsewhere in Hampshire, mostly in villages less than five miles away – especially Mottisfont and Houghton, the Tytherleys and the Wallops – or across the nearby county boundary in Wiltshire. Clearly Broughton in these times was finding its spouses not far away: only 7 per cent of villagers had begun their lives outside these two counties.

Broughton today is a comfortable-looking place with two pubs, where there were once at least half a dozen, and one shop, where there were more than a dozen together with all the traditional village trades of blacksmith, wheelwright, coal merchant, shoemaker, carrier, carpenter, joiner. You got what you wanted to buy in Broughton, and unless you could travel to Stockbridge, the nearest market town, or have a carrier fetch what you wanted, you did without. A station was projected but the line was never built. But like so many such villages, it ceased long ago to be a self-contained place, and its once dominant names too have diminished or died away. Old Broughton names still persist in the village – Arthur, Bailey, Blake, Cooper, Davis, Dawkins, Dumper, Feltham, Gale, Glasspool, Hewlett, Marsh, Musselwhite, Newman, Payne and Pragnell survive, together with later arriving names such as Palmer, but such staple names as Judd, Morgan and Offer are gone from the electoral register.

*

Some 300 miles north-west of here, seventeen miles from the nearest big town, which is Barrow, but only nine miles through alluring country from Coniston in the Lakes, is another Broughton, part of Furness, a tract to the north side of Morecambe Bay, for long part of Lancashire yet always distinct from Lancashire. Now by government fiat it has become part of Cumbria, the former Cumberland and Westmorland, to which by its nature – and most of its predominant family surnames – it more truly belongs. Here at the gate of the church of St Mary Magdalene one is met by a row of tombstones of Tysons, drawn up like some kind of reception committee, impressing on the wayfaring visitor that Tyson was one of the most important, if not indeed the most important name in the town. As it still looks to be now, when right in the centre of town is a shop which still parades the name Tyson's, at a time when in so many other places the old local family shops now bear such unlocal legends as Co-op – or more often have gone altogether.

I call this Broughton a town; it's nowadays more often designated a village, but it has the sense of a town all around it, most of all in the square built in the 1770s by a lord of the manor who had been greatly impressed by the new squares of London and thought his Broughton deserved the same. The story the churchyard tells here is at once the same as that of Broughton in Hampshire, and yet instructively different. The Furness graveyard is as full (or rather fuller, since this is a larger community) of clusters of names. But apart from Carter, one of those names that occur all through England, the names most prominent in the churchyard here barely appear in Hampshire, and the Hampshire names are strangers in Furness – which make it all the more striking that the names Robinson and Cooper, populous in nineteenth-century Broughton, Hampshire, were topping the charts in Furness at the start of the twenty-first.

Here, as in much of the north, men's names tend to reflect those of their early forebears: Dickson, son of Dick, a short form of Richard; Dawson, son of Daw, a short form of David; Casson, the son of Cass or possibly Catt; Frearson, which probably meant the son of a friar – such things did indeed happen, though the name may only indicate some kind of looser connection with friars. Around half the top nineteenth-century names in Broughton in Furness belong to this group, those deriving from a family forename. Broughton, Hampshire, by contrast, had a higher quotient of names such as Carter and Cooper and Offer that end in -er, suggesting that their original names derived from the occupation or office of those who acquired them; Offer is taken to be a corruption of the French name for a goldsmith, Orfevre.

In Furness, as in Hampshire, the 1851 census finds most people living close to the spot where they were born. The total of those born in Broughton fell five short of 50 per cent. The true figure, though, was probably higher; until recently the town had been part of the parish of Kirkby Ireleth just to its south, and some who said they were born there would in fact have been born in what was now Broughton. Most of the rest of this population came from other settlements in Furness, from elsewhere in north Lancashire, or from the neighbouring counties of Cumberland and Westmorland.

*

In some churchyards names are more tightly clustered than they are here: dramatically so in a place like Bettyhill, on the northern coast in Scotland, where around the abandoned kirk of St Columba there's something close to a full house of Mackays, reflecting the use by clans of a single name. The odd Munro or Macleod must feel like an interloper. In the churchyard at Arthuret, a sweet spot in the hills above the Cumbrian border town of Longtown, you will find memorials to the Bells and Armstrongs and Littles who for centuries dominated life in this part of the land, all outnumbered by the graves of the Grahams, whose uncompromising ascendancy no other name here could match. In the churchyard of the hilltop village of Elmdon in Essex, where my brother and his widow are buried, I have often noted how many plots are the province of Hammonds, a name which academic research has established was for a time by far the most abundant in the village. But a sampling of further places called Broughton, to add to those in Hampshire and in Furness, provides a more representative sample of the pattern that most churchyard browsers are used to.

Broughton, Huntingdonshire – now Broughton, Cambridgeshire – is a pretty and prosperous-looking place with church, green and pub (there used to be four, at least) where three lanes meet. This is not nowadays, if it ever was, a place for excitements. When I last looked at its website, a section headed 'News' said that there wasn't any. If you called it placid, it's unlikely that anyone here would complain. The pub looks inviting; the green looks useful. There's a stolid brick building which used to be Broughton's pound, a place where stray cattle were put in the charge of an official known as the pinder (if you meet a person called Pinder, remember that conduct of a village pound may have generated it). A bubbly stream runs behind the green and the pub to emerge at either end of the village.

This Broughton is full of reminders of the Broughton that used to be. A house called the Old Library is next door to one called the Old Rectory (the village, like so many, no longer has rectors); across the way is the old school – now a village hall. Round the corner, facing the pub, is a cottage called the Old Brewhouse; next to the pub is Blacksmith's Cottage, presumably the site of the forge.

It would, by the look of things, be hard for the poor or otherwise carless to live here now. The shops have gone, even the last survivor, the post office – though a Tesco van, busy as a pollinating bee, was circulating there when I visited. The regular bus has expired. Around the church of All Saints, celebrated for a medieval wall painting depicting the day of doom in which nameless souls go down to perdition, are the final resting places of Allpresses, Beards, Colberts, Hempsteads, Hitchcocks (though part of this name on this gravestone has crumbled away), Hows (who seem to have been a prosperous lot: the former Nonconformist chapel just out of the village centre was built in the 1860s by G. How, Gent), Hubbards, Newells, Pains and their cognate Paynes: all characteristic names of nineteenth-century Broughton. The overspill graveyard, a little way up School Lane, displays the names that were dominant in the twentieth. The Allpresses and Colberts here are outnumbered by Ashbys (Ernest Alfred Ashby, carpenter and wheelwright, died in 2005 at ninety-five), Bryants and Peppers.

Here, too, there is diversity in the sources of names. The first Allpress was most probably an old priest. The first Beard is likely to have been a man who wore one, though the name might also derive from a place called Beard in Derbyshire. Colbert comes from a personal forename which may have meant cool and bright. Hempstead is traced to a place name, as is Ashby. Hitchcock, like most names ending in -cock, is a diminutive, from Hitch, a pet name for Richard; Hubbard derives from the personal name Hubert, and Pain and its variants from the forename Pagan, originally suggesting a rustic rather than a heathen, which long ago fell out of use. Bryant comes from Brian, a name still with us. The original Pepper probably sold the stuff. The unostentatious name Newell is probably a form of the upmarket surname Neville, which a Norman family brought with them from Calvados. The original How may have lived near a hill, though there are place names in several counties which might also explain it. But this, more than most of my Broughtons, has failed to cling on to most of its classic surnames. There are still Peppers here, but the 2010 electoral register fails to muster the Allpresses, Colberts, Hitchcocks and Pains or Paynes of the churchyard.

*

It is just over a hundred miles from here to Broughton, north Lincolnshire, though you can if you choose make a mild deviation to take in another Broughton, close to Kettering in Northamptonshire, a place that owes its appeal to warm orangey stone, where St Andrew's churchyard, together with an extension, parade its once formidable contingents of Essams, Thompsons, Birds, Eastons and Pulvers. The Lincolnshire Broughton, seventy miles further north, used to be identified as Broughton near Brigg, but by the 1901 census the younger town had outgrown the old, odd and attractive one. Again there's a difficulty here with nomenclature: this Broughton was officially designated a town in the 1970s, yet still in the centre, around the church, it feels more like a village.

The place began in a quiet way on the great Roman road known as Ermine Street, but grew bigger, but certainly not more beautiful, through the nineteenth century as workmen's houses were run up at speed to accommodate the arriving workforce for the great iron- and steel-works of Scunthorpe, Appleby and Frodingham in the second half of the century. One road in expanded Broughton is known as Harris's Dream, but there's little that is dreamy about this village.

At the church – again St Mary's – with its grizzled tower with an outside turret staircase attached, a lychgate erected by her children on her death in 1934 commemorates a notable benefactor, Eliza Ball Holt. Close by are imposing memorials to other Holts, one a master mariner and African merchant of Liverpool. It's perhaps another sign of the prominence of the Holts that their gravestones still stand when most of the rest have been swept out of the churchyard. Some stones have been neatly stacked along its south wall. Here, as well as some further Holts, are Metcalfes, Lammings and Smiths, Nixons and Parishes; also Birds and Thompsons (names that also occur in Northamptonshire at the other end of the East Midlands region).

Holt is one of those pesky names which has no clear source. It could come from the quite common place name, Holt; it may indicate a man who lived near a wood. Metcalfe probably comes from meat calf, though here again there is ambiguity: did Metcalfe look after calves or was he a butcher? Smith, of course, is unmysterious, though the trades of smith had many variants: goldsmiths, silversmiths, whitesmiths and others, as well as blacksmiths. Nixon, like Thompson, derives from a parent. Parish may have come from that ancient institution, the parish, though some Parishes like to claim a connection with the principal city of France. Bird was most likely a nickname for someone who looked or behaved like a bird, though one modern source suggests it may have developed from a Middle English term for a woman; women, it seems, have been talked of by men as 'birds' for longer than they might think. As for the churchyard clearances, I asked the priest in charge, David Eames, who superintends this village together with those of Scawby, Redbourne and Hibaldstow and who came to open the church for me, why that process was ordered, but he was new to the place and did not know the reason.

A mile or so away, on the old Roman road, is a smart modern cemetery, a suitably peaceful spot for remembrance and reflection, and full of heartening evidence that the clustering of names persisted here well into the twentieth century; sometimes names that had always been in this Broughton, like High, Hare, Stothard and Neal, sometimes those of latecomers to the village. Graves is one name that recurs. Johnsons abound, and Robinsons, as they do across much of Britain, alongside others with equally ubiquitous surnames like Jackson and Marshall, and Cook. Electoral registers show that by the second decade of the twenty-first century the dominant names here were mostly those that were dominant throughout England and Wales. Robinson, Smith, Clark or Clarke, Taylor and Johnson made up the first five, with Wilson, Thompson and Brown thereafter. And yet in this much expanded community some of the old distinctively local names still thrive. Stothard is safely in the top ten. Bowers, Graves, Green and Foster still make a sturdy showing. And here and there you will still find Hares and Neals and Parishes alongside more recently prominent Broughton surnames such as Ladlow, Hickabottom and Traves.

*

And here, 150 miles away to the west, and a little south, is a churchyard full of Williamses, Joneses, Hugheses and Reynoldses, Davieses and Evanses, along with Prices and less predictably, once

again, Jacksons. One of the saddest graves in the cemetery is
that of Robert Jackson who died in 1894 at the age of sixty-seven,
having lost in succession his daughter Sarah, ten months; son
Thomas, six; Martha, daughter, ten months; and in the same
year, 1871, both his wife Jane and son Joseph, again at ten months.
Three years later, a further son, Samuel, died aged nineteen. To
this melancholy catalogue is appended these words:

> We cannot, Lord, thy purpose see
> But all is well that's done by thee.

Nineteenth-century families were schooled in resignation.

Jackson is by no means a name confined to this territory, but
the rest of them suggest we are now in north Wales: as indeed
we are, though some of these surnames usually considered quint-
essentially Welsh also flourish on the English side of the border.
Surnames came later to Wales than they did to much of the
kingdom, and when they did begin to blossom they were mainly
confined to names derived from forefathers: not in the form
familiar in northern England, where the suffix -son is tacked on,
but using the final possessive 's'.

The deriving of surnames from a limited number of forenames
produces some odd effects for which Wales is famous. I once
saw a British film comedy in which crowds were seen converging
on Paddington station on the day of an international rugby match
at Twickenham. 'Would Mr David Jones from Wales please come
to the stationmaster's office,' the station announcer intoned;
whereupon the entire assembly turned in its tracks to respond
to the summons. The pattern is also, perhaps, regrettable. Earlier
surnames which might have survived in Wales, north and south,
were effectively crowded out, though some are here in this
churchyard. Such names, like Price, are contractions of an earlier
form which denoted descent: Bevan from ap Evan, Parry from
ap Harry, Powell from ap Howell, Price from ap Rhys, Pritchard

from ap Richard, Pugh from ap Hugh. ('Ap' means 'son of'; 'daughter of' would be 'ferch' or 'verch'.) This late conversion to surnames and the blanket adoption of standard ones also explains why, as we shall see later on, Welsh names score so highly in the overall table of most common surnames throughout the UK (see Appendix 1).

This churchyard, serving both Broughton, Flintshire, and its neighbouring village of Bretton, may once have been a pleasingly tranquil spot. But it's sandwiched now between two main roads that converge on the edge of the village of Broughton; close by is a roaring roundabout, so that the whole place is subjected to what sounds like the grossly magnified buzz of some demented beehive. Could they come back, these Joneses and Williamses and occasional Prices would surely find their village unnerving. Apart from the church and the churchyard and a building across the way that was once the post office – it's now a shop that specialises in ladies' formal dress and hat hire – there is little that would remind them of the Broughton they knew. Halfway down one of the principal roads, close to the Offa's Dyke pub (not that we are anywhere near Offa's Dyke), the modern school, modern clinic and modern library, there's a cottage so much older and prettier than anything else that it looks as if it had been borrowed from a museum.

The rest is all newish brick housing, mostly semi-detached, perfectly decent and decorous but with not the slightest flavour of Wales. We're only four miles or so from the boundary with England; barely a word of Welsh, I was told, gets spoken here. The village shops too do not hint at earlier origin or resonate with a sense of their localness: Co-op, Village Balti, Elysium (tanning, beauty and nails), Wash Tec (sales and repairs), Post Office (sweets and newspapers), Hammers and Tongs, (ironmongers), Broughton Fish Bar (fish and chips, Chinese and fast food takeaway), Amanda's Hair and Nail Studio and Simply Drinks.

What brought this new Broughton about was the establishment at the southern end of the old Hawarden airfield, right by the cacophonous roundabout, of a factory building planes for Hawker Siddeley early in the Second World War – transmogrified now into the home of Airbus UK, which has recently opened what is claimed to be the biggest new factory in Britain. An enticing lane wanders into the countryside at the western end of the village, diverging from the main road by a now abandoned Primitive Methodist chapel of 1880, into a place called Old Warren, and beyond it, Warren Mountain, said to be haunted by a priest known as the Floating Vicar. This was the main road through to Buckley, but was blocked off when the roads around here were modernised. Otherwise the village has become a kind of Anywheresville.

Yet though so much of the population is new, and the flavour of Wales so elusive, there is one firm link with the Broughton of earlier days: the dominant surnames. Electoral registers (which cover a wider area than the Broughton of the census returns, and take in more than 3,500 voters) show Jones way ahead of the rest, with Williams, Davis/Davies and Hughes also in the top five (the other name here is Smith). Within the next ten places come Roberts, Edwards, Evans, Thomas and Griffith/Griffiths. And though names that end in 's' are not guarantees of Welshness – they are also prevalent in English border counties like Herefordshire and Shropshire – the older Welsh names such as Price, Powell, Pritchard and Lloyd are still high scorers too. That the place has diversified is clear from some of the newer surnames – and from forenames like Giuseppe, Suresh and Jacek, which one used not to find very readily in this part of the world; also from the fact that the top five names account now for just 11 per cent of the total and the top ten for 15 per cent. Even so, there is reassuring evidence here of a continuity not otherwise always apparent in this area.

*

It is over 200 miles to the last of my Broughton burial places, in what was for centuries Broughton, Peeblesshire, but is now more prosaically Broughton, Borders, a place whose present tranquillity hides a turbulent past (see Chapter 5). Unlike the others, the graveyard here is not attached to a working church but surrounds a dead one – the remains of the original parish church, replaced in 1803 by a doggedly graceless brick building down the main road. The old church is tucked away up a pleasant lane that rises into the hills that surround the village. Here, apart from a congregation of Smiths – a surname even more familiar in Scotland than in England, and most common of all in the Shetlands – are characteristically Scots surnames: Newbigging (from a place name, probably one in Lanarkshire), Masterton (thought to derive from a place near Dunfermline), Sandilands (from a place in Clydesdale with that kind of soil), Somerville (in various spellings – a name derived from a place near Caen that reached Britain with William I, or soon after), Thomson (self-explanatory) and Veitch (perhaps from 'vacher', a dairyman). Here too are Armstrong (from a nickname unsurprisingly meaning strong in the arm), Anderson, Lawson and Watson, which are all patronymics: all four names are strong in the Borders, but stronger in Scotland than in England.

Were this graveyard seventy miles to the north, beyond the Forth and the Clyde, you'd expect a solid platoon of Macs; but Macs belong to the Highlands, not to the Borders. The saddest story here, as grievous as that of the Jacksons in Flintshire, belongs to the Smiths. Agnes Smith, wife of John, the schoolmaster here for thirty-six years, died in 1880 at seventy-six, having lost Margaret, eleven months; William, five weeks; Agnes, sixteen months; Janet, eighteen years; Elizabeth, thirty; and William, aged seventeen, before John died in 1871; and finally another son, James, though he made it to a relatively ancient forty-seven. By 2010 the only dominant name here is Brown, accounting even so for only 3 per cent of entries on the electoral register. But the

next names in line nearly all have a good Scottish flavour about
them: Fraser, Gordon, Stewart. And the Mac contingent has
notably increased.

*

Such is the testimony of the churchyards. But gravestones, though
eloquent, do not tell the full story of those who lived in these
places and the names by which they were known. Many died
unrecorded. Others were buried out of the village, returning
perhaps to the places where they were born. Many, if they
worshipped at all, did so outside the parish church, perhaps at a
Baptist or Methodist chapel, perhaps at a Catholic church.

Some of the grandest families preferred to go to their rest in
rather grander localities. Others were memorialised inside the
church, where the tributes inscribed on their plaques were safe
from the weather. Their memories were even perpetuated with
an effigy, like those of the mighty Andersons of Broughton in
Lincolnshire, who not only superseded the previously dominant
Redfords but removed their predecessors' effigies to a less elevated
part of the church to give greater prominence to their own. It's
inside the church that Broughton in Hampshire remembers its
Hattats (a name that reference books do not explain, though it
may have to do with the making or wearing of hats or with
people who lived by a hill), once, along with the Dowses –
Thomas Dowse in 1601 established the village school – and
Thistlethwaytes, dominant families here. (Not every Hattat was
grand: in 1827 a Wiltshire Hattat was convicted at Winchester
assizes of stealing sixty-one sheep, and sentenced to death. 'He
bowed to the vast crowd assembled to witness his execution,'
the *Devizes Gazette* reported, 'and quietly resigned himself into the
hands of the executioner.')

Inside the church of All Saints in Broughton, Cambridgeshire,
are commemorations of Holdiches, Hempsteds and of Robert

Hodson, an eighteenth-century rector, and George Allpress, rector's warden for the last decade of his life. Some lives are rewarded in churches not just with a plaque but with a stained-glass window, such as that in the church at Broughton in Furness commemorating the incumbent, Frederick Amadeus Malleson, who restored it. Other incumbents are also recorded here, but pride of place, as you'd expect, goes to memorials to the inter-woven Gilpins, Sawreys and Cooksons who were Broughton in Furness's lords of the manor.

But above all, many who were buried in places like these have no memorial: they died unrecorded, as Gray, contemplating the heaving turf at Stoke Poges beneath which, each in his narrow cell, the rude forefathers of the hamlet slept, was plainly aware. No storied urns, no animated busts, for them – not even the smallest stone to mark where they lay and where by now must have mouldered away in Hampshire and Furness, Huntingdonshire and Lincolnshire, Flintshire and Peeblesshire. Gravestones were too expensive. Those who want to trace the names that once flour-ished in all these places, and many hundreds of others like them, must therefore look for them in records that until very recently had to be hunted out from churches and libraries, but now, merci-fully, can be summoned up in a twinkling on a computer screen. Above all, they will need to investigate the findings of the succes-sive censuses that span the seventy years from 1841.

The testimony of the scribes: surgers, stayers and sliders

On Sunday, 6 June 1841, the village's census enumerator – a creature not seen before in this part of the world – was to be spotted knocking on doors along the main street of Broughton, down Dog Lane, up the Queenswood road and the Horsehay road, ascertaining the surnames, forenames, ages and counties of birth of the people he found there. No doubt some grumbled about it, as they grumble about censuses still. But this first full national census was, compared with its successors, a rudimentary exercise. It did not record the relationships of those sharing a surname under one roof, so that some who look like married couples might equally have been brother and sister. It asked, were you born in this county? Rather than, as later, where were you born? In a place like Broughton in Hampshire, perched on the edge of one county with another three miles away, the lack of greater precision clouds the picture.

These things were better ordered in 1851, when those who knew where they were born – some had forgotten, others had never known – disclosed them to their invigilators. By 1911, where the sequence of published censuses ends, additional questions established how many children a couple had had, how many were still alive, at home or elsewhere, and how many had died. The continuity of the record is complicated by the fact that sometimes the boundaries of enumeration districts changed, making comparison near impossible (this is the case with Broughton in Furness, as the table in Appendix 2 shows). There are also, as we shall see, errors and illegibilities in census returns, and even more striking, sometimes quite ludicrous, errors in some of their modern transcriptions.

Yet for all their defects, the censuses take us beyond the pictures that churchyards present, introduce us to people the spread of whose surnames we would otherwise never know, and begin to answer the question: how and why did these clusters of names occur? The tables in Appendix 2 show the predominant nineteenth-century names in each of these towns and villages. These were not, it needs to be emphasised, the socially and economically dominant names in the village. In terms of status and influence, those who topped the charts were far behind families like the Sawreys (later the Sawrey-Cooksons) who were lords of the manor in Furness, or the Mallesons, the head of whose household had once been tutor to Tennyson's children and was now Broughton's vicar; and in Hampshire, well below its Hattats (though they were gone by the early years of the nineteenth century) and its interwoven Steeles and Tomkinses, or in Lincolnshire, the mighty Anderson clan.

One might add to this list the names of families which, though not especially numerous, had a sizeable impact on village life, like the Hinwoods, in Broughton, Hampshire, whose surname became one of true local consequence since it appeared above the door of one of the village grocers and one of the village butchers. The name Hinwood seems to have developed from Henwood, which probably came from a place name possibly meaning high wood or even hen-wood. These Hinwoods now have a street in the village named after them. An open space and playing field on the way to the village's overspill cemetery is named for the Fripps, who provided the land: never one of the largest village families but clearly people of local importance – even if their surname, according to the *Oxford Dictionary of English Surnames*, may have derived from a word that meant a dealer in old clothes.

So, though the churchyard at Broughton in Hampshire finds us clusters of Doswells and Morgans and later of Davises, it undervalues what might be called the engine room of the village: families who mostly entered the nineteenth century as agricultural labourers and were still agricultural labourers at the end of it, like the Judds and the Rogerses – the scarcity of Judds in Broughton churchyard perhaps reflecting the fact that this family were Baptists rather than regulars at St Mary's. (The name Judd may derive either from Jude or Jordan.) The Gales are better represented, but the churchyard alone fails to portray how numerous they were in mid-century. The patterns of surnames in my collection of villages with the name Broughton are set out in Appendix 2. Here, the Gales emerge as the family at the top of the tree in the first year of census, numbering forty-four, seven ahead of the Coopers, thirteen ahead of the Judds and Rogerses, fourteen ahead of the Morgans. These five names accounted for more than 17 per cent of the village: add the next five names, and the ten cover more than a quarter of Broughton's population. Or, to put it perhaps more graphically, if in 1841, four years into the reign of Victoria, the year that the railway from London to Bristol opened, the year that Britain acquired Hong Kong, you saw a fellow-Broughtonian trudging along the main street, emerging heavily laden from one of its shops or arriving for a convivial evening at one of its pubs, there was a better than one in four chance that he or she belonged to one of the families in the top ten bracket. That, like so much else, would change as the century progressed.

In the centre of Broughton in Furness, a more isolated and self-contained place, the figures for 1841 are still higher: five names – Dixon, Tyson, Atkinson, Casson, Dawson, all with the -son suffix so prevalent in these parts – provide 23 per cent of population. Add the next five surnames – Simpson, Bellman, Nelson, Carter and Crosby (jointly with High) – and there is an almost 40 per cent chance that someone met in the street would have one of only ten names. The clustering of names in Huntingdonshire is also striking. Here five names – Maile (or Male), Pain, Hitchcock, Hubbard and West – account for 24 per cent of the population in 1841, a figure that unexpectedly is even slightly higher in 1911, by which time these top five names have all been supplanted: the most dominant surnames now are Clark/Clarke, Wright, Cross, Munns and Colbert. Yet all fall way short of Broughton in Flintshire where in 1841 ten names, seven of them ending in 's', make up well over half the population. That circumstance, along with the predominance of Welsh names in the national charts (see the tables in Appendix 2), again demonstrates how sparse the spread of surnames was in this region.

As the century advances, the roads have improved, the railways have set up in business (by 1861 the Broughtons in Furness, Peeblesshire and Flintshire had their own stations) and people are becoming more mobile, looking for broader horizons. The pattern begins to shift: the numbers of those born outside the community rises, men and women look further afield for marriage partners, and the clusters loosen – though by less than you might expect. These Broughtons neatly bear out a rule expounded by some of the expert surname analysts who come into this story later, notably David Hey, Emeritus Professor of Local and Family History at the University of Sheffield: the popular notion that, apart from the nobility and gentry, people rarely moved out of the place they were born in is false. People in early Victorian Britain moved about more than is mostly presumed. But they tended not to move far. For most, the nearest market town was the limit of their aspirations, the edge of their world. As Hardy says in *Tess of the D'Urbervilles*: 'To persons of limited spheres, miles are as geographical degrees, parishes as counties, counties as provinces and kingdoms.'

*

Yet even the census returns cannot alone tell the whole story. Parish records before the census began show that some familiar names of the nineteenth century were rooted in these villages long before. Numerically dominant names in Broughton, Furness, in the records of the seventeenth century are Askew (sometimes Aiskew), Barker, Casson, Hartley, Jackson, Pritt and Towers. In the early eighteenth, they are Addison, Atkinson, Brockbank/ Brocklebank, Carter, Casson, Dixon, Gawith, Gilpin, Newby, Pritt, Stephenson, Tyson and Wilson. Several have dwindled away by the time the censuses start. In Hampshire, there's a greater conti- nuity between late-eighteenth-century names from the parish records and those from the years of census: Gale, Judd, Mersh, Morgan, Rogers and Woodford persist, though the once dominant Hattats expire. What extinguished this Broughton surname was a lack of sons to sustain it: a process somewhat cruelly known to those who study these things as 'daughtering out'.

Taking the various sources of evidence together, it becomes

still more clear that most of the families in these villages fell into one of three categories: the *surgers*, unknown in the village in one generation, numerous in the next; the *sliders*, who fall away and in some cases disappear altogether; and the *stayers*, mostly agricultural families, who have much the same solid representation in the village throughout.

In Hampshire, the notable *surgers* are the Davises and the Lansleys (Lansley may come from the old personal name of Lanceley). Two clutches of Davises move into Broughton during the 1850s. Thomas and his wife Jane, from Wiltshire, arrive to take over a farm. They bring with them their niece, Jane Offer – a surname long established in Broughton. The other new Davises, James, a coal merchant, and Thirza, from Dorset, arrive with son Sidney and daughters Mary and Emily. By the time the census taker notes them down in 1861 they have added four more children: Thirza, John, Eliza and James. Though farmer Thomas and his wife Jane have already gone, a village not long since devoid of Davises suddenly sports enough for a football team.

Ten years on, James and Thirza, now nearing fifty, still with Thirza, John, Eliza and James, are now augmented by Emma aged eight and Ida aged three. Shift a further ten years on, and James and Thirza are still in residence with four children. But now they've been augmented by a new crop of Davises, also from Dorset: Frederick, a widower, with his daughters Mary, Lucy and Charlotte, all born in Wellow, Wiltshire. Frederick is a carter, and has two under-carters living with him, one of whom is an Offer, born in Broughton. The Davises' connections with the Offers suggest that, as often happened in villages, a family's choice of a new place to live could be influenced by having relatives installed there already. It may very well be that this new Dorset household was related to the one that preceded them some years earlier. The census that records them both is silent on that. It's the kind of information that only compilers of family trees or village historians would have the time to resolve. Where such work has been done, it has consistently illustrated a tendency for people to move to communities containing kinsfolk they knew already.

By 1891 James is dead. Thirza stays on as a widow, with two of her children, James and Emma. All the others have left home. Frederick has remarried – his new wife is Martha – and they have living with them in the village his daughter Charlotte and a grandson, William. Ten years later, at the start of the new century, Thirza, now nearly eighty, has with her two of her children, Emily and James. Fred, Martha and William form a second household. And a third family of Davises, again recent immigrants, has also appeared in Broughton. William, thirty-nine at the time of the census – again from Dorset, so quite possibly related to earlier migrants from Dorset – and his wife Maria, from Lockerley, Hampshire, a few miles from Broughton, are about to revive a surname which might otherwise have been fading away. By 1901, two sons and a daughter have been born to this couple in Broughton. And ten years later, in the last of the censuses now available, the household has grown to nine – at a time when to have seven children, once usual, is becoming more remarkable.

Thirza is dead in 1911. But remarkably, five of her children now live in Broughton, three having returned in the past decade, underlining the fact that returning to the place where you were born is a consistent pattern in these villages. Elsewhere in Broughton, the name continues to spread. In 1911, David Davis, a shepherd from Wiltshire, and Mary, his wife, have arrived with their children Lily and Fred, while William, a carter, and Mary, his wife, have moved in from the nearby village of Houghton with a son and two daughters. So after fifty years, Davis has become the biggest name in the village – five descended from the first set of the Davises who came from Dorset, the rest all reinforcements. They are just by a nose ahead of another surger surname, Lansley.

The 1841 census here picked up a single Lansley: Frances, aged twenty-three. None was found in 1851 or in 1861, but the 1871 invigilation uncovered a sturdy contingent which has moved here from Mottisfont, just down the road. George, a journeyman carpenter, and Hannah, his wife, have arrived with five sons – James, Alfred, Walter, George and Albert – and one daughter, Emma, to whom they have added in Broughton three further sons: Herbert, Frank and Edward. To have eight sons strongly suggests that a family's surname will leave its mark in a village; and a ninth son is added just in time for the 1881 census. By 1891 George and Hannah, now sixty, have only two children at home: their sons Albert, now twenty-eight, and William fifteen. But the young men's elder brother James has married Charlotte and started a family of his own: one son and three daughters. Walter, married to Annie, is also augmenting the stock of Lansleys, but all three of his children are daughters, who cannot be expected to pass on the name.

Ten years later (1901), Hannah is dead. Her widower George is living with Edward, his thirty-one-year-old son, who has returned to the village, and Edward's wife Jane. Edward's brother Albert is also there, as a lodger. Walter and Annie, the ones with three daughters, have added a further daughter, and there's a boy in this household too, at last, but he is a nephew. Harry, the son recorded with James and Charlotte in 1901, is no longer listed, but they do have a son called George. Just possibly the Harry of 1891 is the George of 1901. These things happen: the Tom Gale whose gravestone stands at the gate of St Mary's Broughton was christened Henry William.

To keep the surname alive, the Lansleys need all the sons they can get and their younger males have failed to match the productivity of George and Hannah. Two more of the sons of George and Hannah are contributing to the family pool: Frank has married Edith and Herbert has married Annie; each has one child, but each is a daughter. There are two further Lansleys still living in Broughton: Caroline and Alice, daughters of James and Charlotte, are in service at other houses.

In the final published census, 1911, George has joined Hannah in a world beyond census taking, but five of their sons remain. Walter and Anne still have a daughter, Edith, with them. Herbert has taken over a pub called the Plough. His brother Albert is living with them. Edward now has two sons. William, who had left the village by 1901, has returned (that pattern again), is married to Alice, and has a daughter called Gladys. George has married Annie: they have a daughter called Ivy and a son named, unusually, Percival. There are thus five Lansley households in Broughton, all there simply because some half a century back George and Hannah, patriarch and matriarch, had chosen to come a couple of miles or so from Mottisfont and make their home here.

The surgers would have been avidly talked about in the village. The arrival of an unfamiliar surname always set off speculation. In George Eliot's *The Mill on the Floss*, Mr Tulliver's sister notes that he has acquired a new neighbour. '"Why, Pivart's a new name hereabout, brother, isn't it?" she said: "he didn't own the land in father's time, nor yours either, before I was married."' But the decline and sometimes extinction of once famous names was a topic that people mused on too. These are the *sliders*; one or two of whom are by 1911 better described as the disappeared-altogethers. That must have been all the sadder because some of the names that are dwindling away are the ones with the richest local flavour, such as Pragnell, Offer and Tubb. We can start perhaps with the Pragnells, never quite so fecund here as they were in the neighbouring villages of East and West Tytherley, but conspicuous in Broughton under the names of Pragnell, Prangle, Pragnele, Prangnell and Prangnele – with families switching from one to another in between censuses.

It's a name that has been in the village at least since the hearth tax of 1665, which two Pragnell households, both spelled that way, were well enough off to pay. Aside from a scattering of singleton Pragnells whom the census does not explain, there are three households here in 1841: William, presumably a widower, with his daughters Sarah and Ann (she is only ten months old, which makes it likely that her mother did not survive her birth); then William and Hannah Pragnell with two sons and a daughter; and finally Thomas and Mary, spelling their surname (for now) as Pragnele, recently married with a one-year-old daughter, Selina.

For Thomas and Mary Pragnell, daughters outnumber sons (there is only one son, who seems to have died early) so their line will not continue. The survival of the line of William and Hannah looks more assured. William has died by 1851, but Hannah is left with two sons, Henry and George, and by 1871, Henry has four sons of his own. This strain of Pragnells seems to offer most hope for the survival of the name, in its various forms. Yet by 1881 only the aged widow Hannah and Henry's son James, a boarder with a separate family, are left of this original household. Henry and Ann, whom I cannot trace in any 1881 census return, seem to have been overtaken by one of those disasters which sometimes blighted or even wrecked such working-class families, usually because they had run into serious debt. Frederick, their youngest son, is in Stockbridge workhouse, where fellow inmates from Broughton include a Blake and a Judd. I have not been able to find the rest of the family, but by 1891 two of the sons are working for the railways, one in Hampshire and another in Surrey, while a third is an officer of a workhouse in London.

As so often happens in these records, the decline of original families is masked in the overall figures by new arrivals. There are three new Pragnell households on the edge of the village in 1881, two of whom have come from the neighbouring village of East Tytherley – so again, it's tempting to assume that they were related, though without an assiduous search through birth certificates one cannot be sure; each has four sons. Yet ten years later all these newcomers have gone, one lot to Mottisfont and one to Houghton, again tiny distances; and the few of this surname who now remain are far too old to inject any further Pragnells into the village.

Surnames are a sexually transmitted condition and, in terms of surviving names, men will always do best. Women perpetuate, sometimes at the cost of their lives, surnames other than their own: Sarah Judd provides three boys and five girls who swell the surname of their father, Charles Cooper. The fate of the Offers is a clear case of the danger, as it was seen by people who treasured their surnames, of consistently having daughters rather than sons. The trail in the censuses begins with three households, headed in 1841 by James and Sarah (née Frayle); Charles and Ann; and Mary, a widow aged forty-seven. Her son Charles will in the 1850s marry his cousin Mary: seven children will be born of this marriage, five of them girls. James and Sarah will have six children, and four of them will be girls.

So the chances that this name will survive in the village look dim. And sure enough, from 1871 onwards the Offers are in retreat. By 1891, there is one married couple left, with three daughters and two sons neither of whom will stay in the village. In 1911 one of the daughters, Lottie, is still close to Broughton – but she's in a place which over the years has been only too well known to the Offer family: Stockbridge workhouse. The name Offer only survives in Broughton because Beatrice, now twenty, has found work with Tom Gale's widow, now Mrs Glazier, at the Tally Ho! pub.

But by now, there aren't many Gales left either. Theirs has been a spectacular fall. The parish records from 1815 on are full of people called Gale, and in 1841, when the first census is taken, there are forty-four of them. They divide into nine main households, some of whose heads will surely have been related. In 1851, when the census information is fuller, one can distinguish several households that look capable of packing the village with Gales for years to come. There are Silas and Maria, his wife (recorded as Martha in 1841), who have three daughters, but sons are going to come later. There is Sarah, widow of Henry, who has succeeded him as publican at the Tally Ho!, the inn which he had been running since 1832. She has five sons in residence as well as one daughter. Then there are George Gale, carpenter and wheelwright, who was born in the nearby village of Houghton, and his wife Jane, from Wallop a few miles north of here, who also have five listed sons, all born since they came to Broughton. Charles Gale, one of the village butchers in 1841, has died, but has left behind at least four sons. One of them, Amos, has taken over his father's business and will be a big name in this village for much of the coming century.

In 1861, the Gales are still doing well, with sons still outnumbering daughters, though Amos is still unmarried at thirty-eight, as are his brothers Thomas at thirty-three and Francis at thirty. But by 1871 there has been a conspicuous dwindling – partly because one of the principal Gale families has deserted Hampshire for Kentish Town, but partly too because sons have failed to have sons of their own. Amos, the village butcher, is married at last – to Ann from Gloucestershire, in 1862 – but nearly a decade of marriage has brought no children and since Ann is now forty-nine that seems unlikely to alter. And by 1881 the village has lost all but six of its Gales. Only the Tally Ho! Inn, where Tom Gale (the one whose gravestone is by the church gate) is now living with his aunt, the widow Martha who has come to take over the family pub, is maintaining the surname's continuity.

Tom leaves for Wales and gets a job in a colliery in Llantrisant. He and his wife Elizabeth come back to the village to take over the pub after the death of Aunt Martha – only for Tom himself, as we've seen, to die soon after her. Dr Robert Parr, who came here in 1962 to work with the resident general practitioner, and remained here looking after its families until his retirement, incorporated some of what he had learned in an affectionate book called *The Hampshire Broughton; a Social History of a West Hampshire Village*. It used to be said, he records, that Tom Gale's widow Elizabeth had wanted Tom's gravestone close to the Tally Ho! so she could keep an eye on him. But as he says, that could be put the other way round, with Tom adroitly placed to keep an eye on Elizabeth, who had very soon married a man ten years her junior called Charlie Glazier, an ostler at another pub in the village. Under their supervision the business would soon go bust, though the pub was saved for posterity. The 1911 census lists Charlie, now thirty-two, Elizabeth, forty-three, her two children from her marriage to Tom – Ada Beatrice and Henry William Tom – still at the pub, with her two very young daughters with Charlie Glazier, and a servant called Beatrice Emily – the last, as we've seen, of the Offers, just as they at this stage look like the last of the Gales.

This brings us, finally, to the *stayers*: effectively the core families of nineteenth-century Broughton. A conspicuous case is the Rogerses. They number thirty in 1841: there is still a solid contingent of twenty in the last available census, that of 1911. A key figure here is Stephen, a village blacksmith, who appears in the 1841 census as a boy of fifteen living with John, aged twenty – presumably an older brother. Not all the early Rogerses persist, but the name will be saved for the next generation partly by Stephen, who by 1861 is married to Eliza Arthur and has sons aged fifteen and two; partly by Thomas, son of the late George and Ann Rogers, who is married to Betsy and has a young son and daughter; and partly by new arrivals, fulfilling the consistent pattern that as one family's departure reduces the stock of the surname, another, possibly related, comes along to sustain it. There are still twenty Broughton Rogerses in the census of 1911. It's clear that a family that looks from the overall totals to be made up of stayers has needed the transfusion of new arrivals to keep its name on the Broughton map. Even so, twelve of these twenty are traceable back to Stephen.

The Coopers are also high scorers – less so as the years go by, but still numerous enough at the end of the census years to qualify as a solid Broughtonian surname. Of those still there in 1911, Henry and Fanny and their son Albert can trace themselves back to Thomas, one of thirty-three Coopers logged by the census taker in 1841.

Another category of stayers are the Judds. In 1841 there are four main households, headed in order of age by Charles and Mary, Thomas and Eliza, Stephen and Elizabeth, and William and Mary. The line from Thomas and Eliza runs right through the century, mainly thanks to his son Charles, nine in 1841, who marries Charlotte (née Woods) sometime in the 1850s and soon begins to father multiple Judds. Neither the census nor the parish records alone catches all of them. Together, they show that Charles and Charlotte produce eight sons and three daughters in just over fifteen years.

By 1901 Charles is dead, but Charlotte has, somehow, survived. Two of their sons live with her: of the others, one has three children, a second has two. Another household is headed by Alfred and Emma, whose children look likely to have been the cousins, at several removes, of the brood produced by Charlotte and Charles. If so, that would make the Judds the prime Broughton example of a highly continuous village core family, the sort of family so often assumed to symbolise the steady continuity of families in a Victorian village, though, as this section has shown, quite often wrongly so. While Judd girls, as noted above, were helping perpetuate the Morgan and Cooper dynasties, other village girls, particularly Charlotte (née Woods), were augmenting the Judds. It was fitting that these two families should have inter-married, since across all the years of the censuses, the Coopers come second only to the Judds as populators of Broughton. Edward, a glazier, and Elizabeth Cooper, according to baptismal records, have contributed five boys and three girls during these seventy years, while Thomas and his wife Anne have brought eight boys and five girls to the font.

Watching these families waxing and waning, certain threads become obvious. If a name is going to last in a village, the family needs a good crop of healthy sons. Those sons need to stay, and they need to breed the next generation. An instructive case here are the Woodfords – once, perhaps, dwellers at the edge of a wood, though it's also a familiar English place name – who provide the village with shoemakers. They are good at producing sons as well as shoes. Baptismal records show Henry and his wife Catherine, née Taylor, bringing fourteen children for baptism: eleven are boys. That would seem to predict a Woodford-packed future for Broughton. Yet some sons fail to produce any children, and more seek their futures elsewhere. So their numbers drop, and in 1911, the last available census, only a small and ancient contingent remain. Andrew is seventy-one: he was once married to Eliza but they had no children; then she died. About a decade ago, he married Faith, but she was past child-bearing age. Mary Ann, widow of the shoemaker Josiah, is seventy-seven; Jane, widow of Thomas, is seventy-two; and Frederick, married twenty-two years ago, lives apart from his wife. He's the youngest among them, at fifty-six. Daughtering out is not the only road to elimination.

*

Furness replicates the pattern in Hampshire: surgers, sliders and stayers. The Butterfields and the Barrows, and especially the Thackerays (who first appear as Thackrays) and later still the Hadwins, are surgers. The Butterfields, whose name does not appear at all in early parish records, begin to proliferate in the 1850s and continue to multiply. This surname can be relied on to produce large families. The patriarch of this Broughton clan, James, died in June 1891 at the age of seventy-four and his tombstone in the graveyard at St Mary Magdalene tells a story that no census can. Here are James and the wife who died two years before him, Mary, and with them a poignant succession of children: Joseph, died in 1855 at fourteen months; John in January 1859 at thirteen; Mary in December the same year, at thirteen; Henry

in September 1871, at six; another John, named for his dead
brother, in November 1887 at twenty-six; Joseph, again named
for his dead brother, in March 1890, also at twenty-six – all to be
mourned, along with his wife, by James. So many children born;
so many dead in infancy or at a time when their lives should
have just been beginning. One reason perhaps why Butterfields
favoured large families. That the father survived to the age of
seventy-four when so many in the family died so young is part
of a steady pattern. The parish records chart many deaths in
early infancy but also a sturdy collection of people who lived
beyond ninety. According to Wallace Greenhalgh, Broughton's
historian, the longest life recorded on the churchyard gravestones
is that of Anne Watters, widow of William, a surgeon. He died
in 1767 at seventy-eight; she lived on for almost a quarter of a
century, dying in 1791 at a hundred and four.

This being a more isolated, self-contained village, newcomers
do not soar so easily to the top of the charts as the Davises and
Lansleys do in Hampshire. And at the other end of the scale,
the surnames Crosbie (or Crosby), Nelson, Carter, Coward
and, perhaps most strikingly, Newby are on the slide as the
century progresses. These names survive into twentieth-century
Broughton – but all are diminished. The reasons would seem to
be those already familiar: a shortage of sons and in later years
the reluctance of sons to marry. The 1891 census finds three
brothers called Simpson living together in Broughton in Furness.
James is sixty-nine, Thomas sixty-six, Robert forty-seven. None
has married; none so far as one can discern has furnished the
town with further Simpsons.

You can see the tendency to produce children of one gender
only at its most dramatic where a household that's full of sons
lives next door to a household that's full of daughters. Here is
a group of houses in Dog Lane, Broughton, Hampshire, in 1881.
In the first live the Gilberts: James, his wife Jane, daughters Ann,
Ellen, Kate and Emma, but no sons. Next door are the Fays:

William, his wife Ann, and sons Arthur, Felix, Harry, Fred and Walter – and daughter Lily. And beyond them, some Lansleys, here spelled Lanseley, whom we've already met: George, his wife Hannah, who in time will have produced nine sons – one of whom, Walter, breaking the pattern, will by the turn of the century be the father of four children, all daughters.

Far to the north in Furness, there's a family whose record must greatly have heartened those in the town who clung to the old-fashioned teaching that all things come to those who wait. Here in 1881 we find the household of Robert and Frances Barrow. Robert, born in a hamlet called Brow Edge near Cartmel, some twenty miles from here, is a wood-hoopmaker, which has long been a common occupation in this part of England, though it will not remain so much longer. Frances was born out on the Cumberland coast at Whitehaven. Their family began with five successive sons, the oldest of whom is now fourteen, the youngest, six. But then came a run of three daughters, the youngest just two months old when the census taker arrived on their doorstep. Within the next decade, they would bring the scores almost level with a fourth daughter; after that there would be one further daughter and one further son. (But this teaching does not always apply. The Leicester University genetics expert Turi King cites the more recent case of a couple in Birmingham who only abandoned their hopes of having a daughter after producing eleven sons.)

As for the stayers, the pattern in Furness confirms what Broughton in Hampshire revealed: some, the Tysons especially, are helped to retain their pre-eminence as new people with the same surname come in to replace the ones who've moved out. The pattern among the most prolific names in this Broughton varies from surname to surname. Atkinson fathers tend to come from outside Broughton; more outsider men of this surname have come to join Broughton wives than the other way round. Among the Dawsons, couples where the man comes from

Broughton outnumber those where the wife was born there. The
same is true to a lesser extent of the Tysons. Among the Dixons
the continuity of families is striking, with roughly four times as
many households where one or both parents come from
Broughton as households where neither does. Most villages, I
suspect, would show the same kind of diversity.

Two very early names are, like the Atkinsons, rescued from
decline by new arrivals. One is Postlethwaite (the name comes
from a habitation in nearby Millom; -thwaite is a common place
name ending in this part of the world, and -postle may come
from apostle), which appears in the parish records in the seventeenth century and is probably a much older Broughton name
than that. Another old established name here is Whineray, which
appears in several forms. There's a patch of land in Broughton
that is still known as Whineray Bank. Whinnerah occurs in the
parish records of 1667. The chain of three censuses from 1841
finds no Whinerays, however spelled, in Broughton. But the
Whinerays revive, and the census of 1901 shows them back in
residence at Whineray Bank.

There's perhaps a fourth class to add to surgers, stayers and
sliders, which one might call the just-visitings. These people, like
the Reverend Frederick Amadeus Malleson, born in London, vicar
here from 1870 to 1897, friend and editor of John Ruskin, trans-
lator of Jules Verne, bring unusual, even exotic names into a
small town or village, but before long often take it away again.
They have come from a greater distance away than almost anyone
else in the community and though one or two may stay, most
are never likely to do. When the railway comes to a village, new
surnames come with it: at first those of contractors and builders
and layers of track, then those of stationmasters and staff; but
many of these will move on, taking their surnames with them.
In the 1850s a family called Starr, not a familiar name in these
parts, arrives in Broughton, Furness. Richard, who's thirty-nine,
and his wife Eliza, ten years younger, were born in Sussex; their

three oldest children in Maidstone, which the census taker also assigns to Sussex, although, then as now, it's in Kent. But Richard is an engine driver, and sure enough, ten years later, the Starrs have moved on.

Sometimes newcomers, importing fresh surnames, arrive at the end of a life elsewhere, settle in for retirement, but do not live long. Broughton in Hampshire was home for a time to a couple of brothers called Lermitte, who arrived with a reputation for philanthropy in the London village of Finchley, and were soon making some mark in the life of the village. Broughton in Furness attracted painters – some, like J. H. Crossland, good enough to have their work shown in the Royal Academy. The name Brontë was here for a while: Branwell Brontë arrived to tutor the sons of Robert Postlethwaite, but did not stay very long. One notable incomer, born near Preston – he became that town's MP – who chose to make a permanent home in Broughton in Furness had the simple surname Cross, but was known by a grander title: Lord Assheton. He served as Disraeli's Home Secretary, settled in Broughton, built a house there and died a viscount at the age of ninety, in 1918. His memorial in the churchyard of St Mary Magdalene leaves no room for doubt about his importance.

Throw in the other Broughtons, and a clear set of rules emerges. What is overwhelmingly clear from this evidence is the localness of surnames – a few, like Carter and Walker, occupational names, or Jackson, Thompson and Johnson, names that come from descent, crop up in most of them. That occupational names, headed of course by Smith, are so generally prevalent is hardly surprising. Every village needed its smith, as it needed its baker and carter, its wrights and its clerks, and, by deduction, must have needed its coopers and turners, since they rate so high on the national scoreboard – just as every village had its crop of descendants from Jack, John, Will and Richard; and every village had a wood and a hill nearby. So it's not surprising to find almost all of these names among the top fifty across Britain (as listed in Appendix 1).

But the essence of places like these six Broughtons was the surname that belonged here and hereabouts rather than anywhere else. Broughton, Northamptonshire, is perhaps the richest example. The Lentons were the undisputed kings of the village surname – alone of all the families in my Broughtons, they came top of the census table in 1841 and again in 1861, were still at the top in 1881 and there again in the final published census of 1911. But not far behind came its Hights and Sails (later more often Sales) and its Jacques – sometimes Jaqueses or Jacquets – and its curiously rhyming Tilleys, Dilleys and Lilleys, together with its Lillemans. (Since the suffix -man usually indicates someone in service, the Lilleys may perhaps have liked to think that these Lillemans had once been their dutiful servants.) In 1911, by which time the world was becoming more intermixed, four names dominated at Broughton in Lincolnshire: Stothard, Barley, Brocklesby and Codd, which you would not encounter just anywhere. But the Hares who were once supreme in this village have faded away, and the coming family now are the Graveses. Broughton, Cambridgeshire, seems to have more than its fair share of monosyllables – Male (or Maile), Pain (or Payne), West, How, Muns (later Munns), Beard, Cross, Hawks, Moles, Ayres – almost as if people thereabouts did not want to open their mouths for too long for fear of catching something unpleasant.

Again, there is a variety of sources here. Lincolnshire's Codd is the most contentious. A man with a cod-like shape? Or a bag-like shape, since Codd may also derive from a word for a bag; the original Codd may have made them? A fishmonger? A short form of Cody, itself a derivation from the Irish O Cuidighthigh? Or perhaps a man of notable sexual prowess (we are asked to think here of 'codpiece')? Cambridgeshire's Male (or Maile) is more unequivocally taken to represent extreme masculinity. Muns is almost as mysterious as Codd. It's mostly construed as meaning 'monk'; also as 'moon' – but that too may mean 'monk'. One nineteenth-century analyst derives it either from the personal name Edmund or from a Norman name, Mohun, as locally corrupted. Ayres, which elsewhere appears as Ayers, suggests a man who has come by or is expected to come by, a fortune; in other words, an heir. Moles is a nickname, which may come from the burrowing creature or from a conspicuous spot or blemish. Stothard is said to mean a herder of bullocks or oxen or possibly of what one source calls 'inferior horses'.

These villages, too, as the tables in Appendix 2 show, confirm the pattern of Broughton in Hampshire and Broughton in Furness, with surnames that surge, stick or slide away. One name prevalent in Broughton, Borders, but little known through much of the kingdom, is Newbigging – a name which may derive from any number of farmsteads bearing this name in Scotland, but in this case is likely related to one at Carnwath in Lanarkshire. The surname that stands out in Broughton, north Wales, is Crofts. Although, like so many others in this part of the world, it ends in 's', the *Oxford Dictionary of English Surnames* suggests that it derived from a village called Croft (there are several in Britain) or from someone who lived near a croft. Whatever their derivation, the Croftses soar easily here above the Joneses, Williamses and Davieses of almost every Welsh village.

*

Once the published census stops in 1911, the ebb and flow of surnames becomes harder to plot. There are various sources, all of them useful, but none straightforward and none as informative as a census. Telephone directories, once distrusted because only better-off people had phones, grew more widely representative, though now there's a new kind of omission, since the better off frequently keep their names out of directories. Parish records only capture the names of those who subscribe to the parish.

There is still a big pool of people who come to church to be baptised, married or buried, though not for its other purposes; but the names of a growing segment of the population will never appear in church records. Then there's the electoral register, for which anyone over voting age is required to submit information – though too many, especially since Margaret Thatcher's poll tax, don't, while children are wholly excluded.

In our restless, unrestricted, traipse-about age, when a plane can sweep you from London to New York in far less time than it took at the time of the 1841 census to journey from London to Bath, it is hardly surprising that village names are no longer as clustered as they once were. As we've seen in Hampshire and Furness, names that once seemed the core of any community may by now have disappeared from it entirely. Yet despite the way the late nineteenth, twentieth and early twenty-first centuries have so vastly altered the way that we live, you will still find clusters of names persisting in the places where they began. In 2012, Paul Barker, the writer and broadcaster on culture and society who once edited *New Society* magazine, published a book about the place he was born in, which he called *Hebden Bridge: A Sense of Belonging*. For this he interviewed a woman called Mrs Durancyk, whose Polish husband, now dead, had served in the British army. Barker (it's a north country name, which could mean a tanner or a shepherd; most prevalent in the Pennines but making the charts in Furness too) told her he'd remembered her daughter from school partly because her name was so memorable. 'Yes,' she replied, 'not Greenwood or Sutcliffe.' Barker's village has swarmed with Greenwoods through the centuries. One of the definitions of 'local' in Hebden Bridge, he says, is 'anyone who has a Greenwood or Sutcliffe in their family background'. But his own name Barker was predominant here as well, as was Ashworth: both his mother and the mother of the Hebden Bridge girl whom he married were born Marion Ashworth. Whether the same will be true a generation from now is uncertain. In 2013, Ancestry, the biggest of the many organisations providing essential material for students of family history, produced an analysis built on comparing returns from the 1911 census with new material obtained from the Office for National Statistics. This listed among names that had markedly declined, Sutcliffe, Greenwood, Butterworth and Kershaw, all familiar names in the Pennines. Clegg, too, is on the slide.

There are other ways, too, to catalogue local surnames still concealed in the later censuses. Some of the local histories published for the millennium, with the help of one of the most thoroughly justified uses of lottery money, began to fill in the picture of village names in the twentieth century. In the Wiltshire village of Worton, where I once lived, the community put together a book of reminiscences, one value of which was that it charted where the village's growing contingent of incomers had arrived from. But there's also an example, unique in my explorations, though no doubt to be found in the growing data banks of oral history, which shows what a lot can be learned by talking systematically to people who lived through the years in places like these. It comes, by a pleasing coincidence, from the village in whose Hammond-packed churchyard my brother and his widow are buried: Elmdon in Essex.

It happened at Elmdon because Elmdon is close to Cambridge, and a notable anthropologist who had worked for most of her life in Africa came to live in a cottage in Elmdon. Audrey Richards was by now ensconced in the Department of Social Anthropology at Cambridge. She and a colleague, Edmund Leach, later Provost of King's College (which appointment removed him from further work on the Elmdon project), hit on the notion of applying their practised techniques to a study of a suitable village. This one was chosen partly because Richards lived there, but also because these researchers were impressed by the high proportion of Elmdoners who appeared to share the same surnames. Teams of students were sent to interview as many as were ready to talk (not all, but enough) about their recollections of village families, occupations, allegiances and names. The results produced three books: one – *Some Elmdon Families*, by Richards and her colleague Jean Robin – for village consumption, and two more to carry their findings to academia.

The community these books portray is not as entirely harmonious as townspeople often imagine that village life must be. What for centuries had been a simple agricultural village, where farm work was the lot of most families, was evolving by the time their investigations began as assorted newcomers moved into Elmdon, sometimes from neighbouring villages but many from places further away. Some of these newcomers, like Audrey Richards herself, practised trades which had never been part of Elmdon culture – sometimes involving daily commuting to Cambridge or, increasingly, even to London. Some of the newly arrived could not conceal their contempt for the slow, unadventurous, small 'c' conservative ways of the villagers, while here and there longstanding villagers viewed the newcomers with an equal distrust or disdain.

The anthropologists quickly picked out a group of core Elmdon people who regarded themselves as the 'real' Elmdon, even excluding some who had lived in the village for many years but who did not share its most hallowed surnames. The high numbers of Hammonds I noted when first visiting Elmdon churchyard in the early 1960s seems to have been a general matter of wonder. Theirs was one of four surnames that the researchers identified as core families, along with the Reeveses, the Hayeses and the Hoys. The Reeveses were in fact far newer in Elmdon than some of those, like the Greenhills and the upwardly mobile Gamgees (a corruption of a name that began in Italy), whom they regarded as not true core families, though their numbers were bound to impress. The Hammonds multiplied because six brothers stayed in the village rather than looking for work elsewhere, and produced new generations of Hammonds. Five were farm labourers all their lives. They did not have to move out, as so many of their contemporaries did because jobs were too few to go round; these men found work for each other.

One farmer assured a Cambridge researcher that if you met a villager in the street, there was a 50 per cent chance that person would be a Hammond. The aura of the core families was all the greater, these studies showed, because a woman who married into a different family would still be recalled and spoken of by her maiden name. Once a Hammond, whatever it said on the marriage certificate, always a Hammond.

By the 1960s the proportion of Elmdon residents who had been born in the village had fallen to 40 per cent, and the number of marriages in which both bride and groom were from the village had fallen to 8 per cent. The shops were going; the pubs would go, too, before long – though more recently an agreeable new one has opened. In 1964 the most numerous name in the village was Starr. One of the Hayeses had married a man of this name and brought him and his name into the village. It was noted too that where in the nineteenth century you needed to stay in or near the village where you were born to keep in touch with your wider family, now the car and the bus and the telephone serve that purpose (social media were, when Audrey Richards's students were combing through Elmdon, still undreamed of). The village, as the place to which you belonged, was now in a sense replaced by the wider neighbourhood – what David Hey calls the 'country'. That concept, he says, is familiar in the novels of George Eliot and Hardy, indicating 'a sense of belonging not just to a particular town or rural parish but also to a wider district in which families had friends and relations and people with whom they did business'. The changing pattern of surnames is a telling demonstration of that. Astonishingly it was said that when the Elmdon project completed its work, there was not one Hammond left in the village. But there are Hammond graves in the churchyard today whose death dates indicate a continuing presence of Hammonds well into the twenty-first century, and the 2011 electoral roll for Elmdon encompasses three. The name Gamgee, I'm happy to say, also survives.

3

Translocations

Surnames on the March

'I dare say it's a French mouse, come over with
William the Conqueror.'
Lewis Carroll, *Alice in Wonderland*

New blood on Quaker Street

Among the Addisons, Atkinsons, Cassons, Carters and of course
Tysons who recur in the parish records of seventeenth-century
Broughton in Furness – and also in the bloodstained history of
its Peeblesshire counterpart, as chronicled in Chapter 5 – is a
surname whose unravelling requires no detective skills. Fleming
(sometimes spelled Flemming or Fleeming) means somebody
out of Flanders. It has been estimated that around a third of
William I's conquering army were Flemings, and in the subsequent
600 years there were three substantial waves of immigration from
that region. The first occurred in the reign of Henry I, who
initially encouraged it. But English merchants resented the
competition, so Henry packed many of the newcomers off to
an area of south Pembrokeshire bounded on the northern and
eastern side by a line, known by the Anglo-Saxon term *Landsker*,
that the Normans had fortified. Its occupation by the Flemings
established this territory as 'a little England beyond Wales',
sharply different not only in its softer landscape but in language
and culture from the rugged lands of Welsh Wales beyond.

A sizeable number remained in London. But Henry II, again responding to the protests of London merchants, ordered them out. Rather than return to Flanders, many migrated to other parts of this island, mainly to Scotland, but in what is now Cumbria too. They left no great legacy of Flemish surnames behind them, settling on the whole for established local names, though in early years the designation 'Fleming' was all that was needed to pick them out – and yet also the way they spoke counted. At the height of their unpopularity, Flemings in London were hunted by mobs who ordered them to say 'bread and cheese'. If it sounded like 'brod' and 'caisse' they would be set upon and possibly slaughtered.

In the fourteenth century, impelled perhaps by the admiration for strivers that motivated government then as now, Edward III welcomed them back, and the sixteenth century brought further arrivals. Their migrations were sometimes a response to religious persecution, but more often what drove them was the scent of commercial advantage and the promise of a road to prosperity: much the same forces that all through recorded history, not least in our own day, have brought new accents, new cultures and, in one form or another, new names to the British Isles.

But then most of our names relate to invasions. The Flemings are far from unique. Even the Celts, whom we tend to think of as Britain's oldest inhabitants, began elsewhere. The romantic nineteenth-century tendency to imagine them as some kind of monolithic community, united by one language, one culture – as still allegedly evident in what metropolitan arrogance terms the Celtic fringe – is no longer widely accepted. The Celts of this so-called fringe – Scotland, Wales, the Isle of Man and, in England, Cornwall, to which they were gradually driven back – had much in common but much that was different too. The language, though its various exponents can still hope to understand each other, divided into separate strains. In some parts of southern Scotland, the common language was Welsh.

The surnames that came from original Celtic forenames took different directions too. A name that begins with the prefix 'O' will most often come from Ireland, which has its Macs and Mcs too, but on a more modest scale. Macs and Mcs are far more common in Scotland where 'ó' and 'Ó' are few. There are, though, fewer around in the British Isles than there once would have been. Names modulate, and ó Murchadha (sea-battler) turns into Murphy, ó Ceallaigh (bright-headed) into Kelly, ó Suilleabhain (dark-eyed) into Sullivan and ó Maioilriain into Ryan. There are Anglicisations too, as, for instance, Mac Gabhann gives way to Smith. Kellys are famously frequent on the Isle of Man, but you don't expect to find many in Cornwall, where the sturdy remaining crop of surnames is crowded, as tradition has long maintained, with Tres, Pols and Pens.

The Romans made little lasting contribution to British surnames. The Angles and Saxons who settled here from the fifth century onwards and came to dominate what we now call England had a decisive effect on the language that we now speak. In *The Adventure of English*, Melvyn Bragg says that all but three of its hundred most common words come from Old English; the three exceptions – 'they', 'their' and 'them' – come from Old Norse. Among the most preponderant surnames in Britain an echoing influence is clear. Names you used to see on the shop-fronts in any substantial town, Smith and Brown, Taylor and Wright, White, Green and Hall, come from Old English – though not always exclusively so. It would not be for several centuries that they modulated into surnames.

Some three centuries later, the Scandinavians came here, again from differing homelands and favouring different destinations. They headed for Orkney and Shetland, the Western Isles, Skye, West Lancashire, the Wirral and parts of Cheshire, Anglesey (now Ynys Mon) – some from Norway, some from Norway by way of Ireland and potent numbers from Denmark, thrusting so deep into Anglo-Saxon heartlands that Alfred, knowing he could not expel them, created the territory, across what is now the East Midlands and East Anglia and northwards into Northumbria, that became the Danelaw.

Each contingent of new arrivals left its mark on the pattern of English place names, and so in time on the pattern of surnames. Names ending in -by, in -thorpe and in -toft, in -thwaite, -holme and -dale and -wick help distinguish the names of the Midlands and north as sharply as do surnames that end in -son. As so often in these explorations, you need only look at places called Broughton to see that process at work: apart from its profusion of names ending in -son, the record at Broughton in Furness repeatedly turns up names such as Newby, Holme (or Holmes), Barwick, Croisdale, Postlethwaite, Satterthwaite and plain unpreluded Thwaite.

The Normans have left us with a legacy of directly inherited names, though not all have the connection with 1066 that those who possess them like to imagine. Powerful families such as the Courtenays did not arrive until almost a century after the Conquest. Once much-consulted lists of men who came with the Conqueror, especially the Battle Abbey roll, have proved to be totally unreliable. Indeed, the eminent surname expert David Hey says only people called Malet, Mallet or Mallett have an undisputed right to make such a claim.

But aside from that, there are numerous names with a clear Norman origin, not least because so many are traceable back to Norman place names: D'Arcy and Mandeville, Beaumont and Balliol, Harcourt and Fortescue, de Vere, Neville, Sinclair, Vavasour, Talbot and Warren, most of them conspicuous at some time or other in English and Scottish history, hint at unconfected Norman origins. Some of what are often regarded as names of Scandinavian origins are also hybrids. The name Williamson ends in -son, but its William belongs to the Conquest and the rapid adoption of Norman forenames rather than English ones which followed. There's another element of hybridity, too. The

Normans themselves were relatively recent arrivals in France. Their name means 'Men from the North'; at one remove, they too were Viking invaders of England. So the Norman legacy is more complex than is sometimes supposed. Yet it has this indispensable element: we owe the very existence of surnames in Britain to the invading Normans; it was they who introduced the transmissible surname to Britain.

*

The Normans were not the last to come to Britain in search of new lives and new homes, though those that followed came, like the Flemings, peacefully and in restricted numbers. The Normans came not just for conquest but for enduring settlement. Those who followed the Flemings, especially the Dutch who arrived in significant numbers in the sixteenth century (the Flemings and Dutch had a sought-after expertise in techniques of drainage), settled not just in London, as every wave of newcomers did, but in Norwich, Colchester and the larger and more successful towns of the south-east.

The sixteenth century brought the first of the Protestant families from France who became known as the Huguenots, a term whose meaning remains mysterious, though it may be a mixture of the personal name Hugues (Hugh) with the German *Eidgenoss*, a confederate. The first decisive factor here had been the event in 1572 that became known as the St Bartholomew's Day massacre, when thousands of French Protestants – there are no reliable numbers – were slaughtered by Catholic mobs. In 1598, the Edict of Nantes offered them protection and established their rights, but that was revoked in 1685, prompting a still greater exodus. Charles II offered them sanctuary and up to 50,000 responded.

Like the Flemings before them, they brought with them a tradition of striving and marketable skills, especially in the weaving of silk. They also brought a wealth of distinctive surnames. Some were dropped in favour of English versions: a Joliefemme translated himself into a Pretyman, a Taillebois into a Talboys, a Brasseur into a Brassey, a Lefevre (though many Lefevres remained) into a Smith. Many others were preserved and became an established part of the panoply of English surnames. In an article for *History Today* in 2012, Robin Gwynn, director of Huguenot Heritage, suggested some possible modulations: Boulanger into Baker, Barbier into Barber, Delacroix into Cross, Forestier into Forrester, Reynard into Fox, Le Cerf into Hart, Mareschal into Marshall, Le Moine into Monk, de la Neuvemaison into Newhouse, de la Pierre into Peters, Blanc into White, Dubois into Wood.

It seems clear that some of the names fondly traced back to the Huguenots have in fact no direct connection. But some eminent names in modern-day Britain can be fairly safely classed as of Huguenot origin, including Romilly, Labouchere, Chenevix-Trench, Bosanquet, Courtauld, Tizard, Garrick, Olivier and Portal – taking in all kinds of expertise from political and religious office through finance, business and industry, science, warfare and the stage to reading the TV news and inventing the googly.

The district where initially these newcomers were most tightly clustered was Spitalfields, east of the present site of Liverpool Street station in London, which through several centuries has furnished a kind of anthology of London immigration. On its most famous street, Brick Lane, there is a building that has been successively a Protestant church, a synagogue and a mosque, serving first the Huguenots, then the Jews, and latterly Muslims originally from the sub-continent, chiefly Bangladeshis. But the catalogue of Spitalfields immigration goes even wider than that. At one time it had a sizeable Irish contingent too, and it now has a developing community of Somalis.

Some of the most famous names in British Jewry left their mark here – a Rothschild was president of its Jews' Free School, an institution essentially created by a great headmaster called Moses Angel (born Angel Moses, but he transposed his names after his father was disgraced). But most of the newcomers never aspired to the affluence or influence of such people. The fact that immigrants arrived in such numbers and settled so closely together ensured that these new communities were adhesively compact, and able to recreate the manner of life of the places, from patterns of language to traditional occupations, from which they had come.

Yet the tightly packed families of late-nineteenth-century Spitalfields were far from being Britain's first Jewish communities – though they were perhaps the most colourful and, the most vibrant. Jewish settlement had begun many centuries earlier, certainly round about the time of the Conquest, and, in a few scattered cases, probably before it. And though some always railed against their presence here – especially churchmen who blamed them for killing Christ, and much more the envious City of London, where most of the newcomers settled – the Jews for the most part had kings on their side. Two factors worked in their favour. They were moneylenders at a time when canon law forbade the lending of money for gain; and the money they made from usury, which could be substantial, was there to be taxed, often at exorbitant rates. Ask the barons for money and they might retaliate with demands for concessions; ask the Jews and any demands they made would be modest. So William I wanted them here, and William II possibly even more. According to the chronicler William of Malmesbury, the king at one point demanded that a debate be held between his own churchmen and the Jews, declaring that if the Jews won, he would convert to Judaism.

That the Jews were a fecund source of finance is clear from the history of such notables as Aaron of Lincoln, who was rated at the time of his death (1185) as the richest man in England. Other prominent figures were, like Aaron, designated by the places to which they belonged: Aaron of York, Moses of Lincoln, David of Oxford, Hamo of Hereford. Others were identified by the names of their fathers: Josc fil' Isaac, Hagin fil 'Rabbi. Very few, then, would have had transmittable surnames. Through the course of the thirteenth century, their predicament – always precarious; they were there on sufferance – worsened. Increasingly they came under attack from murderous mobs and more and more they found themselves oppressively taxed. Under Henry III, they found themselves paying heavily for the building of Westminster Abbey. Important towns like Bury St Edmunds and Leicester began to expel them, and in July 1290, Henry's son and successor, Edward I, ordered them out. For 400 years thereafter they were officially banished, though in fact some desperate refugees from persecution and wholesale expulsion elsewhere in Europe found their way into England.

Their official exile ended with the coming to power of Oliver Cromwell, who became aware of how much their Jewish populations were enhancing the rise of continental towns such as Amsterdam. The prohibition on Jews settling in England was not rescinded: it was merely no longer applied. From then on, the Jewish population of England burgeoned. The old animosities flared up from time to time, but again successive kings set out to gain from their presence. Jewish finance helped put William III on the throne in place of James II. Once concentrated in London, they established new communities in other prosperous towns. Around the end of the eighteenth century there were probably between 6,000 and 8,000 Jews in England, mostly in London; by the middle of that century, the total had reached something like 50,000 – and most had been born here. That continuing growth was accelerated by the flight from Russia and Poland in the 1880s as their freedom to live as Jews, or even in time of pogrom to live at all, was savagely diminished by Tsarist governments. It was people like these who took refuge in Quaker Street, Spitalfields, huddled together in often unsavoury tenements, and because of their very profusion, importing the way of life they had known in their native lands, as so lovingly portrayed in the novels of Israel Zangwill.

There were two main strands of Jewish relocation in England:

the Sephardis, who came mostly from Spain and Portugal, and were more sophisticated and more well-to-do, more likely to find their way into the higher echelons of English society, and longstanding users of surnames; and the Ashkenazis, originally from Germany, but now refugees from the countries around it where they had so numerously settled. Their communities had remained largely strangers to surnames until in the last years of the eighteenth century and the early decades of the nineteenth, government after government across Europe required their adoption, sometimes allowing a choice, and at others, imposing them (some of the methods they used are described in Chapter 7). Those coming to England without surnames, like the greater numbers who went to the United States, were now bound to adopt them. Where Sephardic Jews often owed their surnames to their places of origins, Ashkenazim were more likely to have names they had chosen for their decorative properties, like those that begin with Rose- or Gold-. Thus the surname Ashkenazi, indicating a place of origin, is a Sephardi not an Ashkenazi surname. Rothschild, the name of one of Britain's most affluent and influential Jewish clans, is, however, Ashkenazi.

*

To assess how migrants brought in new names to augment and enliven our national stock, I looked at the record the census taker made when he turned from Grey Eagle Street into Quaker Street in 2 April 1911. His spelling and comprehension skills were about to be taxed to the limit.

> **48**: three households, 17 people. The Goldsteins, Marks and Annie, three children, and a servant called Polly Fosh. The Kensoffs, Abraham and Rachel, four children. The Suffesteins, Max and Fannie, three children. All six parents born in Russia, all ten children in London.

50: The Weiners, Judah, a tailor, and Rebecca, both born in Russia; five children all born in London.

52: three households, 16 people. The Herrings, Samuel and Deborah, Russian born, three children born in London. The Stoloffs, Berrolf and Becca, Russian born, two children born in London; also Max Iron, boarder, born in Russia. The Levys, Abraham and Kitty with four children: all born in London, but the parents look to be second-generation immigrants and Abraham is probably the son of a man next door.

54: The older Levys: Lewis and Sarah, born in Poland; two sons in their twenties, born in London. The Goodmakers, Morris and Leha, and a seven-year-old daughter, all Russian born, plus a daughter born in London.

56: three households, 15 people: the Nakovitches: Russian-born parents whose forenames are not given, born in Russia; six children. The Luekses, Moritz and Adela, both born in Austria; three children born in London. The Marchinskys: the widow Millie and her son Solomon, both born in Russia.

58: four households, 21 people: the Millions, Harris and Jessie, and Harris's sister Deby, all born in Russia; a two-year-old daughter, born in London. The Molinskys: Milly, Russian born (her husband is away), four sons and a daughter born in London. The Orlins, Harris and Gittel, born in Russia; four sons and a daughter who have also come from Russia and a son and daughter born in London. The Rukins, Davis, born in Russia, and Deborah, born in Austria.

60: a household of Jablonksys and Lazaruses. Deborah Jablonksy, a grocer, whose husband is absent, with three Jablonsky schoolchildren and three older children surnamed Lazarus, presumably from a former marriage; Deborah was born in Russia, the rest in London. The Godfrieds, Lazarus and Jannie, born Russia and a one-year-old son born in London. Also Henry Lyell, grocery assistant.

62: three households, 15 people. The Reubens, parents born
in Russia as was their 15-year-old daughter; three subsequent
children born in London. The Littlebaums, the parents born
in Russia, two children born in Cardiff and London. The
Lyonses, Sophia, whose husband is absent, and a son and
daughter, all born in Russia: a son-in-law and a nephew,
both Levy, make up an all-Russian household, the largest
in this collection.

At this point the census taker crosses the road and resumes
his note-taking on the other side. The families in the first houses
here conform to the same pattern. Parents and often some
of the children are immigrants, mostly from Russia, but most of
the children have known only England and specifically London.
Most work in tailoring or cabinet-making, some are shoemakers
and some work for furriers, though Harris Orlin's occupation is
listed as 'bottle washer'. At number 47 are two Klatzkins, born
in Russia; four Zuravitskys (he and his wife and his mother from
Russia); four Novogrodas, a Cohen, a Stolbof and a Merkin. Next
door, nine Kiesners, all from Austria; and two Golinskys and a
Bass, all from Russia. And beyond, at 43, eleven Berliners: Lazarus,
from Russia, and Polly, from Poland, with five sons and four
daughters.

Here the pattern abruptly changes. From number 41 onwards,
the names are English, though in a substantial number of cases,
with a hint of Irish origins in surnames like Dacey and Sullivan.
Employments are on average more menial than those of the
immigrant Jews, though some Jewish occupations would have
meant cramped and unhealthy working conditions and no
great income. Some are market traders or dock labourers,
others are listed as box-maker, chocolate-moulder, hawker,
pedlar, charwoman, ironer. And compared with the immigrant
families, a strikingly larger number of their children have died.
Four out of ten children of the Lockharts at 41 have died (Charlotte

Lockhart has also lost her husband: she is thirty-three years old);
five of nine Cooks have died at number 39. Only one of four
Newman children has survived. Samuel Howard, at number 60,
has eight of his children dead, out of ten, and the Woolgars,
next door, in their sixties, have lost four of their seven. The
widow Emma Lewis, who is fifty-one, has seen the deaths of six
of her ten children. Among immigrant families only the
Lezarovitches, who at 42 and 40 have lost three of nine children,
and the Pogalankos, at numbers 40 and 38, who have lost three
of ten, have been as severely afflicted, but there are still four sons
to pass on the surname.

Nearly all those households in the English–Irish group are
London-born, though sandwiched between them are two unexpected couples. Among sixteen people crammed into number 25
are Morris Steinochneider, a Russian-born hawker, and Dinah
Wakeman, described (a rare event in a census) as his mistress;
and the Lindicks at 21, both Russian-born.

Then from number 13 we are back with immigrant Jewish
families: the Mundlacks (Russian), the Rosenbergs (Russian), the
Browns (Russian, but the name has been Anglicised); the Anes
and the Josephs (Russian), the Hoffmans (he from Romania, she
from Russia), the Schneiders and Jacobses and Kochinskys and
Goldbergs and Savins and Jubiks and Bernsteins, Cohens,
Lachinskys and Ritterbunds, all Russian; the Pollocks, who despite
their name are Russian, as are the Sackoffs, the Gorallicks, the
Hymans, the Pogalankos, the Myerses, the Grandishes and
the Oppenheims, who came to Spitalfields via Glasgow and
Manchester. The Lezarovitches are recent arrivals from Romania.

In all, there are thirty-four houses in these two groups where
surnames indicate immigrant families, in which are fifty-six
households composed of 318 people. Almost a quarter of all men
and women living in this street, both in its immigrant and its
English/Irish segments, have come from Russia, bringing with
them surnames, almost all Ashkenazi, some of which, given the

pattern of subsequent movement to outer suburbs, can be expected in time to spread across what is now Greater London too. In the 2011 census, the Jewish component in the borough of Tower Hamlets, of which Spitalfields is part, is extremely modest: 0.5 per cent of all present. In 2011, the highest concentration of Jewish people was in the London borough of Barnet, which includes Hendon and Golders Green, at 15.2 per cent, a long way ahead of Hackney (6.3 per cent), Camden (4.5 per cent) and Harrow (4.4 per cent).

For Ritterbund, read Begum

Hitler's assault on the Jews brought further waves of refugees to Britain before the Second World War – to London, but not only to London. Manchester and Leeds especially had long housed large and vibrant Jewish communities: Jewish families founded many of their most substantial businesses. Sir Montague Burton, 'the tailor of taste', born Moshe Osinsky, was a refugee from Lithuania who came to Manchester in 1900 and started as a pedlar there, built up a network of shops, and became a manufacturer employing thousands in his factories in east Leeds. The tightest clusters of Jewish families in that city were at first in an area known as the Leylands, in the north-east corner of the city centre. As families grew more affluent, they moved out to form new communities on or close to the Harrogate Road which runs north out of the city; first in Chapeltown, where a grand synagogue was built in 1932, supplanting the former chief synagogue in the middle of town at New Briggate, and then through Chapel Allerton into Moortown, Moor Allerton, and finally Alwoodley. In Leeds, if you live in Alwoodley, it is taken to mean that you've made it.

Some names by now were Anglicised, particularly those which had seemed to say German as well as Jewish (see Chapter 7). A good source for Leeds Jewish surnames is the records of its Hill Top cemeteries where the most prominent include ones you'd expect and some you might not. Here Sephardi and Ashkenazi surnames mix. Among the most conspicuous are Abrahams, Benjamin, Bernstein, Black, Cohen, Freedman, Frieze, Goldberg, Goldman, Goodman, Harris, Hyman, Levi and Levy, Marks (Marks and Spencer began in Leeds), Rosenberg, Simon and Taylor. Some, like Abrahams and Benjamin, are distinctly biblical: Cohen and Levi often, but not always, refer to priestly castes; Freedman too comes from an Ashkenazi word for a priest; Frieze may indicate an origin in Friesland. The prefix Gold- means the same as it does in English; the same applies to Rose-. Hyman comes from an Ashkenazi given name, Khayim, and Marks from the German name Mark. Taylor is quite often an Anglicised name adopted in migrant communities.

Where Leeds and Manchester particularly attracted Jewish incomers, port cities like Bristol and Cardiff were always favoured destinations for immigrant communities with their crops of imported names. By the early twentieth century, Tiger Bay in Cardiff alone had over forty separate contingents from Europe, the Middle East, Africa and the Caribbean. As a west coast port, Liverpool was the first landing place for many Irish migrants, and though Irish names today are scattered throughout the country, the greatest concentrations are in Merseyside or close to it. This explosion began in the late eighteenth century. On the evidence of a city directory, the number of distinctively Irish names in Liverpool rose from fifteen in 1766 to eighty in 1781. A steady inflow developed into a flood through the great potato famine of 1846–52. It was estimated that in 1846, more than a quarter of a million disembarked here from Ireland, though more than 100,000 continued their journeys, mostly to America. Many of those who went no further found poor lodgings and impoverished lives in the areas around the Vauxhall and Scotland roads.

This was one immigrant group which did not swiftly set about changing its names. At the 1881 census the most common names in the city were Jones, Smith and Williams, but fourth in line was Murphy, the name of nearly 1,800 inhabitants, and sixth, with 1,600, was Kelly. According to the analysis of the census by British Surnames and Surname Profiles, names particularly concentrated in Liverpool were Kehoe, Melia, Sinnott, Kinsella, Bolger/Bulger, Maher, Kearns, McCabe and Redmond. One recent estimate suggests that three quarters of people in Liverpool have Irish origins.

There are many guides to Britain's top surnames on the internet, some with marked variations from others, but the most up-to-date list is still dominated by names – Smith and Jones, Williams, Brown, Taylor and Davies – which were top in the 1850s. The only change in the top ten since then is that Wilson has edged out Roberts (see Appendix 1). Lower down, though, the names have been churning, with new ones from migrant communities beginning to make their mark. On the latest available survey, the name Patel (a predominantly Gujurati name, implying a landowner or village chief) has risen to fortieth place. Ahmed (derived from Mohammed), Ali (Arabic: high exalted, protected by God), Khan (a great ruler: from Turkey or possibly Mongolia) and Singh are also advancing. Singh has two functions: it can be an honorific or nickname as well as a surname. Mohammed fails to make the list only because it has so many variations: those in London include Mahmad, Mahmed, Mahmood, Mahmud, Mahmuud, Mahmout, Mahomed, Mohamas, Mohamed, Mohammad, Mohammed, Mohamood, Mohamoud and Mohamud. It's another sign of our changing times, however, that the name that has most advanced in the decade to 2012 is Zhang.

Because migrants seek the security of living close to each other, their names tend to occur in tight geographical clusters. You can see this if you plot the whereabouts of Patels in two cities with high populations from ethnic minorities. Of the sixty-two Patels I found in the Bradford directory, twenty-nine were living in postal district 7, to the west of the city centre, and five more beyond it in Clayton. The Patels of Blackburn are even more tightly concentrated, with sixty-seven out of ninety-one to be found in postal district BB1 south-east of the centre and all but one of the rest in BB2.

But though Patel is the name people most often cite, others outnumber it in areas of high immigrant concentration. Four names that comfortably outnumber Patel in Bradford are Ahmed, Ali, Hussain and Khan. Again they are clustered in particular postal districts, but not always in the same postal district. Immigrants arrive from different areas and settle in different places. District 8, north of the centre, off Manningham Lane, has the most representatives from all five surnames, followed by district 7, west of the centre, and district 3, to the north-east. The Khans are strongest in districts 3 and 8; the Hussains in 3, 8 and 9 westward from Manningham; the Ahmeds and Alis in 8 and 9. The concentration of Patels in district 7 alone is unusual. But districts 1, 4 and 6 show no sizeable clusters of people from the sub-continent, and district 10, north-north-east around Idle, shows none at all.

In the 2011 census returns for Tower Hamlets, of which Brick Lane is part, the proportion of residents of Tower Hamlets describing themselves as Muslim was 34.5 per cent; almost a quarter of residents there had a main language other than English, though this was lower than Waltham Forest where the figure was 27.4. That implied a crop of appropriate surnames, and the electoral register of 2011, a hundred years after the last available census evidence, abundantly confirms that. Quaker Street is once more a mix of names familiar and unfamiliar (though becoming less unfamiliar) but with names that appear to derive from the Indian sub-continent accounting for as many as three quarters of them. English names like Nelson and Tomlinson are there, along with others that suggest other countries of Europe, but the most numerous now are the names you would expect in streets so close to Brick Lane. Begum is the most prolific, followed by

Ahmed, Miah and Khan. No sign today of all those thronging Jablonksys and Jubiks and Ritterbunds.

Yet these are only a few of the migrant arrivals who have brought fresh surnames to Britain. Material from the 2011 census, published late in 2012, shows how heavily communities from many lands have established themselves in big British cities. Manchester now claims to compete with London for the title of the most cosmopolitan of British cities, with 150 separate languages said to be spoken there. But there's still nothing to match the numbers in London.

Many immigrants like to live close to people from the same homeland, as the Russian and Polish Jews did in Spitalfields – even if, when better settled, they like to migrate to less disadvantaged addresses. Korea, with whose surnames I opened this book, is sturdily represented in the south-western suburb of New Malden; a fact which burst on the world outside Malden when joyful celebrations took place to celebrate South Korea's success in reaching the semi-finals of the 2002 World Cup. The *Daily Telegraph* reported:

New Malden has never seen anything like it. World Cup fever Korean-style – a mixture of extreme passion and extraordinary politeness – erupted in the Surrey suburb yesterday as South Korea knocked Spain out of the tournament to enter the semi-finals.

The streets of New Malden, known as Little Seoul by the 10,000 Koreans who have made it their home, were filled with shouting fans as soon as the ball from the winning penalty hit the back of the net.

Waving flags and banging on traditional pok drums, they danced in the streets and filed around the fountain roundabout on the High Street, which had already been temporarily closed to traffic by the police.

All around the chant of 'Dae han minkug' or 'South

Korea, South Korea' could be heard, as fans waved their
flags, men in red bandannas jumped up and down.

The three local celebrators whom the *Telegraph* stopped in the
street for interviews all had the surname Kim.

Similar large-scale arrivals were already well known elsewhere
in London: the Turks, for instance, in Hackney and still more in
Haringey, their presence sometimes evident in the names above
shop doors. The biggest surge in arrivals from any single country
recorded in 2011 was the Polish contingent, up nearly 900 per
cent in a decade. Polish newcomers appeared to be more scattered: specialist Polish shops opened up in a string of boroughs.
But here, too, there were favourite destinations, headed by Ealing,
Haringey, Brent, Hounslow, Waltham Forest and Barnet, with
new surnames to swell the phone book and, for a time at least,
to baffle the locals.

*

To get the full panoply of surnames in London I took a telephone
directory covering the capital and opened a page at random. It
would not be right to suppose that new names are usurping the
place of traditional ones, since names which have always dominated these pages do so still: it's just that new ones have joined
them. Among those with numbers enough to occupy one or
more pages, unshared with any other surname, I found:

Adams, Ali, Allen, Anderson, Bailey, Baker, Barker, Bell,
Brook/Brooke, Brown, Campbell, Clark/Clarke, Collins,
Cook/Cooke, Cooper, Davies/Davis, Edwards, Ellis, Evans,
Graham, Gray, Green, Griffith/Griffiths, Hall, Harris, Harrison,
Hill, Hughes, Hussain/Hussein, Jackson, James, Jenkins,
Johnson, Jones, Kelly, Khan, King, Lawrence, Lee, Lewis,
Macdonald and variants, Marshall, Martin, Mason, Miller,

Moore, Morgan, Morris, Murphy, Murray, Newman, O'Brien, Palmer, Parker, Simmons/Simmonds, Simpson, Smith, Spence/Spencer, Stewart, Sullivan, Taylor, Thomas, Thompson, Turner, Walker, Ward, Watson, West, White, Williams, Wilson, Wood, Wright, Young.

But here, in all its colourful glory, is my list of names from page 708 of the 1997 all-London phone book. Many are multiple entries, and the highest scoring of those are shown with their totals in brackets. (As with all these lists of surnames taken from phone books, mobile phone numbers are excluded to avoid duplication.)

Hlamyo, Hlavacek, Hlawaty, Hlongwane, Hl-Zawahy, Hmura, Hnablett, Hnatiw, Ho (114), Hoa, Hoad, Hoadbo, Hoadley, Hoadly, Hoaglang-Grey, Hoahing, Hoang (97), Hoar, Hoare (144), Horeau, Hoare-Temple, Hoarty, Hoath, Hoather, Ho-a-Yun, Hoban, Hobart, Hobb, Hobberstad.

The following page includes 233 Hobbses and 74 Hobsons, and closes with Hobstetter, Hoca, Hocalar, Hocaoglu, Hoccum, Hoces, Hoch, Hochar, Hochauser, Hochberg, Hochberger, Hochbergs, Hochdorf, Hoche, Hocherman, Hochfeld, Hochhauser, Hochleitner, Hochnauser, Hochner and Hochnetz. The Qs are a joy. Also the Zs, culminating in Zzaman, a name that might have been contrived to be last in the book – and possibly was.

Sweet are the uses of diversity.

4

Excavations

Why is our Name Bultitude, Mummy?

'Sir Jasper Finch-Farrowmere?' said Wilfred.
'ffinch-ffarowmere,' corrected the visitor,
his sensitive ear detecting the capitals.
P. G. Wodehouse, 'A Slice of Life'

Into the valley of doubt

But what do they tell us, all these assorted names from the standard British repertoire, Norman and Viking, long or short, simple or double-barrelled, alluring or – as we shall see – sometimes vaguely repellent? No one knows for certain quite how many there are in Britain today, though Steve Archer's work on the 1881 census suggests there were more than 400,000 then. How did their possessors come by them? And what meaning did they convey?

In a sense, the correct academic answers here do not tell the full story. If you'd asked in these Broughton villages a century back, you might have been given answers that wouldn't appear in any reference book. These names said more to local people in a time when localness was the essence of life than simply the family to which they belonged; they evoked a man or woman's role in the community. Look up Morgan in *The Oxford Names Companion* and it will tell you the name is an ancient one, to be found most of all in Wales, its second syllable suggesting the old Celtic *cant*, a circle. But in Broughton, Hampshire, the first sense

'Morgan' was likely to convey was 'a carrier'. Not all Morgans were carriers – some were shopkeepers – but the principal village carriers were Morgans. 'Beachem' (which later on became Beauchamp) implied a thatcher. To say 'Hinwood' was to say 'shopkeeper'. The name 'Judd', according to Dr Parr's history of the village, suggested a card, a character, sometimes a bad character: 'they had several black sheep'. They live on, he says, in the village's comic anecdotes.

Like the name Hinwood in Hampshire, the name Frearson in Furness evoked shopkeeping, but because some had grown up in Australia, when so few in the place had come from even as far away as Manchester, it must also have said 'unusual', 'different', 'extraordinary' and 'cosmopolitan'. In many villages, the trade of blacksmith passed from father to son and to grandson. The smith might have been born a Jones, a Taylor, a McGillicuddy or a Satterthwaite; but whatever the name he was born with might be, it now had the smell of the forge about it.

Of course, had you asked some dabbling antiquary like the Reverend Mr Tringham in Hardy's novel, whose unsolicited advice to her father inadvertently determines the tragic fate of Tess of the D'Urbervilles, you'd have got an answer that sounded authoritative. But it still might well not have been right. The onomastic techniques needed to excavate the history and the geography of names simply did not exist in the time in which *Tess* is set. Today, of course, Mr Tringham could have read it all up on the internet: but that, as we shall see, is not error-proof either.

A search for the sources and impact of names begins with the work of anthropologists. If only such folk had existed when names of all kinds began to be used in Britain's primeval periods, we would know a lot more about their significance then, but there's plenty of evidence to demonstrate how primitive societies viewed name as of supreme importance, even of holiness, and we may perhaps be entitled to deduce an early status of surnames in Britain from that.

It used to be the practice, and in some cultures still is, for a person's name to be changed at a turning point in life, much as Abram in the Old Testament is recast as Abraham, and Saul in the New after his vision on the road to Damascus becomes Paul. This reverence for the essence of a name existed in Britain too. The great historian of Anglo-Saxon England, Sir Frank Stenton, chronicled 'the late survival in the north of the belief that the soul of an individual was represented or symbolised by his name and that the bestowal of a name was a means of calling up the spirit of the child to whom it was given'.

What is clear from studies along the line from Sir James George Frazer's *The Golden Bough* to the most recent collections of studies of naming practice in places like Madagascar and the Philippines is that names were believed to be integral to the very essence of those who bore them: so much that in some societies still they must not in any circumstances be revealed, since once your name is known to them, your enemies, and the evil spirits which forever lurk about you, will have you in their power. In Mongolia, a name is entirely personal to its user; if a newcomer enters the community giving the identical name, he or she must find a replacement for it. There must not be duplication. It is also considered wrong to say the name of an ancestor, since this will disturb their spirits. One safeguard in such societies has been to publish a name which wasn't your real one: something obviously ugly or silly would serve.

The same theme is familiar in myth and legend. The knight Lohengrin appears in a boat drawn by a swan to rescue the beautiful heiress of Brabant, Elsa, from her enemies. He only has power to do this if she chokes back her curiosity and never asks him his name. Mocked by her friends for not knowing the name of her lover, she asks him. The swan reappears and sweeps him away. At the other end of the scale, the dwarf Rumpelstiltskin is only safe while the miller's daughter cannot discover his name. When she does, he loses his power over her and destroys himself.

The Greeks used names which also sought to embody some

essence of their possessors – or of what they might one day become. Plato has a dispute between two learned figures divided over the significance of names. Hermogenes holds that names are arbitrary, really no more than labels. Cratylus insists that names must be expressive and meaningful. There are echoes of this debate in much that has been written and spoken about names ever since. Another notable philosopher discusses it in a book by Charles Lutwidge Dodgson:

> 'Don't stand chattering to yourself like that,' Humpty Dumpty said, looking at her for the first time, 'but tell me your name and your business.'
>
> 'My name is Alice, but—'
>
> 'It's a stupid name enough!' Humpty Dumpty interrupted impatiently. 'What does it mean?'
>
> '*Must* a name mean something?' Alice asked doubtfully.
>
> 'Of course it must,' Humpty Dumpty said with a short laugh: '*my* name means the shape I am – and a good handsome shape it is, too. With a name like yours, you might be any shape, almost.'

Charles Lutwidge Dodgson's other name was Lewis Carroll.

It was left to the Romans to systematise naming practice. In time, a man would come to bear three names: praenomen, nomen and cognomen. Thus we get Marcus Tullius Cicero, Gaius Julius Caesar. The nearest to a surname element here is the middle one (Julius). That told you what *gens* or clan someone belonged to. The cognomen narrowed that down to the branch of the *gens* involved: the Caesar branch. The praenomen (Gaius) was the name you were given. His father was a Gaius too.

In Britain before the Conquest, the name that embodies the essence or hoped-for essence of the child to which it was given often combined two prayed-for virtues: thus Godwine invokes the concept of God and friend; Athelstan links 'noble' with 'stone'. And although the old religious veneration has gone, one's name, for long afterwards, is inseparable from one's reputation: 'a good name is better than precious ointment,' congregations were told as the preacher quoted Ecclesiastes, which is much what Shakespeare's Iago says as he tries to unsettle Othello:

> Good name in man and woman, dear my lord,
> Is the immediate jewel of their souls:
> Who steals my purse steal trash; 'tis something, nothing;
> 'Twas mine, 'tis his, and has been slave to thousands;
> But he that filches from me my good name
> Robs me of that which not enriches him,
> And makes me poor indeed.

At about the same time, William Camden was including, among a collection of proverbs in his *Remaines*, the line: 'He that hath an ill name is half hanged.'

The blight on a name will fall not only on the man who incurred it but on succeeding generations. Achitophel in Dryden – written around sixty years after *Othello* – has become 'a name to *all ages* curst'. The fiercest rebuke Tom Tulliver can address to his sister Maggie in George Eliot's *The Mill on the Floss* is to say that she has degraded his father's name. Tess in Hardy's novel tells Angel Clare that she has considered killing herself but denied herself that escape because of the harm it would do to his name. That sense of a name survives. In February 2013, a man called Christopher Dorner, who had been sacked by the Los Angeles police department five years earlier, killed three people and wounded others in a planned act of revenge. He had threatened that he would do so. Accusing the department of racism and deception in his dismissal, he warned: 'You're going to see what a whistleblower can do when you take everything from him, especially his NAME.'

*

The Conquest linked Britain to a pattern of naming already developing on the other side of the Channel in which a name was linked with an identification usually based on a place of origin: de Warenne, de Burgh, de Lacy, de Vere. Thereafter the practice spread slowly and patchily: the upper classes before the lower; the south, especially London, before the north; and Wales last of all. One can watch this process at work in the charts of rectors and vicars that hang in so many churches. Here is a list of early incumbents from the wall of All Saints, Broughton, Cambridgeshire:

1266 Adam de Fenton
1290 John de Sutton
1311 William de Corton
1316 Henry de Benford
1399 Nicholas de Kersyngton
1342 John Horston
1349 William de Buckingham
     Henry Atte Woode
1368 Thomas Cook
1368 Robert de Lynlye or Hinke
1370 Thomas Kymble

Kymble, and all the names that come after it, look like authentic surnames. Horston, thirty years before, may or may not have had an inherited, transmissible name. But Cook looks to be a true surname. The rector is unlikely to have earned a living by cooking, so this cannot be a temporary occupational designation. Robert de Lynlye, like many men of this time, had alternative names. The de Lynlye looks back; the Hinke may well look forward, may instate itself as an authentic surname, as Kymble may well have been. Hinke, a name that rarely occurs nowadays, probably derives from a medieval personal name. Kymble, nowadays more often Kimble, is thought to be a variant of an Anglo-Saxon name meaning 'bold family'.

Why surnames began to spread is no mystery. They did so out of necessity. Their purpose was to differentiate, something all the more urgent when men's forenames after the Conquest dwindled down to a precious few: John, William, Roger, Richard, but not much else. The old composite names of pre-Conquest days, like Aethelred (noble counsel) and Godwine (God's friend), had fallen into disfavour: Norman forenames, as now adopted, offered a much less lavish choice. In his essential book *Family Names and Family History*, David Hey says that poll tax returns for Sheffield in 1379 show 715 men sharing a mere twenty forenames. A third (236) were called John; add William (137) and more than half of these Sheffield men had one of two forenames. So you needed, especially for the purposes of law and other requirements for written records, but also in common intercourse, to find ways of telling one John from another.

That, as we know from Dylan Thomas, and from hundreds of other sources, is relevant still across swathes of Britain. In Wales, where the spread of names is so restricted, one has to find a way of sorting Dai from Dai and Jones from Jones. A BBC local radio station collected a wealth of such names from its readers. A miner was so often absent that he became known as Dai Sick Note. An undertaker in Aberdare was known as Dai Death, and another, in Penygraig, as Dai Coffin. In Llanhilleth, Thomas Thomas was known as Tommy Twice – though a latter-day schoolboy with the same name was called Dai Sat Nav (after the trade name Tom Tom). In New Tredegar, a Jones who lived by a lamp-post was known as Dai Lamppost – by exactly the same process of differentiation that led to one of the fourteenth-century rectors at Broughton in Cambridgeshire being known as Henry atte Wood. There is said to have been a man familiarly known as Dai Bungalow because 'he had nothing upstairs'. The columnist Richard Boston claimed to know of a Welshman who lost all his teeth bar one in the middle on top and one in the middle below, whereafter he was known as Jones Central Eating.

And it isn't only in Wales that such problems occur. There would have been two famous movie actors called James Stewart had one not amended his name to Stewart Granger. The comedian Paul Merton was born Paul Martin but when he applied to Equity they said they already had an actor registered under that name. So he called himself Merton after the part of London where he grew up. The *Guardian* uses two writers called Stephen Moss, and two called Duncan Campbell. In 2013, Leeds United (soccer) and Leeds Rhinos (rugby league) were both being managed by men called Brian McDermott. At one time, Gateshead Football Club, then of the Football League, used to field two players both called Ken Smith. They had to be named on the programme as Ken Smith 1 and Ken Smith 2. (That was before the days when the crowd might have raised the now familiar cry: 'There's only one Ken Smith.' In this case it would have been demonstrably untrue.)

If you did not make the distinction, someone would make it for you. That is what generally happened with nicknames: they were not names you invented yourself. People surely wouldn't have chosen to call themselves Swetinbedde or Gawkrodger (Roger who walked in a gawky way). Names were bestowed for other reasons too: sometimes, perhaps if you brought a newborn child to the church the parson, failing to elicit a surname, might make one up and record it as yours.

Even so, according to *Surnames, DNA, and Family History* by George Redmonds, Turi King and David Hey, a book published in 2011 whose importance will be stressed later on, even outside the north and the Scottish lowlands, people still went without surnames three centuries after the Conquest. The practice came last to Wales, which even after the union with England between 1536 and 1543 continued to go its own way, distinguishing, for example, one of the proliferating Morgans as Morgan ap Llewellyn ap Jevan ap Jenkin. All of these varying practices left a legacy of issues for scholars of various aptitudes to unravel.

And pleasingly, the first in the field, also from the sixteenth century, can still be considered one of the best.

Swimming in uncharted waters

In the south aisle of Westminster Abbey, close to a memorial to the actor David Garrick, just across the way from John Dryden, and within nodding distance of Chaucer and of his own great contemporary, Shakespeare, there's an imposing plaque to commemorate the first notable analyst and disentangler of the mysteries of surnames in Britain. Like his own most famous work, the inscription is written in Latin, which being translated, says: *William Camden, Clarenceux King of Arms, who illustrated the British Antiquities, by ancient truth and indefatigable industry, and adorned his innate simplicity with useful literature, and illustrated his pleasantness of humour with candour and sincerity, lies here quietly, in hopes of a certain resurrection in Christ. He died 9 November 1623, aged 74.*

Since one should not wish to build false hopes among today's onomasticians it ought to be said that he didn't attain this eminence for his studies of names alone. It much more reflects the success of a book called *Britannia*, begun in 1577, the year he turned twenty-six, and completed more than a decade later. It's a kind of inventory of the nation, exploring its history from earliest times but also its geography – augmented in subsequent editions with maps by Christopher Saxton and John Norden. The aim of the exercise, as he explains in a preface, is 'To renew ancientrie, enlighten obscuritie, cleare doubts, recall home veritie by way of recovery, which the negligence of writers and credulitie of the common sort had in a manner proscribed and utterly banished from among us.' He embarked on the project, he says, with a mixture of fear and boldness (no bad blend, I think, for any aspiring writer): 'by the most gratious direction of the Almighty, taking industrie for my consort, I adventured upon it, and with all my studie, care, cogitation, continuall meditation, paine and travaile employed my selfe thereunto when I had spare time'; which spare time must have been limited by his successive employments as teacher and later headmaster of Westminster School, and as Clarenceux King of Arms. He learned both Welsh and Old English. It's a mark of his industry, too, that he has something to say about most of my English Broughtons, some of which he may have charted himself on his extensive travels – undertaken at a time when travel around the land was dauntingly difficult – and some of which would have been gathered from assiduous correspondents eager to contribute to his project.

And when at last all the 'studie, care, cogitation, continuall meditation, paine and travaile' were done, he had still had precious material left which hadn't got into *Britannia*. This he deployed in a further, lighter work which, believing in names free from obfuscation, he called *The Remaines Concerning Britain*: a book full of wisdom, wit and irresistible charm, whose findings on surnames would not be greatly enhanced for centuries afterwards.

His classification of surnames is reflected in modified form in the categories used in standard books and websites today. As I said at the start, the basic pattern is fourfold. Camden has sub-divisions. Where today they would be logged together as nicknames, Camden distinguishes between the kind of name applied to a man by his neighbours – Short, for instance, Tall, Lean or Stout – and what he calls nurse-names, affectionately bestowed on small children which had stuck to them ever since.

Camden is full of good sense. He warns against easy conclusions. He knows that the spread of surnames begins only after the Conquest. Among the Normans, he says, 'it seemed a disgrace for a Gentleman to have but one single name, as the meaner sorte and bastards had'. He tells people with apparently old Norman surnames, who claim to be able to trace themselves back to the Conquest, that they're often deceiving themselves. The direct links they like to parade are too often based on illusion. They're by no means alone in that. 'Some English men and Scottish men', he says, 'like the Arcadians, think their surnames as ancient as the Moone, or at least to reach many an age beyond the Conquest.' Or again: 'Whatsoever some of their posteritie do overweene of the antiquities of their names, as though in the continual mutability of the worlde, conversions of states, and fatall periods of families, five hundred years were not sufficient antiquitie for a family or name, when as but very few have reached thereunto.'

He knows how names vary from region to region, quoting a verse he has heard in Cornwall – now familiar in a different form – as an example of how, as he says, 'In England and Scotland, every town village or hamlet hath afforded names to families.'

> By Tre, Ros, Pol, Lan, Caer and Pen
> You may know the most Cornish men.

He detects – which many twentieth-century writers, with far more research devices at their disposal, confirm – that many names derive from place names that have long since vanished. Who, he asks, would imagine that Whitegift, Powlet, Creping, Trivulet, Antrobus, Heather, Hartshorn and many like them were local names? 'And yet most certainly they are.' He knows that (unjustified pretensions again) some people claim that the names of places derive from their family names, when in fact it was the other way around: 'if any should affirm that the Gentlemen named Leffington, Wilburton, Lancaster or Leicester, Bossevil, or Shordich, gave the names to places so named, I would humbly, without prejudice, crave respite for a further day before I beleeved them.' He knows also that, as he puts it, 'the Tyran Time which has swallowed many names, hath also, in use of speech, changed more by contacting, syncopating, curtelling and modifying them': to which he appends a long list of examples.

Further, he knows that many occupational names refer to

trades that, even then, had already gone: 'neither was there any trade, craft, art, profession or occupation never so mean, but had a name among us commonly ending in Er . . . but some are worn out of use, and therefore the significators are unknown, and others have been mollified, ridiculously by the bearers, lest they seem vilified by them.' (The essentially kindly Camden nevertheless severely disapproves here and elsewhere of people tampering with the names they have inherited.) And he knows that some men owe their names to employers who made names up for them: maritime names, for instance, such as Keele, Ballast, Planke, Fore-decke, Decke, Loope-hole, Rudden, Gable, Misensaile, Capson and Maste.

*

Many years pass before there is any real advance on Camden. 'It is strange how little has been written upon the sources and significations of our English surname,' says the preface of a book on such sources and significations, published in 1873. Much of the enquiry during the second half of the nineteenth century was the work of dabblers, obsessives or propagandists whose findings tended fatally to reflect their preconceptions. Robert Ferguson, mill-owner, Liberal MP for Carlisle, and author of *The Shadow of the Pyramid: a Series of Sonnets*, was a bit of all three. His studies of Northmen in Cumberland and Westmorland reflected an obsession with things Teutonic which led to a book called *The Teutonic Name-System* (published in 1864 and later modified for a more general readership in his *Surnames as a Science*, 1883), of which a later and wiser expert, Ernest Weekley, observed that he seemed to assume that names had leapt straight from the Twilight of the Gods to the London commercial directory. A contemporary of Ferguson was scarcely kinder. 'Like the rest of us who explore the mazes of nominal etymology,' he wrote, 'this author sometimes falls into a bog or quagmire, visible to all eyes but his own.'

This was Mark Antony Lower (1813–76), one of six sons of a man he described as 'a schoolmaster of the old-fashioned middle-class of his profession', who, without being a scholar, 'was a man of varied attainments'. Lower was a respected historian of Sussex, establishing himself with a book which he entitled with his characteristic loquacity: '*Sussex: Being an Historical, Topographical, and General Description of every Rape, Hundred, River, Town, Borough, Parish, Village, Hamlet, Castle, Monastery, and Gentleman's Seat in that County. Alphabetically Arranged. With the Population of each Parish, according to the Census of 1821, and other useful and curious Information. With a correct Map of the County.* By Mark Antony Lower. Printed for the Author, and sold by R. W. Lower, High Street, Lewes; W. Leppard, East Street, Brighton; and all Booksellers in the County. Mdcccxxxi.' 'The registered pedigree of the Lowers of Cornwall,' the bearer of their name writes proudly, 'carries them back to about the time of John or Henry III.' In Sussex, it dates back to around the time of Henry VIII, but unhappily Mark Antony has not been able to link this clan with the older Cornish one. The 2005 edition of the *Oxford Dictionary of English Surnames*, however, links it less grandly with 'ewer', an Old French term for 'a servant who supplied guests at a table with water to wash their hands'.

A teacher, Low Church in religion and radical in his politics, Lower produced two books on names: *Patronymica Britannica*, 1860 – a title knowingly echoing Camden – and *English Surnames*, 1875. An endearing picture of him, classically patriarchal and flaunting the kind of beard you could hide an owl in, can be found in *Patronymica Britannica*. The trouble with Lower is that his well-earned reputation as the historian of Sussex seems to have gone to his hirsute head. This leads him into bogs and quagmires of his own. Ernest Weekley, castigator of Ferguson, tartly remarks of Lower's study of surnames that he's largely reliable so long as he sticks to Sussex.

Lower is sometimes censorious. Like Camden, but much more

sharply, he criticises those, some of whom he no doubt encountered in substantial houses in Sussex, who mess about with their names or invent unlikely sources for them. The name Beauchamp, he complains, has been 'vilely corrupted to Beacham'. This conclusion had perhaps also been reached by a lowlier figure than Lower in the neighbouring county of Hampshire, where a Broughton thatcher hitherto known as Beacham, having married a woman called Harriet Castle, began to call himself Beauchamp, which is pronounced the same way. His neighbours may have thought this an affectation. But Lower would have commended him.

The name Cholmondeley, this author finds, derives from a lordship in Cheshire. 'I cannot refrain from reprobating,' says Lower (whose prose sometimes evokes less Mark Antony than the yet to be invented Pooter of George and Weedon Grossmith's *Diary of a Nobody*), 'the curt and absurd pronunciation of this name.' (Cholmondeleys like to be addressed as Chumleys.) 'It is strange that some of our most aristocratic families who would not willingly concede one jot of their dignity in other respects, should be willing to have their ancient names thus nicked and mutilated.' St Johns, Fitzjohns, Marjoribankses – all are guilty: 'I would fain have the practice refused altogether.' The philosopher Jeremy Bentham also comes in for some schoolmasterly stick: utilitarian and democrat though he was, he had dreamed up a connection with a high German family and even, wishing to shore up that connection, considered buying property that had belonged to them.

Yet one cannot refrain from noting that in his eccentric quasi-Pooterish way Lower did produce something of value that others better equipped would one day build on: a systematic catalogue running to well over 400 well-packed pages of British names and their possible origins, much fuller than his precursor Camden could ever have managed. He may in places have blundered into some of those bogs and quagmires in which he had spotted Ferguson floundering, but at least he was not setting out to prove a preordained case, Teutonic or otherwise.

The next substantial contributor to this enterprise came to the study of surnames with a reputation for scholarship in an area much more remote from this territory than Lower's Sussex: the botany, anthropology and geology of the South Seas. This was Henry Brougham Guppy, named for another notable orator – the celebrated Lord Chancellor Henry Brougham – and author of *Homes of Family Names in Great Britain* (1890). All Lower had to say of the surname Guppy was: 'Perhaps Old French *goupil*, a fox.' Guppy's version is rather more stately. The name Guppy, he says, had for centuries been prominent in Dorset, especially around South Perrott. He does not explain its provenance, but when later discussing the Guppys of Wiltshire traces the name to a settlement in the parish of Mere. One more recent dictionary thinks it may have derived from a Cornish flower or from the personal name Guppa; but clearly not, it kindly adds, from the tropical fish of the same name, since that was unknown in England until the nineteenth century, when it was given the name in honour of the British naturalist Robert Lechmere Guppy, who had recorded it in Trinidad in 1866.

Where Lower was concerned with the history of our surnames, Guppy was much more involved with their geography. He was the first of these experts who consistently and valuably asked: where are all these surnames located? He fitted them into six categories: general names, found in thirty to forty counties; common names (twenty to twenty-nine counties); regional names (ten to nineteen); district names (four to nine); county names (two or three only); and peculiar names, mostly confined to a single county.

Unusually among writers on surnames, Guppy had a political motive for his researches. His purpose was to tell people charged with making decisions about such matters that when drawing boundaries between states or regions they ought to look first

at the patterns of surnames they found there. Had they done
so, he says, the map of Britain would look very different now.
This theory is less fanciful than it may sound. One surname
expert of our own day, Professor Kevin Schürer of Leicester
University, broadly concurs with this finding. Guppy credibly
argues that when you study the surnames, Scotland north of the
Forth and Clyde is a strikingly different place from Scotland south
of them, which more closely resembles the old Northumbria. In
his view there should now be two Scotlands: Caledonia, north
of the two great rivers; and Lothian to the south – though, while
finding that Lothian names are comparable to those immediately
south of the border, he does not suggest that the border be
redrawn.

In Guppy's surname-based Britain, Mercia would return in the
form of the Midlands, plus Cheshire and Lancashire. The lands
south of the Wash to the Solent would constitute Anglia, while
the south-west, transcending mere Wessex and including the
whole of Wiltshire and Gloucestershire, would make up Devinia.
Not only Monmouthshire, in those days administratively separate
from Wales, but the border lands of Herefordshire and Shropshire
would constitute a new and mightier Wales.

Yet Guppy too is the prisoner of his assumptions. The base on
which his general findings are built is fatally inadequate. His analysis
of names is confined first to the yeoman class, as exemplified
by figures like John Ridd in the *Lorna Doone* stories of
R. D. Blackmore – set in Devon, across the country boundary
from his native Cornwall – and to tenant farmers, because in his
view such people are the backbone of good old England: 'greatness,' he says, 'even though it attains a throne, has always
commenced in the field'. And even then, he confines his explorations to names commanding more than 10,000 entries in Post Office
directories. He believed that this covered a substantial proportion
of the whole stock. He assumed the presence of something above
30,000 surnames in a population of 26 million; we now know from

Steve Archer's researches into the 1881 census – a decade before Guppy wrote – that there were in fact more than 400,000.

So Guppy is no stranger to bogs and quagmires. For all that, he had attempted a form of geographical, or, as surname experts might prefer to say, distributional enquiry, recognising the crucial distinction between names like Smith that occurred all over the nation and those confined to particular tracts of it. He too was a praiseworthy pioneer.

*

There's another significant operator in the closing years of the nineteenth century who, although a more eminent figure than any practitioner in this field since Camden, is rarely mentioned by subsequent students of British surnames, since his interest was in a sense incidental. This was Francis Galton, Charles Darwin's cousin, grandson of Erasmus Darwin, a famously comprehensive student of all kinds of science, an explorer of unknown tracts of Africa, and a meteorologist. He was also essentially driven by his own agenda, which came from his expertise in a field which would later move to the heart of the study of surnames – genetics. In Galton's case, that spilled over into more sinister country: the early days of eugenics, a term which he is credited as having invented.

His book *Hereditary Genius*, published in 1869, examined thirty-one peerages all deriving initially from the ennoblement of senior judges between 1660 and 1840. Nineteen of them remained, he said, but twelve were already extinct. The reason, he found, was that peers had this habit of wedding unsuitable women. Eight of these failures had occurred because eldest surviving sons had married heiresses who enjoyed, and could share, substantial money and fine estates – but could not, however, produce children. 'Although many men of eminent ability . . . have not left descendants behind them, it is not because they are sterile, but because they are apt to marry sterile women; in order to obtain wealth to support the peerages with which their merits have been rewarded. I look upon the peerage as a disastrous institution, owing to its destructive effects on our valuable races.'

Elsewhere he sets out what became a classic eugenicist case. 'There is nothing either in the history of domestic animals or in that of evolution to make us doubt that a race of sane men may be formed, who shall be as much superior mentally and morally to the modern European, as the modern European is to the lowest of the Negro race.' On the lowest estimate, he had calculated, our present national ability was two grades below that of Athenians in their heyday – the same margin of difference as that between us and the American Negro. If only that difference could be narrowed! Instead of the paltry six men of the highest grade now to be found in England, we would house eighty-two. What he wrote attracted the attention of the Reverend Henry William Watson, who brought to the argument an expertise in mathematics that even the polymath Galton lacked. Watson asserted that the extinction of the best in our society was not merely possible, as Galton believed, but likely. It took some time for this well-publicised conclusion to be disproved. Galton would have been still more frightened had he foreseen the loss of so many sons of aristocratic families in the First World War, when at one stage the life expectancy of a young officer at the front – and initially most young officers came from upper-class families – was six weeks.

Galton's fear over what he perceived as the steady erosion of the better races was compounded by his alarm at the rise of the worse ones. A lawless, immoral and rapidly multiplying underclass was on the march. In *Inquiries into Human Faculty and Its Development* (1883), he cites a US example, documented seven years earlier by the Prison Association of New York: some 540 individuals directly descended, legitimately or illegitimately, from a man called Jukes, born around 1730 and described as 'a jolly companionable man, a hunter, and a fisher, averse to steady labour, but working hard and idling by turns', of whom 'a frightful number degraded into criminality, pauperism or disease'. 'The true state of the case,' he warns Victorian England, 'appears to be that the criminal population receives steady accessions from those who, without having strongly marked criminal natures, do nevertheless belong to a type of humanity that is exceedingly ill suited to play a respectable part in our modern civilisation, though it is well suited to flourish under half-savage conditions, being both healthy and prolific.'

Before its uglier implications emerged, eugenics intrigued many 'enlightened' people. Shaw, Keynes, Beveridge, Harold Laski, Bertrand Russell and the writer Rebecca West (whose real name was Cicely Fairfield) would at some point espouse, or at the very least flirt with, the doctrines preached by Galton.

*

In the matter of surnames, less exalted figures than Galton had more of lasting usefulness to contribute. One of these was Charles Wareing Endell Bardsley, parish priest (for a time he was vicar of Ulverston, ten miles from Broughton in Furness, so he had a particular taste for the names of that region), serious scholar, author of *Our English Surnames: Their Sources and Significations* (1873), *A Dictionary of English and Welsh Surnames: with Special American Instances* (1901); also of the entertaining *Curiosities of Puritan Nomenclature* – all those seventeenth-century names jampacked with metaphor, of which the most celebrated is probably Obadiah-bind-their-kings-in-chains-and-their-nobles-in-irons Needham. His books also include a history of the town and church of Ulverston and its surrounding areas, in which he says of the Tysons of Furness (whom we met in such profusion at Broughton): 'like a cloud of locusts our Tysons cover Furness from end to end. Yet they have wandered but little. They are only five in the London directory.' And of their neighbours the Cowards: '[their] present orthography is a libel on their category. For the protection of their charge they would have had to meet the wild boar daily.'

Unlike many country clergy who shared his interest, Bardsley was much more than a dabbler. What he wrote commanded the broad respect of most experts who followed him. He too made a lasting contribution to the understanding of surnames, not least because he was first to establish the importance of metronymic/matronymic surnames (both spellings are used), that is, names which come down from women rather than men. A later eminent expert, Percy H. Reaney, singled him out for commendation in his preface to the Oxford surname dictionary: Bardsley, he said, had 'firmly laid the foundations on which future study of surnames must be built'.

He shares Camden's taste for digressions and fondness for lists. He knows of past people called Blackinthemouth, Blubber, Crookbone, Felon, Hatechrist, Mad, Measle, Milksop, Peckcheese, Pudding and Sweatinbed: names that must have developed as nicknames, from conditions most of which one can easily now imagine. As for Puritan nomenclature, his first interest here is in Christian names, at a time when, as he says, 'there prevailed, amongst a certain class of English religionists, a practice of baptising children by scriptural phrases, pious ejaculations, or godly admonitions'. Yet the combination of these with surnames often gives them a still greater piquancy – as with *Hope-for* Bending; *Faint-not* Blatcher; *Clemency* Chawncey; *Weakly* Ekins; *Vitalis* Engaine; *Preserved* Fish; *Replenish* French; *Humiliation* Hinde; *Safe-on-high* Hopkinson (the child died a few days later); *Sindeny* Outerred; *Hope-still* Peedle; *Kill-sin* Pimple; *Abstinence* Pougher; *Battalion* Shotbolt; *Faithful* Teate; *Thankful* Thorpe; *Continent* Walker; *Repentance* Water. Bardsley notes at this point what was then a more recent practice – familiar now but often wrongly supposed to be a modern disease – giving children names that fit or, in practice, mis-fit, the names they were born with: as in *Nothing* and *Something* New; *Christmas* Carol; *China* Ware; *Lemon* Peel; *Salt* Codd; *Cannon* Ball; *Dunn* Brown; *River* Jordan; and the brothers, *Jolly* and *Sudden* Death.

A few years later, the lure of the surname sucked in Ernest Weekley, professor of Modern Languages at Nottingham, author of *The Romance of Names* (1914), and of *Surnames* (1916). If you have heard of Weekley that may be because of a celebrated early-twentieth-century scandal in which he was innocently involved. D. H. Lawrence, who had been one of his students, came to his house seeking advice. There he met Weekley's wife of a dozen years, mother of his three children, six years Lawrence's senior: Frieda von Richthofen. Before long she and the author of *Women in Love* had decamped, taking the children with them. In a letter to Weekley, Lawrence explained it was all Ernest's fault for being Ernest. 'Mrs Weekley,' he wrote, 'is afraid of being stunted and not allowed to grow, and so she must live her own life. All women in her nature are like giantesses. They will breathe through everything and go on with their lives . . . Mrs Weekley must live largely and abundantly. It is her nature.'

Weekley, though apparently not good enough for Frieda, is admirably thorough. He's aware of the bogs and the quagmires and frequently counsels the caution the lack of which, in his judgement, defaced the work of Lower, and even, on occasion, of Bardsley, as well as of amateur Tringhamite dabblers everywhere. His Camdenesque warnings against the dangers of easy assumptions deserved a posthumous cheer from the south aisle of Westminster Abbey. In the Camden tradition, too, he's a puncturer of pretensions, who knows that the forebears of people called Molyneaux, Napier, ffrench and Coke (pronounced Cook) are not as grand as their present owners would like us to think that they were. Molyneaux was a miller; Napier was a man who worked at a napery, looking after the napkins; Coke, sure enough, was a cook. As for ffrench, the name is simply a kind of accident caused by misreading documents in which 'ff' is used to indicate a capital F.

Some who pride themselves on their names might not do so if they knew more about them, while others whose names now seem a little unfortunate may have a greater reason for pride. Kennedy, he points out, means 'ugly head'. Then there's Lush – a name common in Broughton, Hampshire – which, though some of its bearers may not be aware of the fact, implies, as he says, a drunkard. Yet Belcher, a name that few would clamour to get their hands on, derives from the much more enticing Bel-sire.

Weekley isn't afraid to draw on his private passions. He uses the line-up of a rugby XV in a match between the East Midlands and Kent to illustrate the provenance and variety of the English surname. I applied the same technique to David Cameron's Coalition Cabinet line-up of 2010. Some of the results were disconcerting. If we judged them by the origins of their surnames, we would have to think of Cameron as a man with a crooked nose; of George Osborne as a divine bear; of Eric Pickles as one who lived by a small fold or paddock; and of Vince Cable as a rope-maker. As for Chris Huhne, who in 2013 would face a term of imprisonment after a lurid court case, his name is derived from a German word meaning 'giant', 'monster' or 'bogeyman'.

*

The romantic picture of a lone scholar working away in obscurity who, after a long endeavour, brings fresh and lasting illumination is, however, still better exemplified in the author of a vast, learned and unquestionably obsessional book that appeared at the end of the Second World War. That the standard work on the surnames of Scotland should have been published by New York Public Library seems, on the face of it, odd. But George F. Black worked there for much of his life, and the work that became *The*

Surnames of Scotland: Their Origin, Meaning and History began as
a series of pieces in the library's *Bulletin*. Black agreed to turn
them into a book. The result is a work of estimable scholarship
that is also unfailingly entertaining. Some of the most satisfying
entries relate to names now little used or not used at all, but as
Black, again on a path once trodden by Camden, allows himself
to be tempted into yet one more anecdote, who cares?

The richest sequence, which occupies 125 of his 838 pages and
traverses a range that begins with Macabhriuin and ends with
Maczewnie, is his collection of Macs. Macghillesheathanaich, he
discloses, was Anglicised into Shaw (which is scarcely surprising
and over the years must have saved a great deal of energy).
Macgillevarquhane means 'the son of the gillie [a Highland chief's
personal servant] of St Barchan', which makes it sound fairly
exclusive. Macgillivantic invokes an early stammerer. Macmillan
is 'the son of the bald and tonsured one'. Macquaker is 'absurdly
derived by Johnston from the Gaelic Macchuagaire, son of the
awkward, slovenly man', but in fact it's simply a form of Macvicar.
MacWhirr (the name of the captain in Joseph Conrad's *Typhoon*)
is a real surname. On Maclumfa, he quotes a book called *Galloway
Gossip Sixty Years Ago*, by Maria Trotter, Saxton and Robert De
Bruce Trotter, who say: 'another highly respectable and ancient
family, the McLumfas, has become extinct from the same disease
[gentility], and a set of people with the low Irish Downshire
name of McClew has stepped into their stockings'. He does
not explain the name McCririck, but those who follow the
horse-racing coverage on Channel 4 television will be interested
to learn that one was hanged at Kirkcudbright in 1457.

Beyond his Macs are the Maxwells, whose names are not
Norman as often assumed but come from a salmon pool near
the bridge at Kelso. And while we're among the names of famous
newspaper proprietors, Black says Murdoch means a man who
comes from the sea, a sea-warrior. He adds, 'William Murdoch
(1754–1839) inventor of gas-lighting, was proclaimed a deity by

Nassr-ed-Din, Shah of Persia, who believed him to be a re-incarnation of Merodach or Marduk, "god of light."'

Aside from Black and the work of some students in Sweden, the study of surnames seems to become becalmed in the mid-twentieth century. But two books in the 1960s, as coloured as Lower's or Guppy's (or for that matter, Camden's) by the backgrounds and temperaments of their authors, pitch the warmly approachable against the sternly scholarly. In 1966 a woman called Molly Matthews published *English Surnames*, which she followed with an even gentler version for younger readers. Matthews (born Molly Carrington) was an amateur, one of a breed that Weekley warned against, but one suspects he would have made an exception for her. She came from New Zealand to train at RADA, making her stage debut at Haileybury School, where she met and married a teacher called Edgar Matthews. Here she settled into the life of a public schoolmaster's wife. Reading her kindly pages, one can imagine her consoling small boys who have fallen and cut their knees on the rugby field, or have lost some cherished possession, or are simply pining for home. She died in 2008, eight days before she was due to celebrate her 100th birthday, a fact commemorated in the *Financial Times* by its columnist Matthew Engel, who wrote an affectionate tribute to her easy scholarship, her good humour, and her knack of answering questions one had always wanted to ask. Why, for instance, so many Jacksons, Johnsons and Richardsons, Dawsons and Dicksons, yet hardly any Georgesons and Edwardsons? In the days of Richard and John, she explains, royal forenames were copied by lesser folk and gave birth to appropriate surnames. By the time the Edwards came to the throne, and long before the Georges, that pattern was already established. But what Engel particularly savoured was the way in which the study of surnames took her into a wider world. Here, Matthews had said, was 'a chance to listen to the small talk of the Middle Ages, their jokes, their pet-names, the descriptions of six or seven hundred years ago, miraculously crystallised into permanent form'. 'Think about this,' Matthew Engel wrote. 'It IS a miracle.' Yet, again, there are defects here which come from using limited evidence: she bases her research on the 1961-3 London telephone directory, in truth not a broad enough base to reflect the whole country.

No such limitations diminish a book that appeared the following year. Though today in terms of the excavation of surnames it might be seen as part of pre-history, the work in question seems to have been regarded then – and not only by its progenitor – as more like a set of definitive rulings. *The Origin of English Surnames* (1967) was the work of Percy Hide Reaney, one of six sons of a Yorkshire family, who was a senior classics master in a school in Walthamstow, London, until ill-health forced his retirement in 1950. Before the war he had been a recognised authority on place names; he turned to surnames to while away the empty hours of firewatching duty. Even before *The Origin* came out, he had published the first version of a work regularly revised and reissued since as the *Oxford Dictionary of British Surnames*. Reaney (pronounced by him as Rainey, and derived, he says, from a group of stones in the Penistone area of Yorkshire) has only a limited respect for the story so far. Most of his predecessors are swatted away with varying degrees of impatience and even contempt. Guppy, Weekley, and even here and there Bardsley, are pounded for their inadequacy, while various others of greater obscurity not yet mentioned here, such as that wildly eccentric student of almost everything, the Revd Sabine Baring-Gould, are conclusively despatched as if by a firing squad.

Like Camden, Reaney developed a network of correspondents, explorers of nooks and crannies too remote and rarefied even for him; one (whose name was Macqueen: people are sometimes fascinated by surnames other than their own) had spent fifteen years researching the surname Marson. He expertly disentangles names that derive from Old English usage, names of Scandinavian origin, Celtic and Breton and those that come from the Normans.

His range is encyclopaedic. An index of names discussed in the text runs to more than 6,500 entries (and that excludes the ones he considers obsolete). The latest edition of his dictionary, now substantially updated by R. M. Wilson and renamed *English* rather than *British Surnames*, has terser definitions of over 60,000. Though Reaney is consistently dismissive of early practitioners, he acknowledges that much of this territory still requires fuller and deeper exploration – in particular, Guppy's special subject, the locational origin of names, which will constitute, he says, 'a long task demanding patient industry and accuracy and cannot be satisfactorily concluded without the co-operation of philologists, genealogists and historians'. That endeavour was still some way distant when he died in 1968.

Reaney can sound austere. Yet he also touches, more fully than his predecessors, on names as a source of possible shame, noting how 'squeamish' people have taken to spelling Rowbottom as Robathan, or Cockburn as Coburn (the way, of course, that it is nowadays normally spoken) or Glasscoe for Glasscock, quite apart from those that simply delete the -cock at the end of their name. Leger, he notes, may have been Lecher; many a Bullock began as a Bollock (or testicle); such names as Gildynballokes and Strokelady have disappeared altogether; along with some names that were even earthier.

Together his books would dominate the study of surnames for a decade. Yet Reaney was a linguist whose work is almost entirely founded upon linguistics. A new generation of surname scholars, armed with additional methods of investigation, from genealogy through local history into DNA research, would in time subject him to the same kind of doubting or even dismissive scrutiny he had visited on his predecessors in this endeavour. Though noting more often than not that he did as well as he could have with the techniques then available, these experts warn against turning to Reaney for unconditional truths. Towards the end of the century, the whole pursuit of the history and geography of surnames was being transformed, both through advances in academic analysis and through greater and more enthusiastic public engagement – to a point where it does not seem too fanciful to talk of a British surnames industry.

The tears of Jeremy Paxman

There were two main themes to the new growth industry that sprang up around the study of surnames in the closing years of a millennium which had seen this interest in them develop and burgeon: the academic and the popular, with money playing a growing role in linking them. The engine room of the academic strand was Leicester, where in 1965 – two years before Reaney published his apparently definitive work – the university began a programme of historical and genealogical research, thus adding two essential new disciplines in a world until now dominated by linguistics. At the forefront of this new approach was Richard McKinley. His *A History of British Surnames*, published in 1990, drew on material accumulated in previous decades, some of which was contained in a series of books on names in specific counties: Norfolk and Suffolk (1975), Oxfordshire (1977), Lancashire (1981) and, on territory once commanded by Lower, Sussex (1988). On the way he corrected many false assumptions in earlier books. But perhaps his most important teaching, which would become almost a leitmotif in subsequent surname books, was – to summarise, in my words rather than his – essentially this: that the more we know about surnames, the more we know how much we don't know about surnames.

The deeper you delve, the more complicated your findings become. 'A large majority of surnames', McKinley writes in his *History*, 'can be satisfactorily explained, but out of the great number and variety of surnames now in use in Britain, there nevertheless remain a good many which baffle investigation and the origins of which have never been convincingly cleared up.' Researchers may find it impossible to discover with real certainty how a particular surname which interests them originated. Indeed, as I worked through McKinley, I began to think that some of his readers might be moved to give up the struggle rather than go on wrestling with so many imponderables, and could even find themselves sliding into a condition which a psychiatrist might diagnose as onomastic despair. With names derived from place names, for example, even when they are plainly detectable as such, there's the problem that so many places have the same or similar names. There are fourteen places called Aller in Devon alone; while many more places that may once have furnished surnames have long ago disappeared off the map. As many as 3,000 villages failed to survive the Black Death. No doubt aware of the danger of emphasising the complexities, or pointing out the many bogs and quagmires which lie in wait for researchers, McKinley at one point appeals to them: don't be deterred – stick at it.

McKinley joined the department at Leicester when it opened in 1965, retired in 1986 and died in 1999, but his work at Leicester was continued, often by his old pupils. The funding for the university's surname survey has ceased, but new enterprises are flourishing, especially in the brave new world of DNA testing for surname, of which more below. Just up the London Midland line at Sheffield, a separate tradition began in the Department of Local History under the guidance of its Professor – now Emeritus Professor – David Hey, a product of Leicester, who established its Names Project Group. Hey was concerned with extra-mural activities, which gave him more freedom to develop new lines of research than would have been the case in mainstream departments tied more closely to a curriculum. His wise and accessible book *Family Names and Family History*, mixing the fruits of scholarship with practical guidance to would-be participants, was published in 2000.

Hey is a Yorkshireman, as is George Redmonds, another Leicester alumnus, and they found their native county, along with

Lancashire over the Pennines, especially rewarding for the way
that old names survived and the concentration of names within
these counties. Hey shows that 30 per cent of all people called
Levick (a name that may reflect descent from somebody
called Leofa or may suggest connections with a bishop; the bishop
in French is *l'évêque*) listed in phone books in 1986 lived in
Chesterfield and Sheffield. Of 456 people called Drabble (which
may derive from an old proper name or may, less enticingly, have
first been used to describe some kind of slattern) found in the
phone books in the same year, 234 lived in adjacent districts of
Yorkshire and Lancashire. For all those ancient animosities that
disrupted England in the Wars of the Roses and the more peace-
able but still hard-fought Wars of the Roses played out each
summer at Old Trafford or Headingley, people on either side of
the county boundary often share surnames. Yet such exclusive
clusters are by no means confined to the north: of 118 people called
Flippance picked up in the census of 1881, a hundred came from
the Wiltshire village of Pewsey. The name Phaup, George Black
pronounced in his book on Scotland, was now found only in the
vicinity of Hawick. Today, according to the local phone book, there
are two Phaup households left in the Scottish Borders, both in
Selkirk. I have also found one in London. (Phaup derives from a
local place name, Fawhope; Flippance may be a version of Philip.)

Yet again, Hey's book warns that there's also always a chance
that surname research will lead nowhere. Most of all one needs
to be wary of sources that serve up instant solutions. Some
internet sites will offer explanations as if they were undisputed,
when in truth they belong deep down in the valley of ambiguity.
Even surname dictionaries from the most honoured sources
cannot serve up indisputable truths to whoever may consult
them, and some certificates of ancestry offered on the web are
of dubious accuracy. As a general rule, there are no safe short
cuts in this business. This is where a new device comes into use:
the spittoon.

That Teuton-besotted epitome of the surname dabbler, Robert Ferguson MP, had named one of his books *Surnames as a Science*, implying an equivalence that most scientists reading his pages would have found an excessive claim. But now, science is truly involved. The analysis of DNA evidence, initially acquired though the simple process of spitting, is becoming a main player; not a supreme one, but one whose contribution to the unravelling of these mysteries can no longer be disregarded.

This whole new technique was made possible when in 1953 Francis Crick, James Watson, Maurice Wilkins and Rosalind Franklin unlocked the secrets of DNA and of the genetic code which passes hereditary characteristics on from parent to child, and can thus be used as a reliable guide to tracing one's forebears – far more reliable than trying to trace links through blood groups, the practice employed before. It took several decades to fully apply the new methods, but when results appeared they seemed spectacular.

In 1903, a skeleton dating from the Middle Stone Age, an estimated 9,000 years before, had been found in a cave in the Cheddar Gorge. In 1996, the DNA of this 'Cheddar Man' was checked against that of a teacher and pupils at the community school in Cheddar. A perfect match was found – not with a child but with their teacher, whose name was Adrian Targett, who was shown to be a direct descendant through the maternal line. (This itself was unusual: the genetic tracing of ancestors has more often been built on examinations of paternal descent through the evidence of the Y-chromosome.) Targett had many relatives living locally. The implications, newspapers reported, were clear: it might now be shown that substantial numbers of people in large kinship groups in a locality had a history of 300 or 400 generations. And this in turn would undermine the widespread assumption that people in Britain owed their origins largely to successive invasions.

These investigations were taken further by Bryan Sykes,

Professor of Human Genetics at Oxford, who began to describe himself as a 'genetic archaeologist'. Using an even older discovery from Cheddar – a tooth dug up in 1980 – Sykes and his team at Oxford began a series of explorations that started to show that many more people sharing a surname had derived from a single ancestor than had previously been considered possible (though in fact George Redmonds had made this then apparently heretical claim nearly a decade before). Sykes's bestselling book *The Blood of the Isles,* published in 2006, brought awareness of this new pool of research to a wider audience and soon enthusiasts for genealogy and family history were diving head-first into it.

Another powerhouse of this kind of investigation is, as ever, Leicester University, where DNA-related projects have largely taken over today from the traditional forms of research associated with McKinley. Professor Alec Jeffreys, the pioneer in these investigations, confessed that he had a special incentive: he wanted to know if he was directly related to the notorious seventeenth-century hanging judge, Judge Jeffreys. His own methods proved that he wasn't. Professor Mark Jobling and Turi King embarked on an analysis of the Y-chromosomes of 1,678 men sharing forty surnames which included their own, David Hey's and Alec Jeffreys's, and a number of names that occur in my six Broughtons, notably Butterfield and Mallinson (Furness), as well as Smith, which is found almost everywhere.

Men with rarer surnames such as Grewcock, Wadsworth, Ketley and Ravenscroft (the born name of the celebrated disc jockey John Peel) tend, they have found, to share Y-chromosomes that are very similar, suggesting a common ancestor within the past 700 years. One unusual but very familiar name they studied is Attenborough and here almost nine out of ten were found in a random sampling to share the same Y-chromosome type.

There is also continuing collaboration with Ireland, where research at Trinity College Dublin is directed by Dan Bradley, a former colleague of Jobling's. Curiously, names as common in

Ireland as Ryan and O'Sullivan, unlike the ubiquitous Smith in Britain, may derive from a single ancestor. Family histories on both sides of the Irish Sea are interwoven, and a number of volunteers are involved in Dublin's investigations, of whom I am one, having been challenged by Robin McKie, science editor of the *Observer*, who was working on a book called *Face of Britain*, based on a Channel 4 series, to see if we were, as *Private Eye* likes to say, by any chance related. After a certain amount of spitting at the behest of an Edinburgh company, EthnoAncestry, word came that we were. 'Now David has been revealed to be my long-lost "brother",' Robin wrote in the *Observer*. 'Our DNA shows that, between AD 1000 and 1400, either in Ireland or Scotland, our lineages shared a common ancestor, a grandfather of multiple "greatness". Even better, that ancestor turns out to have been a direct descendant of the Irish king Niall of the Nine Hostages, who created a vast fifth-century dynasty around modern Strabane.'

I'm not sure about that 'even better'. Niall of the Nine Hostages is an even more undesirable person to be related to than Alec Jeffreys's hanging judge. Indeed, one reason why, it's suggested, such a large proportion of people descended from Niall was that Niall had exterminated so many other potential progenitors. (The same is said of the very large number of men traceable back to Genghis Khan.) It seems that Robin and I can claim to be related to every Neill and O'Neill together with Gallaghers, Connors, Cannons, Bradleys, O'Reillys, Kees, Campbells, Devlins, O'Kanes and McGoverns. That makes me a kinsman of, among others, such eminent figures as Bernard Gallagher, Martin O'Neill, Tony O'Reilly, Robert Kee, and Ming and Alastair Campbell. It would also allow me to claim royal blood, if I wanted to, which I don't.

That's one of the downsides of all such research, and not just the use of DNA. It may turn up relationships with difficult or dangerous people, or disturbing things about your quite recent family, revealing skeletons in your cupboard considerably less ancient than the one in the Cheddar Gorge. The line you are tracing back may stop very suddenly as it comes across an illegitimate birth. One trawl threw up the name of a sperm donor, to the possible chagrin of whoever commissioned it. There are now commercial organisations offering to do DNA traces, some of which are slow to emphasise the possible discovery of inconvenient facts, while some offer certificates for evidence that appears to be set in stone when at best it may only be tentative. But it's clearly a developing fashion, and has been taken up by a variety of the one-name societies whose activities are described a few pages on.

The use of DNA tracing for genealogical investigation, already gathering pace, was formidably boosted in February 2013 when it was established 'beyond reasonable doubt' that bones found under a Leicester car park were those of King Richard III, slain at Bosworth Field in 1485. His body was said at the time to have been dumped in the River Soar, but fortunately it seems these reports were ill-founded. For some reason the Leicester discovery was hailed as history being rewritten, though the most it could do was to challenge the version of the king portrayed in Shakespeare's play, and that had been done by historians many years earlier, especially in Paul Murray Kendall's account of his life published in 1955. Certainly it told us nothing at all about the greatest riddle of Richard's kingship: whether he was responsible for the deaths of the princes in the tower.

The establishment of a link between the bones and the much vilified king was mainly due to the work of a dedicated groups of archaeologists, experts in the study of bones, enthusiasts from the Richard III Society and others, but what was taken to be the clinching evidence was the confirmation that the DNA in this find matched that of a man called Michael Ibsen, whose mother had been singled out as a clear descendant of Richard's sister. The DNA evidence alone would not have resolved the matter. There were those who warned that such tracing could always have been affected by some non-paternity event: as once sceptic put it, 'there have always been milkmen'. That is a generally necessary warning in DNA tracing, but in this case it did not apply. The Richard III link had been traced down the female line, which meant that no milkman, or other intrusive male, could have had any part in it. That made the Leicester evidence even more persuasive.

*

You can gauge the significance of this broad new approach from a book that appeared in 2011 in which George Redmonds, Hey and the Leicester genetics expert Turi King brought the three essential disciplines of genealogy, family history and DNA research together. This firmly concluded, against most earlier assumptions, that a single distinctive surname may indeed have a single origin. That applies not just to locational names but to nicknames and sometimes even occupational names as well. This is very good news for the burgeoning ranks of one-name societies. If your name is Smith, Brown or Robinson you're unlikely to be related to every other Smith, Brown or Robinson you may bump into. If the name is decently rare, however, your chances are good. 'If we take two men with the same surname from any part of the British Isles,' the book asserts, 'there is a one-in-four chance that they will be related to the extent that they had a common ancestor in the last few hundred years, and that if the most common names are removed the chance increases to 50 per cent.'

Meanwhile a new academic contender has entered the field. In 2010, the Arts and Humanities Research Council awarded £834,350 to a team based at the University of the West of England, Bristol, which aims to produce in 2014 an easily accessible online guide to the origins and meanings of names, built on a database of up to 150,000 surnames, drawing on published and unpublished material running back to the eleventh century. In the summer of 2011, the lead researcher, Dr Patrick Hanks, co-author with Flavia Hodges of *A Dictionary of Surnames* (1989), and his colleague Simon Draper published an account of the new project's work in the magazine *One-Name Studies* which gave examples of the kind of material their online service would be providing. One of their three examples was a surname familiar from newspaper headlines in 2012 when one of its bearers seemed likely to become the manager of the England football team: Harry Redknapp. The earliest bearer traceable was John Redknape, in Norfolk in 1335. They picked it as an example of a name missing from surname dictionaries that had more than one possible explanation. Here it seems is where online dictionaries can score over printed ones; they can be swiftly amended as new research makes the meaning of surnames more definite – or in many cases, no doubt, even more complex.

*

The expansion of academic research into surnames over the past decade has been more than matched by the rise in public enthusiasm. British family trees have become forests as amateur family historians in the United Kingdom and people of British descent in the United States and old Commonwealth countries have fervently trawled the available records and produced results which sadly quite often fail to stand up to professional scrutiny. One librarian in Scotland described to me how people from Australia and New Zealand had come to her office seeking advice on how to improve and extend the family trees they'd already created, only for her specialist colleague to have to tell them that much of their work was wrong and would have to be done again.

These pursuits, even so, have become much easier over the past twenty years, not least in the use of the census and the records of births, marriages and deaths kept in England since the year

1837. Until 2008 this work in England had to be done in London, at an office relocated from the Aldwych to Finsbury. Birth, marriage and death were recorded in bulky files which had to be transported to desks where often the elbows of neighbours would disturb the researcher's calm – most of all when these elbows belonged to agents who, for a price, would dig out your relatives for you. These were men in a hurry, knowing exactly what they were after, impatient of the nervous dithering of amateurs, hauling the chunky metal-edged files off the shelves and crashing them down on the tables before hurling them back into the slots where they'd found them. Yet even the amateurs were not all strangers to violence. Once at Finsbury I heard a dispute developing in the next alcove in which voices were raised and threats uttered when two researchers sought to pull down the same file. After a while the row subsided, whereupon the man working next to me said: 'What a pity. I was hoping there might be a proper fight, like we used to have in the old days. There don't seem to be many fights now they've moved here.'

But that, of course, was before we had Ancestry. With Ancestry at your service you don't have to go to London; you don't have to compete with sharp-elbowed pros and you don't run the risk of a fight. With around two and a half million subscribers, Ancestry, which began in the United States, is the largest family history organisation in the world. It set up its website in Britain in 2002 and now offers its customers more than a billion records. It is not the only such site (more are listed at the end of this book), but it is much the most formidable, not least because it has been established as the official partner of the state custodian of all this precious material, the National Archives. (There are separate arrangements in Scotland, whose National Archives work in conjunction with a company called brightsolid.)

Researchers to whom I talked had mixed feelings about it, as I do myself. They loved the ease of access, and the way the service is constantly being expanded, bringing more and more invaluable information direct to your desk, but they found the rate of error infuriating. Original census records are not always easy to read. Some from the earliest years are faded. Some have words eradicated by big black marks obliterating key words, presumably put there by people checking them. Though most of the handwriting is good and some is beautiful, you find occasional outbreaks of carelessness. As Ancestry says, its transcribers are trained to spot such mistakes. But some conspicuous errors are clearly the work of their own transcribers. I found parents considerably younger than some of their children, sons and daughters given the occupation of 'servant', servants given the surname of the people they worked for, despite the fact that the census enumerators had logged them correctly. People were made to live in places which clearly do not exist. And some of the data given under the heading of occupation were simply grotesque. A man in Broughton in Furness is shown as a 'renal postman'. You could perhaps imagine a renal postman now, as someone delivering kidneys to transplant centres, but that could not have been the case in the nineteenth century. And when you check the original, the writing is faultless: 'rural postman', it says.

Some researchers suspect that the transcriptions are done by people on the Indian sub-continent, in China or in the Philippines. Ancestry says transcriptions are carried out by experts who are trained for up to six months in the relevant skills, though some of the work is done by its Ancestry Worldwide Archives project. It does not say where. It also allows subscribers to suggest corrections, which is easier to do if you are studying records of a particular place or a particular group of families, census by census. Given the wealth of material to be found on their sites, it is plainly unrealistic to hope that checking will eliminate every error. The best rule for using the service is to remember that, should you encounter a renal postman, you need to check what the census taker provided.

Compilers of family trees can also turn for advice to the Guild of One-Name Studies, which is not too solemn, proud or puffed up to use the acronym Goons (even though, one official told me, that may have held back its expansion in the US). Unlike Ancestry, this is a UK venture which travelled west across the Atlantic, not east. But it's certainly transatlantic. Some of the one-name societies, such as the Wingfields, one of the biggest, are based in America and hold their main annual get-togethers there rather than in the UK from where the Wingfields sprang. There are also links with societies overseas. In Germany, one-name studies are known as *Namensträgerforschung*. The Goons use nine categories, more than most others do, to differentiate types of surname: patronymic; metronymic; genitive (Manners, Squires); diminutive (Bartlett); locative toponymic (place names like Stepney); locative topographical (Green, Hill); occupational; post-holder or status (Bailey, Hayward); and nicknames and physical appearance.

I met the organisation's then chairman, a Wiltshire teacher called Kirsty Gray, at a Hampshire Genealogical Society Open Day. On a chain from her neck there hung a label announcing her interest in the name Sillifant and several others related to it (there wasn't room for them all, she said). Kirsty is not a Sillifant, but her great-grandmother was. A few societies prefer to stick close to their core name, but others are wildly liberal. The Palgrave Society, for instance, announces that its doors are open to people with any one of over 100 names, which are listed as:

Pagave, Paggegrave, Paggrave, Pagram, Pagraua, Pagraue, Pagrava, Pagrave, Pagrayfe, Pagrief, Pagrife, Pagriff, Pakegrave, Paldegrave, Palegraue, Palegrave, Palegreve, Palesgrove, Palglafs,* Palgran, Palgrane, Palgraue, Palgraufe, Palgrave, Palgraves, Palgraw, Palgrawe, Palgrawfe, Palgraze, Palgrife, Palgriff, Palgriss, Palgrive, Palgroave, Palgrove, Palgroves, Palgrowe, Palgue, Pallgraue, Pallgrav, Pallgrave, Pallgraves, Pallsgrove, Palmgrove, Palsegrave, Palsgraf,* Palsgraff,* Palsgraue, Palsgrave, Palsgrof,* Palsgrove,

Palsgroves, Paltsgrove,* Paltzgeoff,* Palzgraf,* Palzgraff,*
Palzgrove,* Pargrave, Pasgrave, Paugrave, Paulgraue,
Paulgrave, Paullgrave, Paulsgrave, Paultsgrove,* Pavegrave,
Pawgrave, Pawlgraue, Pawlgrave, Paxgrave, Paygraue,
Paygrave, Peagrave, Peagriff, Peasgrave, Pedgrave, Pedgriff,
Pedgrift, Pedgrifth, Peggram, Pegrave, Pegriff, Pegrom,
Pelgrave, Pelgrift, Pellgrave, Pensgrave, Pesgrave, Pfaltzgraf,*
Pfaltzgraff,* Pfalygraft,* Pfalzgraf,* Pilgram, Pilgrane,
Pilgraue, Pilgrave, Pilgrove, Pilsgrave, Pisgrove, Poldegrew,
Polegrave, Polgrane, Polgrave, Polgraves, Polgravis, Polgreen,*
Pollgrave, Pollgraves, Poulgrave, Poullgreene,* Poulsgrave,
Powell-Greaves, Powlgrave, Powlgraves, Purgrave.

The names equipped with an asterisk are classed as 'dubious',
but the length of this list is some indication of how names
diversify and shows there are more kinds of Palgrave than are
dreamed of in most people's philosophy. I dare say even more
might be admissible. The novel *Armadale* by Wilkie Collins
features an admirable country solicitor called Pedgift: could he
have qualified too?

The Relfs are gathered in an International Relf Society, while
the Carbises have the slogan: 'for all things Carbis'. Some societies have adopted names which signal their commitment to
variety in typographical form, like the Blo(o)r(e)s, while another
designates itself the Stonehewer to Stanier Society. One or two
are proud of a name that others might shrink from: for instance,
the Grubbs. Some Grubbs in Victorian England changed their
surname to the more mellifluous Norfolk Howard; the Norfolk
Howard being a form of grub. Some have produced their own
books, such as *Dead Relatives: the Rise and Fall of the Phillibrowns
in Essex, London and New York City* by Glenda Thornton, and
Sheila Fermor Clarkson's *Over Half a Century of Fermor Family
Cricket*.

Some societies simply swap information; others hold

get-togethers – here, or in the US, or indeed all over the world. Discovering that the Braunds, whose society is spoken of with admiration in Goons circles, were about to hold a Braund weekend in a hotel at Ross-on-Wye, I asked if I might look in on them. They did not reply; a pity, as I might have been able to tell them, though they probably know already, of the Braunds who were blacksmiths at Elmdon for nine generations. I settled instead for a smaller society, whose gathering was more likely to be more representative of the average one-name occasion. These were the Buntings.

*

A sunny Saturday morning in October 2012 and Buntings are flocking into the Colonel Dane Memorial Hall in the unexpectedly pretty village of Alwalton near Peterborough, once in Huntingdonshire, now, since the extirpation of that county, in Cambridgeshire. They number about two dozen: in previous years, they assure me, there had been bigger turnouts but cheap bed and breakfasts have proved to be disappointingly sparse in this district. The organisers have got there early and have posted up family trees of various breeds of Bunting, grown so long that they trail all down the wall and spill on to the floor. The talk of trees at this gathering would hardly seem out of place in a conference of dendrologists. Members have placards around their necks giving their names, most of which are not Bunting, suffixed with place names that show not the towns and villages from which they've arrived, but the location to which their own skeins of Buntings belong. Derbyshire is prominent, but Norfolk and Sussex too, and the area around Romney Marsh in Kent. Hampshire and Northamptonshire also have clusters.

There are Bunting memorabilia on display, with a book of press cuttings and a fact sheet explaining that Bunting was a Teutonic name, derived from a word meaning 'mottled', 'speckled' or 'plaided', which suggests that the name may have begun as a nickname for someone who liked to wear a distinctive costume. It is also linked, however, with the word 'bunt', meaning 'fat' (which may be how the author who called himself Frank Richards came to give the fat owl of the Greyfriars Remove the name Billy Bunter). But a bunting is also a bird, as the Bunting emblem demonstrates, so it could also have come from a nickname initially given to someone small and finchlike. The bird is also displayed on the front of the Buntings' twice-yearly magazine, which is called *Gone a Hunting*, that being where baby Bunting's father has gone in the nursery rhyme.

A few in the group are unmitigated Buntings, born with the name and still sporting it, able to claim it by direct descent. Rather more have acquired it through husbands, or trace it back to grandparents and great-grandparents. Two children are here from Australia with their Bunting father and his wife, who introduces herself as the only non-Bunting of the four of them. The father's links are with the Buntings of Armagh in Northern Ireland, which makes him particularly welcome since information about the Buntings of Ireland is harder to find than information about the Buntings of England, where fuller records are more immediately available. Jerry Green, who maintains their website – his great-grandmother was a Bunting – mentions during the meeting that some of his relatives went to Australia: 'They went *of their own accord*,' he adds. Someone chips in to say, maybe so but quite a few Buntings didn't. But Jerry knows that: he keeps a list of transportees.

Names like Rix, Green and Paine, all strong in this part of the world, are as evident as Bunting today. We would not have been here at all today had not Christine Paine, then Christine Graydon-Tomes, of Lavenham, Suffolk, been intrigued enough by an unplanned encounter with East Anglian Buntings to write to the *East Anglian Daily Times* to ask if there were more around. The name had first caught her imagination when she came across a Bunting great-aunt by marriage, Annie Elizabeth. The response led to a meeting attended by sixteen people at the village hall at Alpheton, Suffolk, and so to the creation of the society. Such chance occurrences swell the numbers of these societies. One of those mustered at Alwalton was a Post Office worker who had encountered the Bunting Society when he saw its name on a wrapper and said: 'My wife is a Bunting.'

Before the main business – the annual general meeting – begins, some of those present introduce themselves and establish their Bunting connections. One academic to whom I had talked for this book had described one-name devotees as fanatics. Yet one could hardly imagine a meeting of devotees less fanatical than this at Alwalton. A touch obsessive perhaps, though no more so, perhaps rather less, than I have found when mingling with birdwatchers, model railway enthusiasts, devotees of old buses, or even those (of whom I am one) addicted to psephology, the study of voting. What in each case has brought them together is a common thread of research, and a pleasure derived from meeting strangers whose interest, even passion, they share. When I asked before the meeting began if such occasions gave them a sense of their Buntingness, they said no, or, more often, not really. And certainly to plug your research into an organisation like this one has the practical benefit of obviating a great deal of vain effort.

Newcomer Buntings, the old hands say, acquire a new optimism and shed old illusions when acquainted with the family trees maintained by Mary Rix, their chairman, who gives the impression throughout the day of knowing every twig of her trees off by heart. Someone refers to a Bunting who was married three times. No, Mary tells him: what he had was three partners. Oh, in that case, says the relative, you can make it four. Her Bunting connection is through her grandmother, Gracenia, a forename as far as she knows unique to the family. 'Everyone who joins the society', she declares at the annual meeting, 'is fixed to a tree in a very short time': a proceeding less melodramatic than it may sound. They can't display all their trees in this hall: in all there are 92 of them, containing more than 22,000 names. Bunting Society members abroad – there are 36 out of 194 overall – are represented today by the family from Australia and by the American Bunting-related wife of a British non-Bunting. Her bubbling enthusiasm confirms what core members had said, that the furthest flung members are often the keenest of all.

I left them discussing subscription levels and whether, the cost of postage having recently risen so viciously, their magazine should transfer to the internet. Some were looking forward to an afternoon ride on the Nene Valley railway; others to further Bunting deliberations until the time came for tea.

Back in Suffolk, where this organisation began, a much more unorthodox one-name gathering had taken place earlier in the year when a committee member of Bungay Town FC of the Anglian Combination and a London advertising man called Bill Bungay decided to stage a bank holiday charity match. Originally it was billed as a game between a team of people called Bungay and Bungay FC ('the Black Dogs'), but in the event two mixed-sex teams composed entirely of Bungays took the field in red and blue shorts with the name Bungay – rather unnecessarily, one might have thought – displayed on the backs. The *Daily Telegraph* reported:

> Bungays from Britain, Australia and America turned up for the match which is believed to be the first in the world using all players of the same name.
>
> The mascot for the match was eight-year-old Carla Bungay and the doctor on hand to treat any injuries was Dr Elizabeth Bungay . . . Retired lorry driver Chris 'Tiffer' Bungay, 57, of Queensland, Australia, agreed to play in the match while combining it with a holiday to visit his relatives in Britain . . . Qualified referee John Bungay, 61, from

Eastleigh, Hampshire agreed to officiate. His two sons Andrew, 37, and Graeme, 34, also attended. All profits from the match – which was drawn 6–6 – went to The Jack and Ada Beattie Foundation, which supports vulnerable people.

*

The biggest boost of all to the blossoming surname/family history industry has come from the BBC, especially through the phenomenally successful series *Who Do You Think You Are?*, launched in 2004, starting on BBC2 but transferred – the ultimate accolade – to BBC1. In its early days, the programme examined both sides of the family, mother's and father's alike. It was seen as social history, from the bottom up, as well as an exploration of family antecedents. As it grew more successful, the pattern changed. Now those featured are all celebrities. Though some of those chosen are famously tough, they habitually gasp and even weep when confronted with the fates of some of their forebears.

The programmes appear to depict celebrities engaged on a personal search for their families' history, but in fact they are following trails laid down well ahead by teams of researchers. They are spared the delays, brick walls and other infuriating hazards which face ordinary mortals involved in this kind of quest. The discoveries which surprise and sometimes distress them are built into the formula. The television chat show host Michael Parkinson, who'd been invited, was told that they wouldn't be going ahead with his story because it wasn't eventful enough. It has seemed in the later years as if producers would never be happy until their subject wept: you could almost hear the whoops of joy when even Jeremy Paxman, contemplating his forebears' tough lives, began to blub. But for spreading the message about how to research your family and where the names in it came from, *Who Do You Think You Are?* has been an unrivalled success.

People watched what was done and then went out and did likewise.

Any doubts that family history has become big business can be simply and swiftly dispelled. Try fighting your way through the crowds that turn up every February for a jamboree now known as 'Who Do You Think You Are? Live', staged on the posh pink carpets of the Olympia exhibition centre, west London. The 2013 weekend has only been opened an hour and the space is seething. This is Friday, so the attendance so far is predominantly middle-aged and elderly: people in retirement with plenty of time to devote to their compelling new hobby, together with knots of enthusiasts who have obviously been at it for years, avidly comparing notes with a great deal of waving of arms and the pulling of sheaves of documents out of bags.

It isn't cheap. Pay at the door and it costs you £22 to get in, which seems on the face of it steep to make the acquaintance of people most of whom are trying to sell you things. But hiring Olympia does not come cheap, and one of the lures of today is the abundance of free, expert and enthusiastic advice you can find on the various stands and in the lectures the bigger companies organise, sometimes with people you've seen on TV. Tony Robinson (rather more *Time Team* than *Who Do You Think You Are?*) is promised this afternoon.

The biggest beasts in this culture have, of course, staked out the biggest territory. Ancestry ('1 billion records, 44 million family trees') has not only a basic stand, but a site (with impressive queues) that offers a twenty-minute consultation with experts, and a sizeable lecture pen, almost full for a session on worldwide records, which has just arrived at Australia. And what does Australia mean in this context? It means convicts, of course. Ancestry, which sponsors this annual show, even provides a members' lounge upstairs. The Society of Genealogists, one of the progenitors of these occasions, has four lecture studios, each with a different programme, some of which promise accounts of celebrities. Others offer help in dealing with that inescapable artefact of all such occasions, the brick wall. Still others take you into more rarefied territory ('Indentured Servants, Shovelled Paupers & Ten Pound Poms: Researching Ancestors Who Were Paid To Leave Dear Old Blighty' by Simon Fowler).

But smaller specialised organisations are here in profusion too: family and local history societies from many if not most English counties, and from Scotland, Wales and Northern Ireland, though they also have shows of their own. They're congregated at the east end of the hall, with scattered among them such famous names as the National Trust and the College of Arms (less stately looking than I had expected) and several local authority libraries and archives. Here, too, are organisations which will sell you a scroll setting out the meanings and origins of your surname, which they aim to trace in ninety seconds (today's featured name is Kwiatosinski, which may have taken rather longer than that). 'An ideal gift', says the Name Shop, 'for the one you love or even your wife or husband.' One can buy a scroll which sets out the coats of arms of a couple just beginning as wife and husband: all yours in a gold-embossed frame for £95. Beyond are sellers of mobile scanners, a stall run by people who have spent twenty-five years researching the surname East, and Methodist Heritage, and the Friends of the Metropolitan Police, and the rather spooky-sounding Deceased Online, a database for burial and cremation records. Further on, you can fork out £2 to check if yours is a genuine Huguenot surname (£3 for two names; all repaid if you buy their CD) and a list of communities where Huguenots settled: mostly London and seaports like Southampton and Bristol and Dublin, but also for some reason Thorpe-le-Soken in Essex, which lurks just inland from Clacton and snooty Frinton and Walton-on-the Naze, towns whose goings on were keenly observed from his house in Thorpe by the novelist Arnold Bennett.

A few of the stands seem to have surprisingly little to do with the business of helping to discover who you may be. The Family

History Press and Life Stories have their customers, but nothing to match the throng that has gathered for Supreme Sausages Ltd (no mention of DNA there). And here is a mini massage clinic which under the legend 'Do You Suffer From Any of the Following?' offers help in dealing with the 'secondary symptoms' of a long string of nasty conditions from 'general aches and pains' through multiple sclerosis, fibromyalgia and ME to chronic fatigue, sleep deprivation and sporting injuries; most, if not all of which must have troubled your ancestors and may perhaps trouble you too. A wan-looking woman lies on a couch, being counselled.

My award for ingenuity, though, goes to the stand which special-ises in the perhaps potentially dry subject of marriage law for genealogists, where key words from this discipline are boldly portrayed on the wall. 'Pre-contract, Lent, Validity, Fertility', one of them says; another reads 'Guardian, Punishment, Fleet Prison, Affidavits, Anglicans, Overseas', and then in big bold italics: 'Gretna Green'. Below that come Dissolute, Dissenters and, just above Nullity and Duress, Broomsticks, and Sodomy. Why broom-sticks, people enquire of Professor Rebecca Probert, who is due, I see, to speak on Sunday on 'Sex, Illegitimacy and Cohabitation'. It used be thought, she explains, that once a couple could marry simply by jumping over a broomstick; and though this has no basis in fact, surprising numbers continue to credit it. A whiff of the naughty is welcome on these occasions. '*And* you get the juicy bits!' says a lecturer elsewhere in the hall, producing a PowerPoint projection headed 'Scandals and Struggle in Church, 1756'.

The western end of this vast Olympia hall pulsates with the unmistakable evidence of the new and ravenous appetite for, and the burgeoning financial potential of, the sub-division of this business which deals with DNA. And you don't have to wait to get sampled. You can start spitting here and now in a decent little cubicle, after which it will take four to six weeks for the findings for which you are yearning to reach you 'in a secure online environment'. Turi King, the DNA expert from Leicester University, who is due to be here on Sunday, talking, of course, about Richard III, says she's often pursued on these occasions by men who hope she can link them with Vikings (a smaller contingent likes to think it may be related to Prince Charles).

Two of the DNA stands feature red hair. 'How red-headed is Britain?' a poster on one of them asks. 'Why is Britain probably [don't you just love that *probably*?] the most red-headed nation, per capita so to speak, on earth?' I see that Alistair Moffat is due to speak on 'How DNA is Rewriting British History'. He is managing director of Britain's DNA, which has won itself some space in the *Daily Telegraph* this week with the story that its DNA samplings of 5,000 people have suggested that a million British men might be directly descended from the Roman legions that came here almost 2,000 years ago. Four million men in England and Wales, it is indicated, carry distinctive genetic signatures which are most commonly found, and are likely to have had their origins, in Italy. 'And although it is impossible to prove whether any individual's genes were introduced during the Roman occupation, and not before or after, researchers estimate that the influx of tens of thousands of soldiers was responsible for at least a quarter of the total,' the paper enthuses.

The organisers of the 2013 show, Immediate Media (formerly BBC Magazines, Bristol), expected the overall attendance figures to top 14,000. Appropriately, the neighbouring hall in Olympia is simultaneously staging the National Wedding Show, promoting an institution for whose future activities generations of family history fans yet unborn will have cause to be grateful.

*

How amazed, I reflected coming away, William Camden and his various successors would be to discover how greatly the public taste for these matters has grown. Yet Camden's warning – 'to find the true original of surnames is full of difficulty' – persists. Will even these new and sophisticated endeavours answer every question brought for resolution? Again, the answer has to be no. Even the newest technologies cannot unravel some of the boggy and quagmirish problems that have even skilled researchers running into brick walls. Indeed, having spent a year in this territory, I am moved to propose a whole new category to add to the traditional list – of locational names, occupationals, parentals and nicknames – one that might be called chronic ambiguities. The more one looks at the record of my various Broughtons, the more the riddles accumulate. Blake is a standard name in Broughton, Hampshire. The familiar explanation is that this surname comes from a nickname for men who were dark and swarthy. But it may also come from an ancient English word meaning pale, wan or white – precisely the opposite. Ashburner, a name that persists for centuries in Broughton in Furness, might mean a charcoal-burner; but it might be a topographical name derived from a place in Lancashire. A name that ends with the suffix -man is usually construed as having come down from a servant – the Lilliemans of Northamptonshire may have worked for people called Lilley – but that too can reflect a geographical origin, as in Manxman. On top of that there are whole quagmirish swamps where what experts like to call non-paternity events are lurking, where, by design or accident, putative fathers are not the real fathers, where adoptions have taken place. To plot the descent of members of royal families is warning enough. Even a cursory tour of the standard reference books confronts you with a series of questions of which these are only a taste.

How much of this matters? The answer is in the eye of the beholder. So many names that have come down to the present day now sound completely arbitrary. You're called Macmillan. You look it up in Black's book, which says it means the son of a bald or a tonsured person. Your father was not bald or tonsured; photographs of your ancestors, arranged in decorous Victorian groups with grandfather, copiously side-whiskered, taking pride of place in the centre, show that he wasn't either.

Nicknames, because they applied to particular characteristic of a particular person, are the least meaningful of the lot. And what about Black, the Scottish surname guru, himself? The original Black may have had the black hair or dark complexion that brought him his nickname, but many others in the family tree may well not have done so. Some Blacks may well have been albinos.

Names deriving from places may tell us more. I'm interested, though not obsessively so, in knowing my distant forebears came from Scotland. But everyone has at the start two parents, which means four grandparents, and eight great-grandparents, and so on until many generations back you owe your blood to thousands of people. In this context, the answer to Juliet's question to Romeo, 'What's in a name?' has to be: sometimes, not very much. But look at the crowds at Olympia, look at the gatherings of one-name societies, and it's clear that for hundreds, even thousands, at other times, a name is of huge significance. It could even, as the lady would shortly find out, be a matter of life and death. And not just in Verona.

5

Confrontations

Surnames that Bark and Bite

'The question is,' said Humpty Dumpty, 'which is
to be master – that's all.'
Lewis Carroll, *Through the Looking Glass*

Names steeped in blood

It used to be said that when John Buchan, author of such red-blooded tales of adventure as *The Thirty-Nine Steps*, used to take his holidays here, this village enveloped in the hills was such a haven of peace that a dog could lie in the sun all morning in the main street of Broughton, Peeblesshire, and not be disturbed. That isn't the case today in what is now Broughton, Borders – Peeblesshire, along with accompanying Roxburghshire, Selkirkshire and Berwickshire, was swept away in the 1970s – but there's still a sleepy feel to it. It has the sense of a village where nothing of much significance has occurred for the past five years. The main news on the village notice board when I was there was concerned with the loss of a dog. The village used to attract a trickle of tourists visiting its John Buchan centre, but in 2012 that relocated to Peebles where there looked to be a better chance of tempting in casual visitors.

This Broughton is perched on the main route from Edinburgh south to Moffat at a point where a lesser road leaves it to run westward to the small Lanarkshire town of Biggar. Dogs would be ill advised to slumber there now. Yet here, and especially in the graveyard around the ruins of the old parish church, abandoned in 1803, with its screen of trees and behind them, the gentle hills, you may feel a sense of kindly protection from the busy boisterous thundering world. Yet note the presence here of a Veitch and a Tweedie. These names are reminders that this tract of Tweeddale, and most of all Drumelzier, a hamlet of no more than 150 people just up the road, were the scene of relentless, perpetually bloody feuds, with the Tweedies and Veitches locked into a conflict fit for a Shakespeare tragedy.

The feuds of the Highlands are famous around the world. Macdonald and Campbell were names far more deadly than anything out of Verona. In places, those animosities linger. Yet the feuds of the border, though less remembered today, were hardly less ferocious and bloody. Indeed, in his rumbustious history of the troubles, *The Steel Bonnets: The Story of the Anglo-Scottish Border Reivers*, George MacDonald Fraser, the creator of Flashman, describes it like this:

> [The border people] were shaped by the kind of continuous ordeal that has passed most of Britain by. The ordeal reached its peak in the sixteenth century, when great numbers of people inhabiting the border territory (the old Border Marches) lived by despoiling each other, when the great Border tribes, both English and Scottish, feuded continuously among themselves, when robbery and blackmail were everyday professions, when raiding, arson, kidnapping, murder and extortion were an important part of the social system . . . It was the ring in which the champions met; armies marched and counter-marched and fought across it; it was wasted and burned and despoiled, its people robbed and harried and slaughtered, on both sides, by both sides . . . Their readiness to slaughter a rival *simply on account of his name* [my italics] was as strong as that of the clans.

Fraser mildly complains that Walter Scott romanticised these times in the Borders. Yet Scott himself writes, in his *Tales of a Grandfather*, of days

> when there was no finding any refuge or protection but in the strongest arm and the longest sword; when there was no raising of crops, no religious devotion, and all the laws of humanity and charity were transgressed without scruple; when whole families were found starved to death, even cannibalism being resorted to, and the whole country reduced to a most disastrous state.

And where in the Highlands they talked of the warring clans, here in official documents they are specifically classed as the warring *Surnames*.

Families lived for their names, and frequently died for them. They employed the methods of gangland. People who lived around Broughton would have known this well, as neighbours of the famously turbulent Tweedies. This was the life, and conceivably also the death, for which young men knew they were destined. It was long a custom in Border country to leave the right hand of male children unchristened so that it might be more readily used against an enemy. The very names of the Borders – Armstrong, Elliot (a name spelled in seventy different ways), Scott (one was known as 'God's curse') – were enough to strike fear across the territory. There's an old Border story of a visitor to Liddesdale who asked why there weren't any churches. 'There's no Christians here,' he was told, 'we's a' Elliots and Armstrangs.'

When the kings north and south of the border and their various agents sought to quell the feuds of the surnames, the methods they used were hardly less brutal. The allegiances of these men were not to the titular rulers of the Scottish and English borders; some surnames switched from one to the other whenever they saw an advantage. When these nominal rulers sought to impose their authority, they often had to enlist the very warlords who were devastating the land. The Roxburghshire warlord Robert Kerr of Cessford, for instance, whom Fraser rates one of the most vicious men in his story, combined his role as ruthless gangleader with those of government warden and privy counsellor.

This would not have struck the surnames or their adherents as in any way incompatible. Like the Provisional IRA in its most powerful days in Northern Ireland, they saw themselves, and were seen by those in their territories, as the agents – the only available agents – of law and order. A blow for a blow, a life for a life, was effectively the only system of justice. Had one surname not punished another, there would have been no punishment. There's a further parallel here with modern gang warfare in London. What's demanded here, and is violently pursued when seen to have been denied, is 'respec'. The Tweedies and Veitches were neighbours in the hills south-east of Broughton, the Tweedies in Drumelzier, the Veitches beyond them in Dawyck. One or other was frequently held to have failed to honour their boundaries. One or other had to be warned that such lack of respect might be fatal.

Both were long-established families here. It's a place suffused in myth and legend. The origin of the Tweedies was said to be this. A crusader returned from Palestine to find his wife, a Fraser, had given birth to a son. He had been away long enough to know the boy could not be his. She told him that the child had been fathered by a spirit, in the form of a man, who had risen out of a pool on the Tweed. The husband was persuaded (he would have been well aware had he denied her claim, the Frasers might have punished his lack of respect), accepted the son as his own, but insisted his name must be Tweedie. (Not necessarily, when it was spelled at all, spelled in this way: early documents include such variants as Twedie, Tweedy, Tweidie, Twedy, Tuedy, Tuedi, Tuedie, Tueday, Tudie, Tidy, Tweedle and Twyddle.)

A latter-day Veitch, Professor John, author of *The History and Poetry of the Scottish Borders*, believed the tradition of feud and the tradition of legend belonged together:

> This district, the land of foray and feud, of hostile inroad from England, and of aggression in return, has been the heart whence strong bold action, the gradual growth of history and tradition, legend, the continuous flow of song, ballad and music have moved the feelings and moulded the imagination not only of the people of the district, but of the whole land of Scotland.

That this Veitch is much praised and quoted in Michael Tweedie's history of his family, published in 1902, serves to confirm that old animosities here had died by the end of the nineteenth century, and certainly one finds Tweedies and Veitches buried closed together not just in Broughton but even more tellingly at the little churchyard in Drumelzier too. But the years of coexistence have lasted only a little longer than the years of enmity.

*

The Tweedies arrived in Drumelzier in the early years of the fourteenth century. Soon they began to proliferate through Tweeddale and the hills above it: the Tweedies of Oliver, the Tweedies of Dreva, the Tweedies of Wrae, frequently up to no good. As Walter Buchan says in his vast history of the county of Peebles, they were 'as turbulent a race of fighting men as ever clove skulls on the Border'. (John Buchan wrote world-famous novels and ended up governing Canada; his brother Walter wrote this excellent but, outside the county, little known history, and reached the peak of his working life as town clerk of Peebles.) These were men who as their power and influence gathered came to see themselves as monarchs of all they surveyed, even when what they surveyed belonged by law to some other surname. They adopted the practice of waylaying travellers through their territory and demanding payments to let them proceed. The story was told in Peeblesshire for centuries of how on one occasion they made these demands of a man who proved to be the king, James V, travelling as he frequently did in a humble disguise, incognito – only for James to summon his entourage, travelling not far behind him, round up the Tweedies and force them into submission.

Some Tweedies were respectable: members of the family held the posts of Dean of Peebles and Sub-prior of Melrose. Perhaps, Michael Tweedie, historian of the family, wistfully suggests, it may have been the case that the family's bad deeds were remembered where their good was interred with their bones. Yet his history from the mid fifteenth century on is thick with trouble: sometimes in petty affrays, sometimes in matters of high Scottish politics. In 1566, two Tweedies, William of Drumelzier and Adam of Dreva – a man once arraigned for lopping the ears off one of his enemies – were implicated in the plot to kill Queen Mary's Italian confidant, David Rizzio.

Their first spectacular quarrel exploded in the 1520s in a feud with another mighty surname, the Flemings. The families were competing for the hand of a wealthy heiress, Catherine Fraser of Fruid. The Flemings wished to marry her to one of Lord Fleming's illegitimate sons, confusingly given the same forename, Malcolm, as one of his legitimate half-brothers, while John Tweedie of Drumelzier aspired to wed her to his son and heir, James. In 1524, Lord Fleming, accompanied by Malcolm, his eldest son, was pursuing his favourite pastime of hawking in Glenholm, now part of Broughton, when they were set upon by a mixed bag of Tweedies: John, the head of the Drumelzier surname, and another John who lived with him, James of Kilbucho, James of Wrae, and young Thomas Tweedie of Oliver. In the skirmish that followed, Thomas drew his sword and did away with Lord

Fleming. Malcolm, who by his father's death became the new Lord Fleming, was locked up in one of the Tweedies' strongholds and told he would not be released until he agreed to his captors' terms, the most solemn of which was that Catherine must marry James Tweedie.

Once free, he repudiated an agreement extracted from him under duress. The government, such as it was, intervened. The families were persuaded to sign a document announcing their reconciliation and their readiness to forgive all previous wrongs. The Tweedies and their closest supporters had to go to the cross in Peebles in their shirts and offer their naked swords to Malcolm Fleming, and even to undertake to be his servants. They were later ordered to found a chaplaincy at Biggar where the soul of the man they had slain could be prayed for and to undertake pilgrimages to the principal Scottish shrines of St Ninian in Whithorn in Galloway, St Duthus in Ross, and St Andrews, while to bring these surnames closer together a Tweedie was required to marry a Fleming. A further humiliating requirement for the Tweedies to surrender lands and fortifications to the Flemings was, however, rescinded.

Low-level bickering between these two surnames continued for years, while the Tweedies also engaged in feuds with the Scotts and the Geddeses, perhaps to punish the Veitches after one of them married a Geddes. But the Tweedies' war with the Veitches was their biggest, deepest and darkest engagement of all – 'a feud', says Walter Buchan, 'beside which the vendetta of the Montagues and Capulets seems merely a slight and elegant misunderstanding'. In 1590, Patrick Veitch, son of William Veitch, known as 'the De'il of Dawyck', was ambushed and slaughtered near Neidpath Castle just outside Peebles by a band of Tweedies headed by James of Drumelzier. The Tweedies were summoned to answer a charge that this action impugned the king's honour. Having ignored it, they were captured and jailed in Edinburgh. But before they were brought to court, the Veitches had taken their revenge, killing John of Drumelzier and Andrew Tweedie in a street fight in Edinburgh. Again, the government intervened, requiring both sides to offer heavy sureties to back promises of good behaviour, but pragmatic calculations prevailed and no action was taken against either side to punish the murderers.

Those charged with maintaining law and order knew very well that if they took resolute action against wrongdoers they might merely inflame matters further. Brutal experience told such people that the rough and ready concepts of justice applied in the Borders were better than no effective operation of justice at all. In any case, those whose duty it was to bring a law-breaking surname before the courts were frequently related to them and for motives either of ingratiation or fear were unwilling to take them on. As the English agent in the Borders, Scrope, said of Buccleuch, who held the law and order office of Keeper of Liddesdale, he showed 'a backwardness to justice, except [that] which was solely to the profit of his own friends'. And as a general rule in the Borders, English and Scottish alike, men who demanded respect for themselves had only a slight respect for the authority of a mere king.

The new century began as the old one had ended. In 1602, just as scholarly Camden was writing the final pages of his study of surnames in London, two Tweedies were named in a declaration indicting thieves and murderers and their associates for inflicting 'wrackful and intolerable calamities' in the feuds they had so long sustained. Again it made little difference, though, unusually, a man called Bateson who had murdered a Tweedie was hanged. Three years later, the restless James of Drumelzier was yet again required to offer an undertaking not to harm Andrew and James Veitch. And again – the traditional duality, a force for evil cast as a force for good – he was also summoned in the rank of baron before the Council and was twice returned to Parliament for the county.

But that did not ensure his safety. In 1607, while he was 'recreating himself after supper' in Edinburgh, he and his friend Alexander Lord Spynie were set upon in the High Street. Spynie was slain, but James survived, to join with eleven more Tweedies, their friends and their servants, to take reprisals. Three years later a petition was raised against James and his allies for waylaying a man called Russell, amputating his fingers and leaving him for dead. Yet that seems to have been the last of the outrages of this most powerful and feared representative of his surname. The following year he accidentally encountered the laird of Dawyck, a Veitch, and agreed with him that their feuding must cease; at which point James's feuding did in fact cease, since Veitch killed him.

His sons immediately swore to take their revenge. James VI, king of Scotland since 1567 and now, since 1603, king of England too, issued from Greenwich a proclamation demanding that Tweedie v. Veitch, which he believed to be the only feud now continuing in the Borders, must be halted and instructing his council to call before them 'the principals of either surname' and order them to cease the violence. As ever, these high commands were ignored. In the following year, James Tweedie's son, also James, was slain by a Veitch in a duel. Yet what the intervention of authority could not achieve, money, or rather the lack of it, could. The Tweedies, mired in debt, were forced to sell their lands and barony. It was said that when John, Lord Hay of Yester, who had purchased the property, came with his son William to claim it, the only Tweedie left in the place was a daughter, whom they found on the hearth, weeping. William went back to console her, and soon they were married. Lord John gave them Drumelzier as their wedding present. So at least in that once mighty power-base there was once more a Tweedie footfall.

'From this time on,' says Michael Tweedie, with an understandable hint of relief at writing a final line to this chronicle of violence and depravity, 'the power of the Tweedies in Tweeddale seems to have been broken . . . most of the family seem to have fallen within the civilisation which was spreading over the country, and to have settled down as gentlemen or farmers.' Before long they were known for their very respectability, holding the posts of provost and treasurer in the county town, Peebles, and taking seats on the council. Parish registers for the late seventeenth and eighteenth centuries show the surname still lavishly present in Broughton and its attendant lands of Kilbucho and Glenholm, in Drumelzier, and beyond it, in Stobo. The Veitches, too, survived here: they were prominent in Broughton Free Kirk, with fifteen of them on the communion roll in 1844. Several had taken up tailoring.

It is all civilisation now. The peace of Drumelzier makes even Broughton feel stressful. Cars hurry through on their important journeys, but in an hour in the village I saw only one other person. A memorial stone for James of Drumelzier, than whom no Tweedie was ever more destructive, has a place at the door of the family vault at the parish church. Beneath the family motto, 'Thol and think' – 'thol' is customarily translated as 'endure' or 'suffer', though sometimes merely as 'wait' – is a tribute in Latin to a life of honour; not one that those who suffered and endured at his hands would have necessarily wished to endorse.

*

All over the north of Britain, and not just in the Borders, a name could strike fear, not just into enemies but into all who lived in terrains where these battles were fought, often in the cause of that name alone. A surname became its own war cry: south of the border, 'a Percy! a Percy!' or 'a Ridley! a Ridley!'; north of it, 'a Douglas, a Douglas!' or 'a Turnbull, a Turnbull!' needed no gloss. Just so had the Syrians, according to ancient texts, once sought to frighten recalcitrant children by invoking the name of Richard the Lionheart, and the French, in the same cause, to cry 'Talbot' at them:

Is this the Talbot so much feared abroad
That with his name the mothers still their babes?
                    Shakespeare, *Henry VI, Part 1*, Act I, scene 4

Names that have marched into dictionaries

A Ridley, a Douglas: in cases like these, a brief procession of syllables can convey a whole world. Chaucer, Shakespeare, Dickens, Brontë; Adam Smith (it is only because he's a Smith that he needs a forename to distinguish him), Beveridge, Keynes; Purcell, Elgar, Britten; Darwin, Newton; Brunel, Watt, Faraday; Marlborough, Wellington, Nelson – most responses to surnames like these will be warm with approval, though some will be quite the reverse: economists such as Keynes are regarded by some as teachers of truth, by others as pedlars of fatal illusion. That applies even more to politicians. In 2002, Churchill came top of a BBC poll on Greatest Britons, but had votes against the famous been permitted, some would have cast them. To most of us now, nearly seventy years on from the Second World War, the surname evokes a national saviour; yet for others, it means a deep-dyed reactionary, a shameless imperialist who would have denied its freedom to India, a man guilty of indefensible conduct from some of the decisions he took, in both the First and the Second World Wars, and in his treatment as a Tory Home Secretary of the miners of Wales. Say 'Thatcher' or 'Blair' – or indeed 'Benn', who was never prime minister – and again you evoke a hero for some, a villain for others.

Had there been a poll to choose the hundred worst Britons, a whole range of equally recognisable names might well have emerged. In 2005 the *BBC History Magazine* published just such a list, though here the choice was left to ten noted historians. Some of their selections were deliberately wayward. One was Thomas Becket, the archbishop murdered at Canterbury. Only a few – King John, Titus Oates, Jack the Ripper (who must have

had a surname, but no one ever knew what it was), Oswald
Mosley – would have figured on most people's lists. Had the
public been given votes, they would no doubt have arraigned,
along with the Ripper, a rich crop of murderers, frauds and other
ne'er-do-wells. Such names as Burke and Hare, Crippen, and
latterly Donald Neilson, Fred West and Harold Shipman, would
surely have figured, along perhaps with such authorised merchants
of death as Judge Jeffreys after the Monmouth rebellion. But here
too there might have been mixed responses to names. Some long
regarded as thoroughly evil – Richard III is an obvious nominee,
but King John across the centuries was hardly better regarded
– have found not just defenders, but champions. Some established
criminals, like the train robber Ronnie Biggs in our own times,
have commanded at least a measure of sympathy and sometimes
affection, rising even to adulation.

*

The classic case here was that of a man who claimed to be Sir
Roger Tichborne, the missing heir to the family's name and
estate. It had until then been supposed that Roger had been lost
on a boat called the *Bella*, which sank on its way from Rio to
Kingston, Jamaica. But rumours began to circulate that some of
the crew had survived and found their way to Australia. His
grieving mother advertised for news of him, and to her delight
there came a response from a man who presented himself as the
missing baronet. His mother was sure he was genuine: the rest
of the family vehemently denied it. His claims came to court in
successive cases: the first to establish the authenticity of his claim;
the second, when the first court had found against him, on a
criminal charge of perjury. The evidence paraded before both at
very great length was persuasive: this was not the true Tichborne
heir but a man called Arthur Orton, once of Wapping, east
London, but more recently of Wagga Wagga, Australia, where

he practised the trade of butcher under the name Thomas Castro. These Tichbornes had long had the reputation of a somewhat exotic family in whose households strange things happened. In the twelfth century Lady Mabella Tichborne, facing imminent death, founded a charity of which her husband Sir Roger disapproved. It was said that she put a curse on anyone who abandoned it: if they did so, the outcome would be the birth of seven successive daughters, which would cause the line to die out. An attempt was made at the end of the eighteenth century to close the charity down, but fear of the curse caused it to be reinstated; it survives even now. In the reign of Elizabeth I, Chidiock Tichborne, a devoted Catholic, was condemned for plotting against the queen and sentenced to be hanged, drawn and quartered. While awaiting death he wrote a poem about his impending death, known as 'Tichborne's Elegy', which caught the eye of several later anthologists.

But now the case of Orton alias Tichborne – in two episodes which lasted from 1871 into 1874 and generated some of the longest speeches ever heard in a British courtroom – made the name Tichborne famous across the globe. When the claimant died in 1898, the *New York Times* recalled that the case had for a time been 'the talk of the civilised world'. All across Britain then and for several years afterwards there were people, especially working men, who took up his cause, not least, no doubt, because working-class radicals sensed an aristocratic conspiracy to do him out of his rights. His lawyer, a wild and eccentric Irishman called Dr Kenealy, was disbarred in 1874 for the way he'd conducted the Tichborne perjury case which he'd helped to make the longest in legal history. But he would not give up the cause, and in February 1875 persuaded the electors of Stoke-on-Trent to return him to Parliament to enable him to keep up the fight for the claimant.

That alone might be enough to have propelled the name Tichborne into the language, but more was to follow. A few years later a comedian called Harry Relph was establishing himself on the London stage. He was tiny (four foot six) and slight, the absolute obverse of the Tichborne claimant, who at the height of the court case was said to weigh twenty-eight stone. And so, as often happens with nicknames, he was given one which represented all that he wasn't: young Tichborne, then little Tichborne, and finally Little Tich. He thus entered the world of the eponym.

*

An eponym is simply defined as 'one who gives his name to something'. Millions are spent every year inventing names for brands, some of them more baffling than alluring (why call a company 'More Than'? – the name RSA Insurance, formerly Royal and Sun Alliance, gave to one of its brands?). The rebranding of the Post Office as Consignia, hailed at the time by the chief executive as 'modern, meaningful and entirely appropriate', is a case in point. It disappeared in a torrent of mockery within a few months.

But others whose names must have seemed at first sight odd have lived to see their eye-catching qualities selling the product. Who would have called a range of food Birdseye had Clarence Birdseye not been in charge? Not even the wackiest branding consultant. Yet today, if you trade in your Hoover to buy a Dyson, if you design a Heath Robinson car and power it with diesel, if you loll on an ottoman while sporting a trilby, if you wear your leotard in a jacuzzi, you are deep in the world of eponyms. These cases, where a single unmodified word says it all, are the purest form of the species. Many more are words derived from a name, rather than using the name alone: Elizabethan, Marxist, Thatcherite. Why, I wonder, does Marxism give us Marxists while Thatcherism gives us Thatcherites? There might seem to be a distinction between cases like Platonist, Buddhist, Marxist, Stalinist, Thatcherite and Blairite, and those like Gladstonian or Churchillian: the latter suggest a tendency, a style, an adherence; the former, a fully logged-on religious or quasi-religious belief. It's instructive that the surname of Tony Benn (a name that, significantly, he had boiled down from the Wedgwood Benn he was born with), who effectively ousted Michael Foot as the most cherished hero of the Labour left wing, spawned an eponym, Bennite, where Foot did not. Even at the height of his popularity, people never called themselves Footites. But there's no consistency here. Why *Christian* rather than Christist or Christite? Invoke a man with a very loud voice and people may say: stentorian. Discuss the harshest of laws and people will call them draconian. It's the kind of response we have come to call Pavlovian.

There are also places named after people: model villages like Saltaire (Sir Titus Salt), Akroydon near Halifax (Colonel Edward Akroyd), Tremadog and Porthmadog in Wales (William Maddocks), Fleetwood on the Lancashire coast (built by a man who had changed his own name from Hesketh to Fleetwood); or sites of an industrial enterprise – Leverburgh (William Hesketh Lever, first Viscount Leverhulme). Most people in Saltaire and Akroydon know how these places got their unusual names – just as Titus Salt and Colonel Akroyd had intended. Elsewhere, however, developers who gave their names to suburbs that they created may be largely unknown to many who live there. Such are *Cubitt* Town in dockland, named after William Cubitt who developed it; *Raynes* Park in south-west London, named after the Rayne family who owned much of the land on which it was built; and *Stone*leigh, just over the border in Surrey, named after a big house in the area called Stoneleigh that was built by a man called Stone. *Tufnell* Park adopts the middle name of the man who owned the land. *Pimlico* may derive its name from a Hoxton brewer whose ales were popular there, though another version says it refers to the Pimlico tribe of American Indians who send timber to the district. But we have on the whole been spared from the kind of surname-based place name that so offended the poet and critic Matthew Arnold when he found them in America: 'What people in whom the sense for beauty and fitness was quick could have invented, or could tolerate, the hideous names ending in --ville, the Briggsvilles, Higginsvilles, Jacksonvilles, rife from Maine to Florida; the jumble of unnatural and inappropriate names everywhere?'

There are of course much older names that derive from the first communities established in Britain, not all of them vastly better than Higginsville. Birmingham is thought to owe its name to a man called Beornmund. At the time of the Conquest, Nottingham was Snotengaham or Snotingaham; it began with a man called Snot. The local council and tourist office must give thanks every day to the Normans under whose influence Snot was supplanted by Not.

Day by day, eponyms range about us and infiltrate conversation. Here is a list of them, mainly pure but some derivative. Warning: not all the names on this list can be trusted.

Bakelite. Bauxite. Biro. Bogus. Boolean. Bowdlerise. Boycott. Brougham. Cabriolet. Chesterfield. Derrick. Everest. Fiasco. Flugelhorn. Gerrymander. Gusset. Hooligan. Parquet. Ricochet. Saxophone. Shrapnel. Sideburn. Stetson. Toupee.

Bakelite is a substance invented by a man called Leo Baekeland. (In this it differs a little from bauxite, where the name derives from the place where it was found; or from kryptonite, which comes from the Greek verb meaning to hide.)

Biro comes from László József Bíró (1900–1985) who gave us the ballpoint pen. Bogus we'll come to later.

Boole was George Boole (1815–64), mathematician, who developed forms of algebra into a system of logic. 'Bowdlerise' derives from the activities of a doctor called Thomas Bowdler, who went through the works of Shakespeare, removing such lines and phrases and words that he thought fell short of

propriety (quite a lot). Captain Charles Cunningham Boycott
was an English land agent ostracised by subordinate landowners
whom he had misused. Henry Brougham, later Lord Brougham,
Georges Edouard Cabriolet and Joseph Aloysius Hansom are all
said to have invented new forms of transportation. A Lord
Chesterfield perfected a new kind of sofa. The name Derrick,
which now implies a form of lifting gear, originally meant a
gallows and derives from a prominent English hangman. The
name Everest was chosen to honour Sir George of that surname:
he did not climb that most famous mountain, but was the first
to map it. The word fiasco refers to an Italian opera director,
Alessandro Fiasco, who was famous for his catastrophic produc-
tions, in one of which – his staging of *Norma* at Padua in 1839
– a large moon made of pewter fell from the flies and nearly
did for a tenor.

A flugelhorn is a trumpet-like musical instrument – but its
name derives from a German word meaning wing. The saxophone
was invented by Adolphe Sax. Gerrymander commemorates
Governor Elbridge Gerry, of Massachusetts, who rigged the
electoral boundaries in his party's interest, producing a shape on
the map that somebody said looked like a salamander. Florence
Gusset, a needlewoman, improved the construction of some
forms of underwear. The Hooligans (though they may have
been Houlihans) were a family in south London, famous for
their unruly behaviour.

Jean-Philippe Parquet laid the floors at Versailles for Louis XIV.
Marc-Antoine Ricochet discovered a way of causing a bullet to
hit an inaccessible target by making it bounce off a nearby hard
surface. Elsewhere on the war front, the English artillery officer
Henry Shrapnel invented a new kind of explosive device. The
word 'sideburns' derives from a soldier called Burnside who grew
his hair that way. The stetson, an American wide-brimmed hat,
was bestowed on the world by John Batterson Stetson. If under-
neath your stetson you wore a toupee, your benefactor here was

a French hairdresser, Maurice Toupee, who devised this appurtenance for himself when he found he was going bald, thus transforming the future of show business. Giovanni (formerly Juan) Vertigo, an Italian born in Spain, gave his name to the fear of heights which afflicts so many, though not apparently him, since he was a high-wire artist.

That leaves us with Bogus, a word, according to Martin Manser in his *Dictionary of Eponyms*, where most of the characters on this list may be found, that may have derived from the name Borghese – of an Italian who peddled forged banknotes in the American West – though it's also claimed to be linked to a machine for making counterfeit coins, or even to have derived from a French word *bagasse* which originally meant 'rubbish'. *Chambers Dictionary* says it's American, of doubtful provenance, and may be related to 'bogy'. Another source traces it to a Harold Bogus – which may, it says, have not been his real name; he used several others – a serial defrauder practising in the US. But this last definition of Bogus is bogus. It comes from a wonderfully entertaining book called *Stipple, Wink and Gusset* by James Cochrane. On the list above, Cabriolet, Fiasco, Gusset, Parquet, Toupee and Vertigo are, as you may have guessed, Cochrane concoctions, along with such ripe inventions as Emmeline Boudoir, the puritan Nathaniel Bigot, Sir Oswald Binge, Frederick Doldrum, Miles Dudgeon and many more. Curiously this book also includes a hangman called Derrick, listed as a fiction in Cochrane but as fact in Manser and *Chambers*.

Playwrights and novelists too have left us with deathless eponyms. We cherish the concept of Malapropism. Jekyll and Hyde are evoked to portray split personalities, to which the word schizophrenic is so often, and ignorantly, applied. Micawber, Uriah Heep, Miss Havisham, are emblematic figures in Dickens, who created a world that's now described as Dickensian. Remembering Pooter in *The Diary of a Nobody*, we find acquaintances, or writers like Mark Antony Lower, Pooteresque. Humpty

Dumpty is constantly called up for comparisons, along with Tweedledum and Tweedledee. There are some names too where an eponym has sprung from a pseudonym. The word 'Orwellian' is endlessly used to conjure up the kind of society depicted in his novel *Nineteen Eighty-Four*. But Orwell's real name was Blair. Had he not adopted a pseudonym, the word we would apply to the bleakest of all imaginable futures would be Blairian.

Names like Macdonald and Campbell, Birdseye and Biro, proceed from nature, from the names that those who wore them were born with. But the impact of surnames affects us in other ways too. Some that, in one way or another, shape the way in which we think about their possessors – especially where their success may depend on box-office appeal – are the products of skilled and expensive manipulation. And still others may shape our behaviour in ways we are hardly aware of – in the images that a name may immediately form in our minds, through the way we assemble in queues, to the way that we choose to vote.

6

Manipulations

Names that Infect the Mind

'Tell me, Baynes,' said Holmes, 'who is this man Henderson?'
'Henderson', the inspector answered, 'is Don Murillo,
once called the Tiger of San Pedro.'
Arthur Conan Doyle, 'The Adventure of Wisteria Lodge'

Masks and masquerades: the starry career of Herbert Charles Angelo Kuchacevich Schluderpacheru

One of the more substantial tombs in the churchyard at Broughton in Hampshire commemorates a woman call Theodosia, a writer of much-loved hymns, forgotten now, but highly regarded in both Britain and America in the early years of the nineteenth century. As one admirer wrote:

> Her hymns are evangelical
> They are of matchless worth.
> They are sung by congregations
> Through nearly all the earth.

She was revered most of all by Baptists. Her father, a timber merchant, was the Baptist pastor in Broughton. It wasn't only her hymnody for which Broughton remembered her. It was also, perhaps even more, for the tragedy that overtook her early in life when, on the eve of her marriage, the man she was about to marry was drowned. Dr Parr, in his history of Broughton, is not convinced this story as told in the village is true, but clearly many people believed it. She is buried, despite her Baptist persuasion, in the Anglican churchyard. Her grave bears the inscription, still just about legible:

> Silent the lyre, and dumb the tuneful tongue
> That sung on earth her great Redeemer's praise;
> But now in Heaven she joins the angelic song,
> In more harmonious, more exalted lays.

But she wasn't buried as Theodosia. That was a pen name concealing her true one, Anne Steele – a form of masquerade much favoured by women writers, some of whom adopted the ultimate pseudonym by displaying no name at all. They come in several varieties, some denoted by other descriptions: pen name (more affectedly, *nom de plume*), alias, *nom de guerre*. None has got there by accident.

★

The actor Herbert Lom died while I was writing this book. He was ninety-four. 'Remember Lom', people said, 'in *The Ladykillers*?' (or *The Pink Panther*, or *Phantom of the Opera* or the three different films in which he played Napoleon); but it wouldn't have tripped off the tongue so easily had he stuck through his long career to the name he was born with, which was Herbert Charles Angelo Kuchacevich Schluderpacheru. Of all the haunts of the pseudonym, none is as thronged as this one, and when you imagine some original names of the biggest stars you can see why they changed them. What about, for instance, *Top Hat* starring Frederic Austerlitz and Virginia Katherine McMath? Norma Jeane Mortenson (from the age of sixteen, Norma Jeane Dougherty) and Bernard Schwartz in *Bus Stop*? Better Astaire and Rogers, better

Monroe and Curtis. A few such stars were born with names any studio might have slavered over: Laurence Olivier, who came from a line of priests genuinely called Olivier, for one, though Vivien Leigh was a confection; she was born Vivian Mary Hartley. Joan Fontaine abandoned the name de Haviland, one that Hollywood might have concocted, though the sister with whom she warred all her life, Olivia, kept the family name. Humphrey Bogart was born a Bogart, but Lauren Bacall began life as Betty Joan Perske.

Likewise one can see why the studio turned Archibald Leach into Cary Grant, and even more why John Wayne was considered a better name for the man we know as John Wayne than Marion Morrison, the one he was born with. Kirk Douglas started life with a Russian name that translates as Issur Danielovitch; Woody Allen was once Allen Stewart Konigsberg. The actress Dinah Sheridan, another star lost to the world in 2012, was marketed by her studio as a typical English rose, a task that would have been rather more challenging had she kept her original name, which was Dinah Nadyejda Mec. The singer Billie Holiday was Eleanora Fagan Gough, a name which seems wildly removed from the sort of life she led and the kind of person she was, and also from her beginnings. Her autobiography, *Lady Sings the Blues*, begins: 'Mom and Pop were just a couple of kids when they got married. He was eighteen, she was sixteen, and I was three.'

The great flowering of popular music in Britain from the 1950s onwards, the unparalleled cult of the pop star, multiplied stage names too. Cilla Black was born White, Elton John was born Dwight. Adam Faith was Terence Nelhams-Wright. An agent called Larry Parnes changed Tommy Hicks into Tommy Steele, Reginald Smith into Marty Wilde, Ronald Wycherley into Billy Fury and Clive Powell into Georgie Fame. Parnes was mocked in a novel by Colin MacInnes, one of the sharpest observers of the pop scene:

'Which of the boy slaves was it swung it? Strides Vandal?
   Limply Leslie? Rape Hunger?'
'No, no . . . Soft-core Granite, I think it was.'
Oh, that one. A Dagenham kiddy. He's very new.'

But the pattern continued, and still does today. Declan MacManus became Elvis Costello; he married the jazz singer Diana Krall (who, in case you wondered, was born Diana Krall). Were he to be resurrected, the German composer Engelbert Humperdinck (1854–1921) would find no doubt to his chagrin that he was now only the second most famous Engelbert Humperdinck, that name having been purloined by Arnold George Dorsey. Prince, born Prince Rogers Nelson, for a time retreated behind a sign he described as a love symbol that could not be spoken; the world was expected to say, The Artist Formerly Known as Prince.

Now and then a name is taken to be a pseudonym only for its owner to assure the world that it isn't. The conductor Leopold Stokowski had to deny persistent rumours that his real name was Stokes, which he had tampered with because Stokowski seemed a more imposing name for a great conductor. But, as his birth certificate showed, his name was genuine; his was a Polish family. The exotic Peruvian singer Yma Súmac, whose range was said to extend beyond four octaves, was pursued by rumours that she had started life as Amy Camus from Brooklyn, which name she had deftly reversed. But Peru was proud of her, and its government formally endorsed her claim to be descended from Atahualpa, the last Incan emperor. The British prima ballerina Alicia Markova frankly admitted, however, that her born name was the inadequately ballerinaish Lilian Alicia Marks.

Where actors and singers have stage names, writers have *noms de plume* – less ostentatiously, pen names. But sometimes writers have resorted to a practice unimaginable among actors and singers by giving themselves no name at all. They remain anonymous. Many now universally venerated would not when they published disclose who they were – women especially. Fanny Burney, Jane Austen ('*Pride and Prejudice*, by the author of *Sense and Sensibility*'), Mrs Gaskell – all denied their earliest readers any hint of their identity. But so among men did Andrew Marvell, Jonathan Swift, Laurence Sterne, Richardson (author of *Pamela*) and Fielding (when he responded to it with *Shamela*), John Locke, Horace Walpole and Samuel Butler ('the author of *Erewhon*'). Sir Walter Scott was billed until his final impoverished days only as the author of *Waverley*. That Thomas Gray was the author of 'Elegy written in a Country Churchyard' was revealed only after his death. Thomas Love Peacock liked to present himself as the 'the author of *Headlong Hall*'. 'I thought', explained this creator of outsize personalities, 'I might very fitly preserve my impersonality.'

Tennyson's *In Memoriam*, which did not disclose his name, was attributed at first to others. Other writers adopted names more convenient for readers to pronounce and remember: Joseph Conrad had started life as Józef Teódor Konrad Korzeniowski. The excitement that anonymity could sometimes cause – one reason, no doubt, why it was resorted to – was demonstrated in recent years when fervid speculation broke out over the author-ship of a political novel based on the Clinton years called *Primary Colours*, eventually traced to a New York and Washington columnist, Joe Klein. The book was published as 'by Anonymous' and Klein at first denied that he was the author.

Women resorting to pseudonyms masqueraded as men: the Brontës, using the names Acton, Ellis and Currer Bell, expected to be taken for men. 'George Eliot' was a specific statement of maleness. Mrs Gaskell began as Cotton Mather Mills, and later toyed with the name Stephen Berwick (her father was born in the border town). Other names – E. Nesbit, J. K. Rowling, or latterly the E. L. James of *Fifty Shades of Grey* – sound resolutely androgynous.

Men adopting female pen names have been much rarer, though not unknown. William Beckford, better known as the author of *Vathek*, had earlier posed as Lady Harriet Marlow when he published *Modern Novel Writing; or, The Elegant Enthusiast; and Interesting Emotions of Arabella Bloomville, a Rhapsodical Romance*. Swinburne, for a work that might have embarrassed his family – a consideration that deserted him through much of his life – hid behind the sobriquet Mrs Horace Manners. But worse dangers lurked than family disapproval. As John Mullan shows in his book *Anonymity* (2008), from which many of these examples are taken, a writer who offended could find himself faced with a duel.

But fear was not always the motivation: sometimes it was more like flippancy. Minor writings might dent a serious reputation. Thackeray kept his real name for his novels, retreating for less solemn occasions into such names as Charles Yellowplush, Ikey Solomons, Michael Angelo Titmarsh, Bashi-Bazook, Folkstone Canterbury, George Fitzboodle, Dr Solon Pacifico and Launcelot Wagstaffe. It was not unusual for writers dealing with different sectors of life to invent alter egos. Lewis Carroll remained Charles Lutwidge Dodgson when practising as an academic. According to the journalist and editor Edmund Yates, Dodgson had first signed his writings 'BB', but when Yates came to publish a poem he told Dodgson he needed something more substantial. Dodgson suggested the surname Dares, after Daresbury in Cheshire where he was born, and then Edgar Cuthwellis, an anagram of Charles Lutwidge; or alternatively, Edgar U. C. Westhill (another). Finally he offered a choice: Louis Carrol or Lewis Carroll. Yates chose the latter. The poet and topographical writer Edward Thomas, whose reputation has burgeoned since Matthew Hollis's life of him, first published as Edward Eastaway.

A generation of crime writers were known to be other people: J. I. M. Stewart (a renowned Oxford academic, author of analytical studies of Joyce, Kipling, Peacock and Hardy), was Michael Innes, Cecil Day Lewis (poet; eventually, Poet Laureate) was Nicholas

Blake. Anthony Burgess published some of his novels under the pen name Joseph Kell, which name he also employed to write a very favourable review for the *Yorkshire Post* of a book by Anthony Burgess. Both names, in fact, were pseudonyms; his real name was John Anthony Burgess Wilson. In our own day Julian Barnes, again anxious to differentiate one kind of writing from another, has published crime novels as Dan Kavanagh; John Banville uses Benjamin Black and claims to be happier when he is being Black than when he is being Banville; while Jonathan Freedland distinguishes between his two lives: on the one hand, as a *Guardian* journalist and broadcaster, on the other as the concocter of bestselling thrillers, by styling himself Sam Bourne. (His agent had felt that his true name sounded too like a pointy-headed operator from a pointy-headed newspaper.)

Recently, there has been what appears to be a new development: publishers or agents advising writers to change their names, in the manner of showbiz people, to something more glamorous. An American writer called Patricia O'Brien had published five novels but her sixth could not find a publisher. More than a dozen, apprehensive because her previous book had not sold well, said no. Her agent told her to find a new name and resubmit the new book. So she changed the name on the title page to Kate Alcott. The rights were sold in three days. In England, a writer called Alison Potter was told by her publisher that her name wasn't grabby enough to appeal to young readers and buyers (though the name Potter on a dust jacket does not appear to turn young readers and buyers off J. K. Rowling). Alison was swiftly cut down to Ali, but the surname was more of a problem. She looked for something suitable in graveyards and on cinema websites, and now writes as Ali Knight.

Lists of pseudonyms and the real names behind them are easily come by. The latest edition of Adrian Room's *Dictionary of Pseudonyms* contains 13,000 examples. What is much more sparsely charted is why those adopting them chose the names that they did, or what others they first considered. Ford Hermann Hueffer, author of *The Good Soldier* and *Parade's End*, changed to Ford Madox Ford because, when he came home after serving in the First World War, he thought his name sounded too German, but also because of his veneration for his grandfather, the painter Ford Madox Brown. Eric Blair, who became George Orwell, fearing his books might upset his family, resolved to take on a mask. His first shortlist, fortunately discarded, included the names Kenneth Miles and H. Lewis Allways. So the kind of world we now call Orwellian, which might – had he stuck to his original name – now be termed Blairian, could even have been Allwaysian, which would never have done. He had also, in his spell as a tramp, used the name P. S. Burton. Having talked with his publisher Victor Gollancz, who liked it too, he settled on Orwell after the river in Suffolk, where he lived as a child, and George because of its Britishness. Though seen as a man of the left, Orwell was always proud of his patriotism – a patriotism not based on the waving of flags but on quiet appreciation for the country to which he belonged.

Some pseudonyms are embodied in law. In the US two crucial cases determining a woman's right to an abortion were listed as Roe v. Wade and Doe v. Bolton. Roe and Doe are what are called 'placeholder names', used in cases where real names are for some reason withheld. It was not until after the case had been settled that Jane Roe in the case against Wade was revealed to be Norma McCorvey. Other names in quite different contexts serve the same purpose. Joe Bloggs was a term often used in Britain to indicate Mr Average, nobody in particular. (It was later snapped up as the name of a clothing company.) People would talk of Charles Farnes-Barnes or Fred Fernackapan where a name was forgotten or did not matter. The name Walter Plinge would appear in the cast list for a part in a play which had yet to be allocated. In the days when rugby union used in its superior way to ban any participant caught playing for money, rugby league sides which tried them out would promise them anonymity, and the team sheets might then have to list one or more players called A. N. Other and S. O. Else.

In national and perhaps even more in local papers, regular polemical columns are given a general name which anyone who contributes can use. The surname selected is designed to give a kick to the copy – John *Blunt* is a typical specimen – usually with a claim attached to the column which proclaims that they Speak Out Fearlessly, or Pull No Punches. Upmarket papers did the same with names like Scrutator or Senex – so much more dignified, that, than Old Man. Individual columnists too write under pseudonyms. The *Daily Express* had for many years a fanciful columnist who used the pseudonym Beachcomber. Everyone knew it was written by J. B. Morton and by Morton alone, but Beachcomber it remained. His opposite number on the *News Chronicle* was called Timothy Shy. 'Shy' (real name D. B. Wyndham Lewis) had in fact been Beachcomber before Morton.

Long names are awkward for newspapers since the by-line becomes too long for a single column. My local newspaper in south-west London some time ago had trouble with a contributor called Rebecca Chaput de Saintonge. The *Daily Telegraph*'s Hugh Montgomery-Massingberd shed his Montgomery. But these changes were not always dictated by limitations of space. John Izbicki, a Jewish refugee from Hitler's Germany, later the respected education correspondent of the *Telegraph*, was delighted to be called in after a month in the reporters' room by his managing editor, 'Pop' Pawley, and offered a pay rise because his work was considered so good. In that case, he asked, why was it that they never gave him a by-line – the name at the top of a story? He narrates what follows in his memoir, *Life Between the Lines*:

Pawley looked slightly startled and his smile disappeared. 'Ah, a by-line. I see. Well, you see, Izbicki, if we were to

give you a by-line, we'd have so many readers writing in to
ask us why we were employing so many – er – foreigners,
people like Loshak and Guy Rais.'

He could have added: Aneliese Schults, Peter Schmidt
and several other *real* foreigners who covered news for the
paper abroad. The difference was that David Loshak, who
was to become one of my closest friends, and Guy Rais
were, like me, Jewish. The others were not.

In the end he wrote a 'splash' – the story that leads the paper
– and so had to be given a by-line. But it still wasn't John Izbicki.
He had mentioned at some point that his second forename was
Howard and his page one report carried the by-line 'John Howard',
as did every other story under his name for around a year. Only
then did a senior colleague persuade the hierarchy that the name
Izbicki was not just decent to place before *Telegraph* readers but
actually, because of its catchiness, potentially useful.

Sometimes the names of authors sound more like pseudonyms
than genuine pseudonyms. Lascelles Abercrombie, Coventry
Patmore, Thomas Churchyard, George Psalmanazar, Hastings
Rashdall, Edgell Rickword, Augustus Montague Toplady: all but
one of these is a wholly natural name. The one that isn't is
Psalmanazar. A successful impostor, who invented a past in
Formosa and published studies of its geography, customs and
language which were mostly inventions, he was befriended by a
Scottish priest called Innes who claimed to have converted him
from heathenism to Christianity and from crime to godly behaviour. He ended his life as a writer of theological tracts. His name
had been invented by Innes. He never revealed the name he was
born with, and subsequent research has left it a secret. Psalmanazar
was in this sense a pseudonym, but it was also his genuine name,
in that it was the only surname he'd got.

The most mysterious pseudonymous figure of all (unless, of
course, you believe that the works of Shakespeare were written

by somebody else), using a name determinedly sexless and face-less, was B. Traven, whose B, like the S in President Harry S. Truman, probably stood for nothing. Investigative journalists spent many fretful months, even years, trying to determine the true identity of the author of *The Treasure of the Sierra Madre*. Was he Ret Marut, a German actor and anarchist who had disappeared? If he was, who had Ret Marut been? Could he really be Otto Feige, from Brandenburg? And who was Hal Croves, who turned up at a meeting the film director John Huston had fixed with Traven, saying he was Traven's representative? Was this, in fact, Traven/Marut/possibly Feige? The speculation helped to build an even bigger audience for Huston's film of *The Treasure of the Sierra Madre* than it might have commanded without it. And then, who was this new mysterious figure – a man who said he was Traven Torsvan, and who seemed to be getting "Traven"'s royalty payments? Was he Traven/Marut/Feige/Croves as well? Before anyone could extract an answer, he joined the ranks of the disappeared. Nearly fifty years on from the death of a man (Hal Croves) who may have been all of them, nobody really knows.

There are other kinds of pseudonym more often described as aliases, some plucked out of the blue, others carefully plotted, adopted by people up to no good. According to Edith Sitwell's *The English Eccentrics*, quack doctors used to parade a remarkable range of unlikely names: Don Lopus, the Illustrious Danish doctor (though 'lopus' sounds more like the sort of disease patients might have asked him to have a look at); Dr Anodyne, at the court of Charles II. John Wilmot, the notorious seventeenth-century Earl of Rochester, practised as such a doctor under the name Alexander Bends, claiming, as so many quack doctors did, to come from the Continent. An enterprising gentleman who appeared in London in the 1780s did not offer specific cures but offered his service as an expert in the Philosophical, Mathematical, Optical, Magnetical, Electrical, Physical, Chymical, Pneumatic, Hydraulic,

Hydrostatic, Styangraphic, Palenchic and Primantic arts. This polymath claimed that his name was Katterfelto.

Others out to deceive adopted names a good deal simpler than these. After the Great Train Robbery of 1963, Ronald Biggs disappeared and began a new life under the alias Terry Cook. In 1974, the Labour MP and former minister John Stonehouse, in financial trouble and (correctly) under suspicion for being a spy for the Czechs, disappeared. His clothes were found on a beach in Miami. He appeared to have drowned. In fact he had gone to Australia, where he called himself Joseph Markham – not an invented name, but that of a recently dead constituent whose papers he used. He then crossed to New Zealand to carry out illegal financial transactions, telling the bank that his name was Clive Mildoon. A teller became suspicious. When Stonehouse returned to Australia a watch was put on him. It was thought he might be the missing peer Lord Lucan, who had vanished after the murder of the family's nanny. Stonehouse/Markham/Mildoon, correctly identified, was arrested, deported to Britain, put on trial and given a seven-year sentence.

In 2002, a Hartlepool man called John Darwin, who had also run into deep financial difficulties, went out canoeing and did not come back. In time, his grieving wife made a claim on their insurance. Darwin, who was in hiding, had adopted the name John Jones, assuming the identity of a child who had died very young. For a time he even surreptitiously rejoined his wife in their family home. The same device was adopted by a succession of police officers, needing new identities to work under cover in the Metropolitan Police Special Demonstration Squad. In 2012, the mother of a boy born in 1985 discovered that her son's father, whom she knew as Bob Robinson but who disappeared some two years after the boy's birth, was in fact Bob Lambert, an SDS officer, married with two children, who had now reinvented himself as an academic. He had used the identity of a boy called Mark Robert Charles Robinson, who as his gravestone in

Branksome cemetery, Dorset, says, 'fell asleep' in October 1959, aged seven and a half. In 2013, a US investigation into alleged money-laundering uncovered an account-holder who used the alias Joe Bogus.

Sometimes, as with Orwell, the choice of a name is long considered; sometimes it's decided by impulse. The actor Michael Caine began life as Maurice Micklewhite. Finding it cumbersome, he began his career using the name Michael Scott. But he wasn't the only Michael Scott in the business, so he cast around for a name that would better distinguish him – and found it on a cinema poster advertising *The Caine Mutiny*. Robert Maxwell, born Ján Ludvík Hyman Binyamin Hoch, but anxious to sound British, took his name from the label on a jar of Maxwell House coffee. At least, that was Maxwell's story. And even though it was one of Maxwell's, it may have been true.

Such names were deliberately chosen. But in several other departments of life, the impact a surname makes may be purely accidental.

The tyranny of the alphabet, or, It's all right for you, you're a Capulet

Here's another answer to the immortal question that Shakespeare's Juliet puts to Romeo – though she might get a different answer from someone called Abercrombie than she would from someone called Zwicker.

'What's in a name?' That rather depends on the letter it starts with. Long condemned for condoning racism and sexism, society now finds itself condemned for alphabetism, too. There used to be issued every year four vast phone books that covered the whole of London, divided into A to D, E to K, L to R and S to Z (a reminder, this, that names do not divide into two equal halves after the middle letter of our twenty-six, which is M: the middle name in an alphabetical list of MPs for 2012 was Jones). Once, there had been a clamour of companies calling themselves by the initials AA or confecting a name such as Aardvark to get to the head of the A to Ds, though by 1984 even these had been gazumped as sharp-eyed entrepreneurs noted that numbers came first.

One can find a similar sense of competition in queues as marshalled by every range of officialdom. In line with what is taken to be the natural order of things, the As are almost always placed first, with those lumbered with names like Young or Zwingli left sulkily at the end of the queue. Enlightened organisers, scenting injustice, will sometimes call the M to Zs first, but that still denies a Zwingli parity with a Matthews.

Some of the screeds railing against alphabetism that are posted on the internet are satirical, but others are entirely serious. The case for a greater equity in the land of the surname is especially pressed by academics on other academics. There are long and scholarly analyses in journals of social science examining the issue, which cite in particular a study in the *Journal of Economic Perspectives* by Liran Einav of Stanford and Leeat Yariv of the California Institute of Technology, Pasadena, the latter a scholar whose name makes him especially well equipped for examining this form of discrimination. These investigators sought, as they explain in their paper, 'What's in a Surname? The Effects of Surname Initials on Academic Success', to marshal evidence 'that a variety of proxies for success in the US economics labor market (tenure at highly ranked schools, fellowship in the Econometric Society, and to a lesser extent, Nobel Prize and Clark Medal winnings) are correlated with surname initials, favouring economists with surname initials earlier in the alphabet. These patterns persist even when controlling for country of origin, ethnicity, and religion. We suspect that these effects are related to the existing norm in economics prescribing alphabetical ordering of authors' credits.' They deal here with economists and econometricists. Other disciplines, they find, are more enlightened: 'Indeed, there is no significant correlation between surname initials and tenure at departments of psychology, where authors are credited roughly according to their intellectual contribution.'

There is evidence, however, of academic economists in their ivory bunkers fighting back, according to Einav and Yariv: 'The economics market participants seem to react to this phenomenon. Analysing publications in the top economics journals since 1980, we note two consistent patterns: authors with higher surname initials are significantly less likely to participate in projects with more than three authors and significantly more likely to write papers in which the order of credits is non-alphabetical.' Einav and Yariv were by no means first in this field. Robert K. Merton (in no alphabetical trouble here, as he was working alone) had explored it in *The Sociology of Science: Theoretical and Empirical Investigations* (1973). Merton had practical experience of problems with names. He was born Meyer Robert Schkolnick, son of a Russian emigré who arrived in the US as Schkolnikoff, and his second wife was a sociologist called Zuckerman. Merton is credited with the invention of the term 'self-fulfilling prophecy', and, delightfully, with a phenomenon which he called 'anticipatory plagiarism', defined as: 'when someone steals your original idea and publishes it a hundred years before you were born'.

The *Journal of Political Economy* took up the baton with a study called 'First Author Conditions' by Maxim Engers, Joshua S. Gans, Simon Grant and Stephen P. King. Note the strict alphabetical order here. Also note that the paper was cited afterwards as by 'Engers *et al*'. It's that *et al.*, the literature suggests, that especially hurts. Who knows which of this distinguished quartet made the greatest contribution? Yet, as ordained by the tyranny of the alphabet, Engers gets a name spelled out in full, where the rest disappear under an *et al.* blanket. In 2009, David A. Lake, of the University of California, San Diego, published a paper entitled 'Who's on First? Listing Authors by Relative Contribution Trumps the Alphabet', which a blogger called Matthew Yglesias enthusiastically (for obvious reasons) placed on the web, prefacing it thus:

Given my last name, I've long been concerned about the last socially accepted form of systematic institutionalised arbitrary discrimination in the United States: Alphabetism. Nobody ever made Matt Yglesias and Rachel Zabarkes sit in the back of the bus, but we sure as hell did have to stand at the end of the line at snack time in school (worse, later she got married and changed her name to Rachel Zabarkes Friedman and briefly worked at *National Review*). By the time they handed me my diploma at college graduation, practically everyone and their families had already scattered elsewhere. And of course if I co-author anything with anyone, my name goes last.

Yglesias adds that as a matter of principle, he tries to list names in reverse order, 'but often find myself over ruled in formal contexts'. Still, at least Zabarkes would have finished ahead of Zuckerman.

Lake is looking at the discipline to which he belongs, political science. He finds it subject to what he calls 'the tyranny of the alphabet' in ways that some other disciplines, carefully listing authors according to the relative values of their contributions, are not. And this may have broader consequences: 'hiring, promotion, and professional distinction are tied more or less directly to perceived scholarly contributions. Although important publications will benefit all collaborators – just as a tide lifts all boats – at the margin there is always some trade off in assessing the relative contributions of multiple authors to any scholarly work.'

Listing names in order of the value of their contributions can, Lake accepts, cause trouble too. It may lead to conflict among participants. His experience, though, suggests that senior scholars who insist upon being first in the list of authors may be made to pay for such arrogance. Their colleagues and their students know who they are and what they are up to, and devalue their reputations accordingly.

Most of the activity in this cloistered sub-division of the human rights movement occurs in the US. But in 2004, another possible victim of alphabetism, Professor Richard Wiseman of the University of Hertfordshire, asked *Daily Telegraph* readers to assess their success rates in their careers, their finances, their health, and their lives in general. Fifteen thousand responded (some indication perhaps of how much such issues are worried over). Those with surnames lower in the alphabet had significantly lower satisfaction scores than those higher up. The pattern was stronger among the old than among the young – perhaps reflecting, Wiseman suggested, the way in which one's sense of success builds up gradually during one's life. But what was he really measuring here? His findings were built not on any objective measure of success, but on the perceptions which individuals held of their own success. The truest deduction might be that it's the sense of success, rather than success itself, which varies according to the alphabetical order of surnames. Because they've so often had to stand at the back of the queue, the Ns to Zs in our society are that much more discontented.

It's possible too that if Juliet were today running for elected office, she as a Capulet would have a lead over Romeo as a Montague. Some electoral authorities in the US became so concerned about the inequity of always printing names on the ballot paper in alphabetical order that they ruled that they should be varied.

It was not until the 1970s that ballot papers in Britain showed party affiliations against candidates' names. Before that, political parties were faced with a temptation which they could not always resist – to pick candidates with names high up in the alphabet, to get them to the head of the ballot sheet. There was, and to some extent still is, a second insidious impetus for a party to pick a candidate on the basis of his or her surname: the chance that the name of a challenger might be confused with that of the favourite. A congregation of Joneses is never unexpected in Wales, so it may have been pure coincidence that a ballot paper for Anglesey at the general election of 1964 offered three men called Jones against one called Hughes. Cledwyn Hughes, the Labour MP here since 1951, was so well entrenched in Anglesey that in effect the contest between the Joneses was only to be runner-up. But what does seem more dubious is that in 1955, Hughes, then a relative newcomer, had been opposed by a Liberal called J. W. Hughes and a Conservative called O. H. Hughes. Only the Nationalist candidate bucked the trend by being called Jones.

The event which finally caused the law to be changed to permit party labels on ballot papers was the contest in the Bexley constituency in the general election of 1970. Here, the Conservative leader and enthusiast for British membership of the Common Market, Edward Heath, was opposed by a fervent opponent of British entry, also called Edward Heath, registered as standing for the Conservative and Consult the People Party. The name had only been his for a matter of weeks; until then he had been James Robert Lambert. The Conservatives stationed people outside the polling stations to warn voters to check very carefully which Heath they were voting for.

Much later, after party labels had been permitted, there were further blatant attempts to confuse. A man called Douglas Parkin, standing as a candidate for a Social Democratic Party set up two years before Roy Jenkins, Shirley Williams, Bill Rodgers and David Owen launched theirs, changed his name to Roy Jenkins to run against the more famous Roy Jenkins, candidate for the SDP, in the Glasgow Hillhead by-election of 1982. The masquerading Roy Jenkins won 282 votes against the 10,166 which carried the real one to victory.

In the following year, a man with a beard attempted to present his nomination papers at Barnet and Finchley, a seat then held by the Prime Minister Margaret Thatcher, whose papers showed her to be a Conservative living at 10 Downing Street. The newcomer's papers said that his name was Margaret Thatcher, that he lived at Downing Street Mansions in Southwark, and that he represented the Conservatory Party. The agent who put in the nomination gave his name as Ronald Regan. The new Thatcher had previously been called Colin Hanoman; the agent, Simon Stansfeld. The returning officer refused to accept the papers. Thatcher and Regan then took him to court, but the judge ruled against them. The case was then hurried through to appeal, where they lost again. That this Thatcher and Regan had stated that their intention was to make the proceedings even more of a farce than most elections were did not deter some who worked through the judgements from coming to the conclusion that the returning officer had been wrong. He had no right to rule out a nomination because it was designed to confuse. In a later case, a court found that a man called Richard Huggett, who had put up as a Literal Democrat against a Liberal Democrat, could not be prevented from doing so. After that, the Electoral Commission was given the power to regulate the use of names on the ballot sheet.

Yet such confusions continue. In 2012, a result in a local election in the Prestatyn North ward of Denbighshire was declared void because people counting the votes had awarded some of those cast for a Labour candidate called Pennington to the candidate the Conservatives fielded against him, a Mr Penlington. There is solid evidence that, especially in elections where more than one candidate needs to be plumped for, there's more in a name than most people suspect. The supreme analysts of voting in British elections, Colin Rallings and Michael Thrasher of Plymouth University, estimate that between 1973 and 2011, some 2,050 councillors owed their election to their high places on the ballot sheet.

The Greeks had a theory called *onomantia*, which held that in any contest the contender with the longer name was likely to win. Though no one would take that seriously now, it's a curious fact that when you take the top two contenders in US presidential elections since George Washington was installed in 1789, the candidate with the longer name has won almost twice as often as the candidate with the shorter one. Perhaps longer names simply sound weightier, more appropriate to the highest responsibilities. It's also a matter of note that of forty-three US presidents, twenty-nine had names which began with a letter in the first half of the alphabet, and only fourteen came from the second half. In terms of the old London phone books, ten were A to Ds, fifteen were E to Ks, the L to Rs had eleven, but the S to Zs notched only a meagre seven. The Greeks would no doubt have built a theory on that.

This is not the only aspect of US life where the A to Ms heavily outnumber the N to Zs. I came by accident across a list which had nothing to do with elected office – a catalogue of 456 astronauts whom the US had shot into space. Of these, 296 had A to M surnames and 190 had N to Zs. It's also intriguing to speculate, in the light of Juliet's question, and of the repeated allegations by way-out Republicans that Barack Obama is a Muslim born outside the US, how Obama would have fared in US politics had his name been just slightly different: not Barack Hussein Obama but Barack Obama Hussein. 'I got my middle name', he said shortly before his electoral triumph of 2008, 'from somebody who obviously didn't think that I'd run for President.'

In general, it seems to be the case that the less that's known about an election, the more likely it becomes that the initial letter of a surname may influence the result. In Australia, where voting is compulsory, there's a tendency, known as the donkey vote, for reluctant voters in contests where preferential voting is used to make their choices in the order the names appear on the ballot paper. Because this was clearly giving an advantage to those with the names at the top of the list, names began to be listed in random order. An American academic called Ward Elliott drew attention to the tendency for seats in the US Senate to go predominantly to candidates whose names began with the letters A, B and C. Analysis of thirty-three candidates successful in the US Senate elections of 2012 fails to confirm that, yet ten of them came in the batch A to D, twelve in the E–K group, but only five among L to Rs and six among S to Zs.

There is evidence, too, that, again especially when little is known about a contest, a name that looks or sounds alien will be held against you. In my own hitherto solid Conservative ward in south-west London, a Liberal Democrat candidate came top of the poll in the local elections in 2010 and ousted a Tory. She succeeded where two other Liberal Democrats failed. It must have helped that hers was a well-known local surname – Mary Burstow is the wife of the local MP, who was re-elected to Parliament on the same day. Three incumbent Conservatives stood in the ward: their names were Graham Whitham, Jonathan Pritchard, and Misdaq Syed Husain Zaidi. This is a ward with very few ethnic minority voters. I leave you to guess the name of the one who was ousted.

The pattern has been clear in general as well as in local elections. In some constituencies with high numbers of ethnic minority voters, a name that chimes with their own is seen as a possibly decisive advantage. In others, such a candidate's name can lower the vote. In the 2010 general election, the swing against Labour was lower in seats where identifiably Muslim candidates ran. In most cases, the name would be the main clue to their Muslim affiliations. Resentment at a Labour government's involvement in the war in Iraq evident five years earlier had receded. An examination by electoral experts from Oxford, Manchester and Essex found that though white voters appeared not to discriminate against ethnic minority candidates generally, they were less likely to support candidates they knew to be Muslim. In most cases, decisions must have been arrived at by taking a guess at a name.

But the negative impact of an unfamiliar name can be detrimental to candidates' prospects far outside the world of elections. In 2009, Nazia Mahmood, Mariam Namagembe and Alison Taylor all applied for identical jobs with companies in seven British cities. The three had a great deal in common: the same education, the same qualifications, the same experience – and the fact they did not exist. They were fabrications in an exercise commissioned by the Department of Work and Pensions from the National Centre for Social Research (Natcen) to test claims that discrimination is regularly practised in favour of white and against non-white job-seekers. The three job-seekers made almost 3,000 applications. Alison's rate of success was one favourable response (the offer of an interview or an encouraging phone call) for every nine applications; for the two with names which suggested a minority ethnic community, the equivalent success rate was one in sixteen. The rate of apparent discrimination was lower in the public sector than in the private.

Nominative determinism: can your name shape your destiny?

There's a further possible implication in Juliet's question: can a surname influence crucial choices you make in life? In 1994 John Hoyland, a columnist in the *New Scientist*, wrote:

> We recently came across a new book, *Pole Positions: The Polar Regions and the Future of the Planet*, by Daniel Snowman. Then, a couple of weeks later, we received a copy of *London Under London: A Subterranean Guide*, one of the authors of which is Richard Trench. So it was interesting to see Jen Hunt of the University of Manchester stating in the October issue of *The Psychologist*: 'Authors gravitate to the area of research which fits their surname.' Hunt's example is an article on incontinence in the *British Journal of Urology* (vol. 49, pp. 173–176, 1977) by A. J. Splatt and D. Weedon. (This really does exist. We've checked it.)

We feel it's time to open up this whole issue to rigorous scrutiny. You are invited to send in examples of the phenomenon in the fields of science and technology (with references that check out, please) together with any hypotheses you may have on how it comes about. No prizes, other than seeing your name in print and knowing you have contributed to the advance of human knowledge.

And of course, plenty of readers did.

Hoyland was not the first to draw attention to what he called 'nominative determinism.' Newspaper columnists, stuck for material in August, had long taken particular pleasure from names that seemed wrong for their jobs rather than right for them, like Doolittle and Dalley for a firm of estate agents, or lawyers called Argue and Phibbs in Sligo and Wright Hassall in England. But they did also pick out names that seemed inexplicably apt, like the Belgian footballer (though here you need the forename as well) Mark de Man.

How else, it is asked by some who parade such discoveries, did a Mr Fromage come to be the head of Danone UK? Could it be more appropriate, considering that he made off with so much of other people's money, that a high-profile US finance wizard and fraudster bore the name Bernie Madoff? Barclays, enmeshed in the Libor rate-fixing scandal, shed one very rich senior executive called Diamond but continued for some time with another who celebrated his opulence (further swollen in early 2013 by an £18 million share award) by appearing at race meetings in a big homburg hat to cheer on the horses he owned, one of which was named Fatcatinthehat. His name is Rich Ricci. When in the spring of 2013 Barclays was setting out to refurbish its image, it was announced that Ricci would also be leaving the operation.

How is it, too, that a man with the surname Judge (Igor Judge, Lord Chief Justice) became not just a judge but the highest judge in the land? What made a man called Brain become a

neurologist? And why should the speediest man on the globe
have the surname Bolt? Perhaps the most persuasive case is that
of gardening writers who tend to have names either directly
related to, or only at one remove from, the subjects they write
about: Loads, Sowerbutts, Flowerdew, Greenwood, Rose and
inescapably nowadays Titchmarsh. A notable firm of London
topiarists was run by people called Cutbush. There are sightings
of barbers called Barber, bakers called Baker, butchers called
Butcher, and claims of dentists called Dentith. A tree expert at
Kew is called David Ash. Guy Poppy is an ecologist at the
University of Southampton. In its first number of 2013, the *New
Scientist* returned, a little apologetically, to this theme, having
discovered an expert on bird disease called Loiseau (*l'oiseau* being
French for a bird), an underwater photographer called Haddock
and a World Bank consultant called Cashin.

I found a carter called Carter in Broughton, Hampshire, and
a clerk called Clarke, but the incidence of nominative determinism in my Broughtons seems minimal and tellingly unper-
suasive. And yet serious people have taken it very seriously. Here
is a great psychiatrist, in a paper on a favourite subject, synchronicity – coincidence or agreement in time – brooding on exactly
this question:

We find ourselves in something of a quandary when it
comes to making up our minds about the phenomenon
which Stekel calls the 'compulsion of the name'. What he
means by this is the sometimes quite gross coincidence
between a man's name and his peculiarities or profession.
For instance . . . Herr Feist (Mr Stout) is the food minister,
Herr Rosstäuscher (Mr Horsetrader) is a lawyer, Herr
Kalberer (Mr Calver) is an obstetrician . . . Are these the
whimsicalities of chance, or the suggestive effects of the name,
as Stekel seems to suggest, or are they 'meaningful
coincidences'?

Can a speculation that leaves a great mind like Carl Jung in a quandary be dismissed out of hand?

Euphony: the accidental music of names

One much less disputable ingredient in the impact of names is the way they sound: their euphony, or sometimes its opposite (for which there is no convenient word: 'cacophony' is too harsh). Euphony is defined as 'an agreeable sound, a pleasing, easy pronunciation'. A euphonious name, like any euphonious sound, is one that people may warm to, even be thrilled by. That happened to an Australian poet – who, significantly perhaps, was also a writer on music – called Walter J. Turner when as a child he opened an atlas. 'When I was but thirteen or so,' he wrote in a poem he called 'Romance', 'I went into a golden land, / Chimborazo, Cotopaxi / Took me by the hand . . .' Later he worked in Popocatépetl as well, but these first two peaks were enough to precipitate him into anthologies. Long before him, John Keats had looked into Chapman's Homer and dreamed of stout Cortez 'when with eagle eyes / He star'd at the Pacific – and all his men / Look'd at each other with a wild surmise – / Silent, upon a peak in Darien.' In fact, it wasn't stout Cortez involved in this comradely stare-in; it was Balboa. But somehow if you rewrite the line its music is diminished.

John Betjeman wrote a poem called 'Dorset' which begins by hymning the county's place names – Ryme Intrinsica, Fontmell Magna, Sturminster Newton and Melbury Bubb – followed in the next verse by Bingham's Melcombe, Iwerne Minster, Shroton and Plush. Each of the poet's three verses ends with names of another kind: with claims that Tranter Reuben, T. S. Eliot, H. G. Wells and Edith Sitwell; then Tranter Reuben, Mary Borden, Brian Howard and Harold Acton; and finally Tranter Reuben, Gordon Selfridge, Edna Best and Thomas Hardy, lie in Mellstock Churchyard now. To which he appends a note: 'The names in

the last lines of these stanzas are put in not out of malice or
satire but merely for their euphony.'

Mellstock does not exist: it's the name that the last of the figures
(some, at the time, not yet dead) whom Betjeman buries in
Mellstock churchyard gave to Stinsford, a village close to Hardy's
Dorset home. There's an echo here of lines from a far less sophisticated poet, his work passed down through generations of rude
forefathers and collected in Devon by Sabine Baring-Gould:

> Tom Pearce, Tom Pearce, lend me your grey mare
> All along, down along, out along lee.
> For I want for to go to Widecombe Fair
> Wi' Bill Brewer, Jan Stewer, Peter Gurney,
> Peter Davy, Dan'l Whiddon, Harry Hawk,
> Old Uncle Tom Cobley and all
> Old Uncle Tom Cobley and all.

T. S. Eliot revelled in names, and not just when he conjured
them up for cats – Growltiger and Grumbuskin, Mungojerrie
and Rumpelteazer, Tumblebrutus and Griddlebone, Macavity and
Skimbleshanks. In his pages we find names whose immediate
music seems to echo nursery rhymes, or sometimes to sail close
to Betjeman. Miss Nancy Ellicott strides across the hills and
breaks them. Mr Apollinax visits the United States, and his
laughter tinkles among the teacups. In a small hotel, Mr Burbank
encounters Princess Volupine, and is smitten.

Likewise, Scott Fitzgerald, part-way through *The Great Gatsby*,
unreels a long catalogue of the people who came to Gatsby's
house in the relevant summer: among them the Chester Beckers
and the Leeches, and a man called Bunsen, and the late Dr Webster
Civet, who recently drowned in Maine. And much later in these
recollections, Beluga, the tobacco importer, and Newton Orchid,
who controlled Films Par Excellence, and Mr Albrucksburger
and Miss Haag, his fiancée, and Miss Claudia Hip, with a man

reputed to be her chauffeur – together with a throbbing host of others, all testimony to the joy that he found in names.

*

But these are poets' contrivances. Euphony, which might be described as a sequence of sounds that makes music, occurs accidentally too. Wressle, Howden, Eastrington, Gilberdyke, Broomfleet, Brough, Ferriby, Hessle, Hull: you don't have to give the terminus its full grand name of Hull Paragon to find this collection of East Riding railway stations a satisfyingly musical incantation. This railway line is still open; its no less alluring continuation through to the towns of the Holderness coast has gone, though that had its music too: Withernsea, Patrington, Ottringham, Keyingham, Rye Hill, Marfleet, Southcoates, Sculcoates, Stepney, Botanic Gardens, Hull. Neither list works as well for travel in the reverse direction.

This accidental music occurs in surnames too. When I was but thirteen or so, and miserably unhappy at boarding school some 250 miles from home, I used to take an odd sort of comfort from roll call: a ritual played out every night about teatime where a monitor read out, in sequences of three or four names, the list of everyone in the house to which we had to answer dutifully: 'Here'. The sequence before and after my name, as usually intoned in order of the year-by-year groups in which we arrived in the house, still stays with me some sixty years later:

> Barnard, Edsall, Stanger, Whipp
> Bartlett, Bate, Challen
> McKie, Banner, Cockburn
> Rawlins, Thomson, Chubb

And so on to Allcorn, Evans, and other later arrivals. No poet would select these names for their beauty. It was rather, I think, the rhythm I found consoling; and also euphonious. Most of all, the trio whose names came just after mine: Rawlins, Thomson, and that final conclusive monosyllable, Chubb. I later began to imagine Sir Rawlins Thomson-Chubb, turnin', as he might say, to pastures new after a distinguished career as a much-decorated senior army officer; red-faced and exuberantly moustached, at ease in his armchair clutching a gin and tonic, somewhere in the bar of a fine hotel in the Far East; an associate perhaps of Sir Stamford Raffles. Raffles's name seemed to me almost as exotic as Cotopaxi and Chimborazo did to the poet Turner. But Thomson on the list from my schooldays left quite early, home-sick I think for Bromley. Roll call was never the same without him.

At about the same time, the names of the Leeds United team I had just begun to support, and liked to recite to myself, had a pleasing flow to it too. They were typically Twomey, Goldberg, Gadsby, Henry, Holley, Browne, Cochrane, Powell, Ainsley, Short and Heaton. (It did not do them much good. At the end of the season they were relegated to the Second Division with what was then the lowest number of points in a season ever achieved in the First Division.)

There have been many such sources of comfort over the centuries. Those endless verses in the Old Testament recording how A begat B and B begat C and there then ensued a festival of begetting right down to the recent past must have given this kind of pleasure to early worshippers, as well as serving that prime purpose of all genealogy, reminding them who they were. But perhaps the feeling of consolation from a mere school register was not so surprising because when one is but thirteen years or so, the memory of nursery rhymes and the music of the names they contain are still recent. Rhyme, rhythm and repetition begin to exercise their power on us early in life. The tales of Wee Willie Winkie, Milly Molly Mandy, Georgie Porgie, Humpty Dumpty, Mary Mary Quite Contrary, Incy Wincy Spider have euphonious names built into them. And though most of these rhymes are ancient, some must come from the era of surnames: the mother who lives in a cupboard is a Mrs Hubbard, the couple who alternate between the eating of fat and the eating of lean are Mr and Mrs Sprat, the girl on the tuffet is the pride and joy of Mr and Mrs Muffet, and the plump little chap pigging himself in the corner is the son of Mr and Mrs Horner. And of course there is Baby Bunting.

That persists in modern concoctions. Middle-class children were helped to feel secure by the unlikely names of 'James James / Morrison Morrison / Weatherby George Dupree' in A. A. Milne's poem 'Disobedience'. Generations of children grew up reassured by the repetition of names like those of the Trumpton Fire Brigade, read out in a daily roll call in the BBC children's television series: 'Pugh, Pugh, Barney McGrew, Cuthbert, Dibble, Grub.' Whatever you thought of the old unreformed contingent of hereditary peers, their names were pleasing to read or to listen to. What joy the upper classes found in naming their progeny! Here are a few of the peers who sat here in 1962, the year in which the decision was taken to add life peers to the chamber:

Brian Stuart Theobald Somerset Caher Butler, Earl of Carrick

Richard Frederick John Donough Le Poer-Trench, Earl of Clancarty

Sheridan Frederick Terence Hamilton-Temple-Blackwood, Marquess of Dufferin and Ava

Arthur Wills Percy Wellington Blundell Trumbull Sandys Hill, Marquess of Downshire

John Clotworthy Talbot Foster Whyte-Melville-Skeffington, Viscount Massereene

Jestyn Reginald Austen Plantagenet Phillipps, Viscount St Davids

Arthur Strange Kattendyke David Archibald Gore, Earl of Arran (who was commonly known as 'Boofy' Arran).

How drab they make the chosen names of some of the life peers who would come to sit beside them: Denis Herbert Howell, Lord Howell; Frank Ashcroft Judd, Lord Judd. Nor did it need a poet to bring together the dazzlingly surnamed, pleasingly un-alphabetical, eminently chantable collection of experts contrib-uting to a paper, 'A Neolithic Origin for European Paternal Lineages':

> Patricia Balaresque, Georgina R. Bowden, Susan M. Adams, Ho-Yee Leung, Turi E. King, Zoë H. Rosser, Jane Goodwin, Jean-Paul Moisan, Christelle Richard, Ann Millard, Andrew G. Demaine, Guido Barbujani, Carlo Previdere, Ian J. Wilson, Chris Tyler-Smith, Mark A. Jobling.

An even more euphonious assembly if you rearrange it to enhance its rhythms, allowing Guido Barbujani, Carlo Previdere, Ian J. Wilson and Chris Tyler-Smith to bring the list to a thumping conclusion. Though, no doubt, elsewhere they have found them-selves reduced to Balaresque *et al.*

But names have a greater, more penetrating resonance on the most solemn occasions. There's a powerful sense of that in a memoir called *Leaving Alexandria: A Memoir of Faith and Doubt* by Richard Holloway. Holloway was Bishop of Edinburgh, but gave it all up as his faith ebbed away. Earlier he had been for twelve years minister at Old St Paul's Church close to the southern end of the North Bridge in the city. Here, at the close of the funeral service, the bodies of the newly dead would be carried down a flight of thirty-three steps to a door on the lower level in Jeffrey Street from which they would be borne away. What affected him most, he says, was that their names were not only on these occasions written down, but read out aloud. And on the anniversary of each death, the names of the dead would be called out again, even when no one was still alive who remem-bered them. 'Sitting in Old St Paul's now,' he writes, 'my religion pared away almost to nothing, I can still remember. I wait for the names to be read out. I remember their lives. I remember their dying. And I remember leading them down those stairs to the long black hearse waiting in Jeffrey Street to take them under the North Bridge to the place of their final resting.' In that same spirit, a revered predecessor at Old St Paul's, whose name was Albert Ernest Laurie, had established a Warriors' Chapel to commemorate the young men of the parish who never returned from the First World War; a place where he could speak out the names of those whose loss haunted him.

You can catch this accidental music on those poignant occasions, of which there seem to be more every year, when the names of the dead from some great disaster of war or peace from First World War battlegrounds to the Hillsborough football disaster are read aloud to a congregation. The value is to bring home the truth that though very large numbers died, this was more than the death of a very large number: it was the sudden irrevocable loss of so many separate individuals, whose names mark out their separateness. The richness of the spread of names in multi-ethnic America makes the recitation of names on anniversaries of the Twin Towers massacre especially poignant:

Gordon McCannel Aamoth Jr; Edelmiro (Ed) Abad; Maria Rose Abad; Andrew Anthony Abate; Vincent Abate; Laurence Christopher Abel; William F. Abrahamson; Richard Anthony Aceto; Heinrich B. Ackermann; Paul Andrew Acquaviva . . .

And so through a matter of hours to the last:

. . . Jie Yao Justin Zhao; Yuguang Zheng; Ivelin Ziminski; Michael Joseph Zinzi; Charles A. Zion; Julie Lynne Zipper; Salvatore J. Zisa; Prokopios Paul Zois; Joseph J. Zuccala; Andrew Steven Zucker; Igor Zukelman.

Some names, of course, sound essentially ugly, though even
then their place in a litany, especially the rhythm they bring to
it, can enhance its music. In an essay on the function of criticism,
Matthew Arnold has a curious outburst brought on by reading
a news report which said: 'A shocking child murder has just been
committed at Nottingham. A girl named Wragg left the workhouse there on Saturday morning with her young illegitimate
child. The child was soon afterwards found dead on Mapperly
Hills, having been strangled. Wragg is in custody.' It was partly
that bleak last sentence that so incensed him – her Christian
name, her sex, denied to her. But most of all he seized on her
surname, almost as if he felt in some nominative determinist
sense that it might have helped drive her to it: '*Wragg!* . . . has
anyone reflected what a touch of grossness in our race, what an
original shortcoming in the more delicate spiritual perceptions,
is shown by the natural growth amongst us of such hideous
names, Higginbottom, Stiggins, Bugg!'

But some Buggs agreed with him. In his endearing memoir *A
Cab at the Door* (1968), V. S. Pritchett recalls an uncle by marriage
called Bugg who liked to claim that the name was traceable back
to that fine old family, the de Burghs. 'This', says Pritchett, 'he
proudly stuck to, but many of his brothers could not stand it.
They changed theirs to avoid low jokes. The news that dear Ada
had married a Mr Bugg sent my mother into fits; and Gran, who
thought second marriages were wicked, grimly called her
son-in-law plain Bugg for the rest of her life, and after a drink
or two would mutter about "the old bugger". It took the kind,
patient man about twenty years to bring her round.'

The comic actor John Cleese escaped being a Cheese because
his father adapted the name on signing up for military service
in 1915. Why should Cheese have been less acceptable? There is
always injustice here. The word 'rose', and the surname that
comes from it, is inherently attractive; but would that be so had
the name bestowed on this flower been 'slurp'?

First impressions: or, mixing with Marquawpunt

There's a further question that some people ask themselves: what psychological impact, if any, does my name have on people I write to, meet in the street, bump into at a party? Some names are inherently more alluring than others. Which of these two would you feel more likely to be drawn to immediately: Janey Graham, or Hepzibah Clutterbuck? John Wright, or Uriah Smellie? Academic research suggests that in any encounter, first impressions do matter. *First Impressions* is what Jane Austen originally called the book that became *Pride and Prejudice*. Often, as Austen instructs us, first impressions are wrong, and get revised on further acquaintance. But maybe first impressions from names do linger until you find a positive reason to drop them. They carry associations they may not deserve. That is certainly true of forenames. A survey of 3,000 teachers in the United Kingdom suggested they were wary of children with names such as Callum, Crystal or Chardonnay. The logic of this, if any, is that parents who give their children such names may not be the best of parents: therefore, their offspring may turn out to be trouble.

The impact comes from the general image a name is thought to convey. As children, we form vivid pictures from the names in familiar stories. What imaginative child could fail to form some picture from Roald Dahl's Charlie Bucket, Augustus Gloop, Veruca Salt, Violet Beauregarde, Bruce Bogtrotter, Miss Trunchbull (with its unsettling suggestions of truncheon and bull) or Mr and Mrs Twit, whose surname so loudly signals: these people are going to be ghastly?

A great deal of research has been done over more than a century to try to measure the psychological response to proper names. In one intriguing exercise at Cornell University in 1916, reported in the *American Journal of Psychology* – which might make a good party game – students were asked what images were suggested by names read out to them. The first time this was done, few agreed in their answers – so much so that the researchers concluded that there was no steady pattern of images. A second experiment on the same lines, however, produced a very different response. A new group examined the names put before them, and this time – drawing not only on these newcomers but also on the re-examined evidence of the first trial as well – the researchers found responses were consistent enough to divide the names they were offered into specific groups. These were given designations such as 'big', 'smooth', 'slow' and 'broad'.

It was the sound of the names that seemed to bring interpretations together – and most of all their initial letters. Start a name with a 'K' and its possessor would be imagined as sappy, active, clean-cut. Start with a 'Sh' or a 'So' and the image was smooth. The result was summarised thus: 'The sound of the word is a determinant of the most fitting person in about 30 per cent of cases and . . . on the whole the correspondence of responses to the same names is considerably more than chance would allow.'

It may have made this exercise more unreal that the names that students were asked to assess were inventions of a rather fanciful kind. They included such mouthfuls as Thaspkuwhin, Chermtyawkov, Marquawpunt, Quajnwmeth and Thubtawicarnth, together with snappier numbers such as Brob, Grib, Stisk, Skamth and Snemth. The fear must have been that if any familiar name was offered, respondents would simply home in on a person of that name whom they had already encountered. Even so, the response on being asked to imagine someone with the surname Quajnwmeth must surely be pure disbelief, coupled perhaps with a fervent wish to be doing something more interesting – and after that, a weary attempt to relate the name to something more ordinary. Murdix, a simpler and not impossible name, was thought to invoke someone shady, sneaky or shallow – even, in the judgement of some of these students, capable of murder. The piece after this in the *Journal*'s report, as it happened, was contributed by E. G. Boring and Amy Luce.

Here, anyway, are three sets of names which may suggest a

great deal, or may suggest nothing at all, in terms of appearance, age, personality and perhaps social class. Some will spark associations with names you already know; but that is how first impressions work:

> Norbert Blume, Caroline Harrison, Philip Hall, Carol Ella, Nikos Zarb, Audrey Henning, Natalie Taylor, Michael Leaver, Carolyn Scott, Mary Whittle, Matthias Wiesner, Peter Mallinson.
>
> Karen Mann, Richard Targett, Lizzie Boulton, Tom Lane, Jim McDonald, Shaun Beale, Bet Hewlett, Tony Smith, Beryl Pratley, Peter Pragnell, James Boggis.
>
> Annie Tooke, Catherine Churchill, Charles Peace, Edwin Smart, Enoch Whiston, Henry Bedingfield, James Dilley, James Simms, John Darcy, John Ralph, Kate Webster, Stephen Gambril, Thomas Johnson, William Cooper, William McGuiness.

You might also try to imagine the personalities of this collection of people, all of whom, oddly enough, you may already know a good deal about:

> Winston Jerome, Clement Watson, Anthony Grey, Harold Belles, Harold Seddon, Edward Pantony, James Cundy, Margaret Stephenson, John Coates, Tony Corscadden, Gordon Souter, David Mount.

Unlike the Cornell collection, these people were or are real. The first group are the viola section of the BBC Symphony Orchestra as listed in 2013. The second group were among prize-winners at a flower show in Broughton, Hampshire (Pragnell is a clue there). The third were all executed in 1879 (there, the clue is Charles Peace). As for the fourth, their forenames give them away. They are Britain's last dozen prime

ministers, but with their mothers' names rather than their fathers'.
How different they sound from the Churchills, Attlees and Edens
of our established history. Winston Jerome is surely one of those
feared West Indian fast bowlers from the age of Marshall, Garner,
Holding and Roberts. Tony Corscadden is a golfer who just
missed out on a place in the European Ryder Cup team.

The opinions of the turbulent radical academic Harold Laski
greatly troubled more sober figures like the party leader Clement
Attlee when Laski took over the chairmanship of the Labour
Party. The right-wing press built him up as a figure of menace.
But how much more frightening he might have seemed had he
taken his name from his mother, and been Harold Frankenstein.

I name this man Pumblechook

There is one field, though, where the choice of a name may be
absolutely crucial to the success of an enterprise, and where first
impressions are not so easy to disperse. Adam was given the privi-
lege of naming the whole of creation – flora and fauna, the beasts
and the fowls of the air, everything under the sun . . . including
his wife. No one since has been given such freedom to choose.
But writers of fiction have the next best thing: a total freedom
(subject only to the laws of libel, which have trapped quite a few
over the years) to invent the names of their characters.

Yet the choice of characters' names, like the choice of the title
to put on a book, can be a matter of anguish. If it isn't, it probably should be. Because there is no English equivalent, the British
use the expression *le mot juste*. It means: exactly the word you
are looking for. What a novelist needs is *le nom juste*, and unlike
le mot juste, you aren't going to find it by looking it up in Roget.
Get the name right, and it will not just engage the reader; it may
even enter the language – becoming emblematic, evoking a character type familiar in real life. Get it wrong, and readers may
turn against a character you want them to like, or warm to one
you want them to reel away from.

Writers deal with this problem in three different ways, though some of them draw on more than one category. They might be termed *inspirationalists*, *accumulators* and *calculators*.

The *inspirationalists* toil not, neither do they spin. A name may come to them out of the blue; they may take it from a passing lorry, an ad on a hoarding, a cereal packet. It may sweep into their consciousness as they walk on the Downs, or ride on a bus. They may pick it up from an overheard conversation.

The *accumulators* trawl for names in places where they are clustered: graveyards especially, war memorials, the phone book, the chronicles of births, marriages and deaths in newspapers. Fielding drew names from subscription lists; Henry James, a writer particularly sensitive to names (but as David Lodge observes, why did he call a character Fanny Assingham?), noted them down from *The Times*. A friend of mine sat next to the prolific writer Alan Plater (and the more prolific you are the more names you are going to consume) at a university degree ceremony. Plater kept scribbling down the names of those collecting certificates. Why? Because, Plater said, he was running out of names for characters and gathered them wherever he could.

Calculators, a rarer breed, will plot their most important characters syllable by syllable, each one put there to help build the image. In a short but instructive book, *The Art of Fiction*, the novelist and playwright David Lodge identifies himself in this group. In a novel, he says, 'names are never neutral . . . They always signify, if it is only ordinariness . . . The naming of characters is always an important part of creating them, involving many considerations, and hesitations . . . For an author to openly change his mind about the name of a character, in mid-text, is a particularly blatant admission that the whole story is "made up", something readers know but usually suppress . . . One may hesitate and agonize about the choice of a name, but once made, it becomes inseparable from the character, and to question it seems to throw the whole project *en abîme*, as the deconstructionists say.'

It isn't customary, Lodge says, for a novelist to explain why a name has been chosen. But fortunately he breaks that rule to explain some of his own inventions, from his particularly satisfying novel *Nice Work*. 'I was looking', he writes,

> for names that would seem 'natural' enough to mask their symbolic appropriateness. I named the man Vic Wilcox to suggest, beneath the ordinariness and Englishness of the name, a rather aggressive, even coarse, masculinity (by association with *victor, will* and *cock*), and I soon settled on Penrose for the surname of my heroine for its contrasting connotations of literature and beauty (*pen* and *rose*). I hesitated for some time, however, about the choice of her first name, vacillating between Rachel, Rebecca and Roberta, and I remember that this held up progress on Chapter Two considerably, because I couldn't *imaginatively inhabit* [my italics] this character until her name was fixed.

He finally settled on Robyn, a familiar form of Roberta, which seemed right for his initially androgynous heroine – with the added bonus that Wilcox, when he first met her, would not be sure if he was expecting a man or a woman.

A lot of writers, of course, find names by all three routes. The epitome here is Dickens, whose novels have been estimated to contain almost a thousand characters. Contemplating his Pecksniffs and Podsnaps and Pumblechooks one senses an inspirationalist here, but in fact he is also an accumulator and a calculator. His happiest names, it seems to me, are those just one step away from reality. Was there ever a real-life woman called Mrs Gamp? The name is real: Steve Archer's analysis of the 1881 census chalks up just one Gamp. Her imaginary friend Mrs Harris has the simplest of names, but Dickens's instincts are sure: to give her a name as original as Sairey's would destroy the relationship. Was there ever a Pumblechook? Or a Sweedlepipe? Or a Mivins? Archer finds none of those. But there were and are names around that make them look just possible.

But he also relies on what might be called nudge names. Murdstone in *David Copperfield* suggests murder, though may also, like Merdle, the crooked financier in *Little Dorrit*, invoke the French word *merde*. Scrooge is a kind of clenched-up, screwed-up name for someone who is screwing everyone under his command. The word 'screw' used also to mean a stingy fellow, extortioner, skinflint, while a now obsolete verb 'to scrouge' (or even 'scrooge') meant 'to squeeze'. Cratchit has to scratch for a living – though a 'cratch' is also a word for that centrepiece of the Christmas story, a manger. The grind in Gradgrind, the name Cheeryble for the good-natured, generous brothers in *Nicholas Nickleby*, Pecksniff combining two unendearing habits for one unendearing man – these and a host of others speak instantly for themselves.

And yet to an extent that is sometimes missed in assessments of Dickens, he was in these matters an accumulator: he kept lists of names he might one day use – some of those listed in appendix 3 are already familiar because he did indeed use them; others so odd (Cay-Lon, Etser, Fennerck, Bandy-Nandy) that one cannot expect even Dickens to saddle a character with them. His list, recorded by his biographer John Forster, can be found in Appendix 3 to this book.

Many names in Dickens that are often assumed to be pure invention were in fact lifted from life. He saw the name Pickwick on the side of a coach run by Moses Pickwick of Bath. In *Pickwick Papers*, Stiggins was a neighbour and Snodgrass a shipbuilder in Chatham. Serjeant Buzfuz's name was a modulation from a real-life lawyer, Serjeant Bompas, some of whose family lived at Broughton, Hampshire. Dorrett (rather than Dorrit) was a fellow debtor of the author's father in prison. The Dartles were a

Rochester family. Edwin Drood was only a step away from Edwin Trood, landlord of a local pub. The name of Joe Gargery, one of the most lovable characters in all literature, was also taken from life. Other names were remembered from accounts books he had kept in early employment.

And finally, as his repeated amendments of names of quite crucial characters show, Dickens was a calculator. 'Like many novelists,' says Alastair Fowler in his richly instructive *Literary Names: Personal Names in English Literature*, 'Dickens needed to determine the names of characters before he could tell their stories.' Martin Chuzzlewit might have been Sweezleden, Sweezleback, Sweezlewag, Chuzzletoe, Chuzzleboy, Chubblewig or Chuzzlewig, until Chuzzlewit pipped Chuzzlewig at the post. He was equally restless in picking titles. '*Bleak House*' was the twelfth name he found for that book; among those he rejected were eight which began with '*Tom All-Alone*', mostly coupled with 'the ruined house' or 'the ruined mill' and several invoking Chancery, including the last but one: '*Bleak House and the East Wind. How they both got into Chancery and never got out*'. *Hard Times* was his fourteenth choice. *A Tale of Two Cities* might have been '*Rolling Years*', '*Rolling Stones*', '*Memory Carton*' or '*The Doctor of Beauvais*'. *Little Dorrit* began as '*Nobody's Fault*'. The name he gave to the book we know as *David Copperfield* was '*David Copperfield the Younger of Blunderstone Rookery (which he never meant to publish on any account)*'.

His calculations engendered his nudge names. His first choice for Murdstone was Harden – with Hard a rather excessive nudge, which may be why he rejected it. David Copperfield had at one point or another been Trotfield, Copperby, Copperstone and even Mag – which became the first part of Magwitch, the prisoner who so terrifies Pip Pirrip at the start of *Great Expectations*. The name of Colonel Chowser in *Nicholas Nickleby* derives from a now obscure word that meant to defraud. As Alastair Fowler notes, Oliver Twist is given a surname that in Dickens's day could evoke a hanging. His true name proves to be Leeford – Lea and Ford, evoking soothing pastoral places. Slurk and Slumkey at Eatanswill both start with 'Sl', which so often tends to suggest something unpleasant, and include a 'k', which often suggests something comic.

The impact of some of his names is harder to judge because they are now so much part of the language. Say 'Uriah' and one image drowns out all others. The original Uriah was a blameless man. In the second book of Samuel, King David, involved in an affair with Uriah's wife Bathsheba, who is shortly to bear their child, arranges for Uriah to be killed in battle. But after Dickens, the creepy hand-wringing villain Heep became the only Uriah who mattered. It set off a general retreat from the name, which has never recovered – so much so that it was a matter of some surprise when a Premiership referee appeared who was called Uriah Rennie. So why was it right for Heep? Uriah, says one analyst, 'forms with Heep a dismal combination, possibly because the muscular activity required of the tongue in the rapid alternation of close and open vowels with the tough medial aspirate'. Or possibly because Uriah echoes 'pariah', just as Heep at this time suggested a dung heap. Say Micawber, which makes such a wonderful fit with the first name Wilkins, and the image you get can only be the Micawber dreamed up by a writer of genius – though possibly coloured by the film embodiment of Micawber by W. C. Fields.

Others among Dickens's creations, though, have less nudge names than dig-in-the-ribs names, some of them so over the top that you feel let down. Lord Verisopht in *Nicholas Nickleby* is perhaps the most frequently cited: M'Choakumchild in *Hard Times*, the Reverend Melchisedech Howler in *Dombey and Son*, nudge you hard enough to knock you over. Wackford Squeers in *Nickleby*, it seems to me, mixes two separate genres, recalling the advice that playwrights used to be given to segregate farce from comedy. 'Squeers' is a cunning echo of words with a nasty taste

– squalid, squat, squamous – but also, given Squeers's unsuitable aspirations to social importance, also of 'squire'; whereas Wackford, by embodying 'whack' as M'Choakumchild does 'choke', is simply farcical. Some even complain, though I wouldn't, about the surname given to the couple in *Our Mutual Friend*, who were

> bran-new people in a bran-new house in a bran-new quarter of London. Everything about the Veneerings was spick and span new. All their furniture was new, all their friends were new, all their servants were new, their plate was new, their carriage was new, their harness was new, their horses were new, their pictures were new, they themselves were new, they were as newly married as was lawfully compatible with their having a bran-new baby, and if they had set up a great-grandfather, he would have come home in matting from the Pantechnicon, without a scratch upon him, French polished to the crown of his head.

Yet other writers, some more austere than Dickens, had revelled in the concoction of ridiculous names, inherited perhaps from the plethora to be found in Restoration comedy: Sir Novelty Fashion, Lord Foppington, Sir Tunbelly Clumsy in Vanbrugh's *The Relapse*, or Sir John Brute in his *The Provok'd Wife*, or Sir Fopling Flutter in *The Man of Mode* by George Etherege (otherwise Etheredge); and even before Restoration comedy, names such as Sir Voluptuous Beast in Ben Jonson. Sir Walter Scott is rarely regarded as a writer of fanciful comedy, yet he introduces names of a wholly fanciful kind: Blattergowl, Douster Swivel, Mucklebackit, Fairscribe, Croftangry, Kettledrummer, Muckle Wraith, Snailsfoot, Quackleben, Sludge – a name that Robert Browning chose for his medium ('Mr Sludge, "The Medium"').

Trollope has taken as much stick as Dickens for excess in choosing names – as with his Mr and Mrs Quiverful (they have fourteen children: geddit?), Dr Pessimist Anticant (thought to be based on Carlyle), Mr Popular Sentiment (Dickens) and at a deathbed, a doctor whom he named Fil(l)grave:

> Dr Filgrave was the leading physician of Barchester, and nobody of note in the city – or for that matter of that in the eastern division of the county – was allowed to start upon the last great journey without some assistance from him as the hour of going drew nigh. I do not know that he had much reputation for prolonging life, but he was supposed to add a grace to the hour of departure.

Henry James regretted some of Trollope's extremes, comparing him unfavourably with Thackeray whom he thought exemplary in the matter of naming – though Thackeray could dream up weird names when it suited him: Sir Huddleston Fuddleston, Kickleby, Gruffanuff, Granby, Tufto. The playwright Harold Brighouse is best known as the author of *Hobson's Choice* (Hobson is another whose name has entered the language: the original Hobson was a Cambridge stable owner who would offer customers choices of which only one was remotely feasible). He too singled out Thackeray in a piece about naming for the *Manchester Guardian*, seeing 'Becky Sharp' as a masterly blend of the commonplace with the indicative (that's to say, the nudging).

Perhaps those so rebuked for making names too fantastical envied the freedom of writers who by the nature of what they wrote could drift as far away from reality as they liked. Thomas Love Peacock peopled his books with satirised characters, who most of the time can be found strolling through delightful countryside, talking; dallying in delicious glades, talking; or sitting around in the house over dinner and late at night, talking and drinking. Wherever they are, like the voice of prayer in the hymn, they are never silent. His names are wonderfully inventive and beyond academic complaint. A characteristic collection of Peacock people gathers in the first of his novels at *Headlong Hall* as guests of Squire Headlong: Marmaduke

Milestone, the picturesque landscape gardener; Mr Cranium and his lovely daughter Cephalis; two very profound critics, Mr Treacle and Mr Gall; and two multitudinous versifiers, Mr Nightshade and Mr Mac Laurel. Late arrivals include Mr Cornelius Chromatic, most profound and scientific of all amateurs of the fiddle, and the dilettante painter Sir Patrick O'Prism.

In further novels 'by the author of *Headlong Hall*' (though Peacock revelled in names he did not want the public to discover his own) we encounter such memorable people as Scythrop Glowry, the Hon. Mrs Pinmoney, Harum O'Scarum, the Irish landlord, the Reverend Mr Portpipe and Sir Telegraph Paxarett ('I am a moderate man; one bottle of Madeira and another of claret are enough for me at any time'). Likewise Stella Gibbons in her matchless *Cold Comfort Farm* (1932) can populate her rural disaster scene with characters called Amos Starkadder, Mark Dolour and Ada Doom – or back in civilised, all-mod-cons London, Mr Mybug and Dick Hawk-Monitor – and no one is going to object.

Where objections do occur, however, is when blameless, or sometimes relatively blameless, people with particularly distinctive names find these same names applied to fictional characters. Ian Fleming called one of his juiciest villains Auric Goldfinger, thus violently affronting the architect Erno Goldfinger, and no doubt other real-life Goldfingers too. Erno was soon afflicted by calls in the hours of sleep by people claiming to be agent 007. He objected, with reason, that he had been targeted. Like Auric, he was a British-naturalised Eastern European and Soviet sympathiser, though he was 6ft 2ins against Auric's 5 ft. Fleming is thought to have been taking a form of revenge: he greatly disliked houses designed by the architect which had sprung up close to his Hampstead home. Erno sued and, to Fleming's disgust, his publishers Jonathan Cape agreed in an out-of-court settlement to make it clear in future editions that all characters in the book were purely fictitious.

Such cases have sometimes occurred without any hint of

malicious intent. The classic case, which all young journalists used always to be warned about, is that of Artemus Jones. In 1910, a young reporter on the now-forgotten *Sunday Chronicle* decided to spice up a story by introducing a fantasy character called Artemus Jones, engaged in some kind of hanky-panky with a woman in Dieppe. He thought the name so unlikely as to be safe. Unfortunately for him and his newspaper, there *was* an Artemus Jones, a lawyer – who oddly enough had worked for the *Chronicle* long before this reporter arrived. He sued, and though the *Chronicle* fought the case all the way to the House of Lords, he won and the paper had to pay him substantial damages. The courts ruled in each case that, as witnesses had attested, some people reading the story assumed that the real Artemus Jones was involved.

In an erudite piece in the *Guardian* in 2006, the celebrated literary sleuth John Sutherland lined up further examples. In 1974, the novelist Tom Sharpe had invented a TV presenter whose name proved to be that of a man who worked for the BBC. He sued; the book was withdrawn; the publishers paid serious money. Two years later, the novelist Piers Paul Read had given an unsavoury character a name that proved to belong to a real-life peer. And now, a crime writer, Jake Arnott, had featured as a villain in his new novel a former big band singer called Tony Rocco. A blameless real-life former big band singer called Tony Rocco sued him and won. The novel was pulped, to re-emerge with the character's name amended, no doubt after long research, to Tony Royal. All of which, Sutherland said, underlined the wisdom of Arthur Hailey, author of *Airport*, who checked the names of his characters against the two million contained in the Manhattan phone book.

*

The struggles to find *le nom juste* that afflict great writers throng around lesser ones too. As they did around that Stakhanovite toiler (Stakhanovite is an eponym for someone who won't stop working: taken from the name of Aleksei Grigorevich Stakhanov (1906–77), a Russian coal-miner) Charles Hamilton, who was Frank Richards when he wrote about Greyfriars, but when writing about other schools for the same or for other employers, was also Hilda Richards, Martin Clifford, Owen Conquest, Winston Cardew and nearly a dozen others. In these various guises he was computed to have written a million and a half words a year for around thirty years. Still, once he had filled up a fifth form or a Remove, that would see him through for years on end, since Bob Cherry, Harry Wharton, Billy Bunter and comrades at Greyfriars, Tom Merry and the monocled Arthur Augustus d'Arcy, second son of Lord Eastwood, a kind of proto Jacob Rees-Mogg, at St Jim's, never grew any older.

Most of these names – Cherry, Wharton, Nugent and, nudgiest of all, Johnny Bull – suggested a healthy, imperial Englishness, while exotic Overseas was represented above all by that cheery fracturer of the English language, Hurree Jamset Ram Singh, Nabob of Bhanipur. Intriguingly, the bounder of Greyfriars, Vernon-Smith, is double-barrelled, while an 'out-and-out worm' at St Frank's is called Snipe.

The staff have catchy names too – most of all Quelch (Quelch is a real name, listed by Lower, who explains it as a northern guttural version of Welch or Welsh; I have also come across people in a present-day phone book called Squelch). Bunter, the most memorable of all his creations, may possibly derive from Dickens where in *Dombey and Son* a character is described as 'a regular Bunter'. One definition of the noun 'bunt' is 'the bagging-part of a fishing-net, a sail etc.' or as a verb, 'to belly, as a sail'.

Hamilton/Richards became involved in a curious spat with Eric Blair/Orwell (product of a grander school than Greyfriars – his was Eton), who accused him of encouraging snobbishness and cheap patriotism; to which he retorted that 'it is an actual fact that in this country at least noblemen generally are better fellows than commoners. My own acquaintance with titled Nobs is strictly limited; but it is my experience, and I believe everybody's that – excepting the peasant-on-the-land class, which is the salt of the earth – the higher you go up in the social scale the better you find the manners and the more fixed the principles.' And in something close to an echo of Francis Galton, despairing of the waning away of eminent English surnames: 'The fact that old families almost invariably die out is proof of this; they cannot and will not do the things necessary for survival.' All this is chronicled in a wonderfully entertaining book by E. S. Turner, *Boys Will Be Boys.*

The boys and girls of Greyfriars and St Jim's and the rest – though these schools seemed capable of attracting the sons of nobility – were hardly in the same league as those foregathered in the opening pages of Anthony Powell's great twelve-volume epic, *A Dance to the Music of Time.* Powell, by the way, pronounced his surname 'Pole', which some Powells do and a great many others don't. The Thatcher government had a senior adviser who liked people to call him Pole; the Blair government had a senior adviser who insisted on Powell to rhyme with 'trowel'. They are brothers.

The school, here, though Powell never specifically says so, is Eton, which Powell attended himself, along no doubt with the prototypes of Charles Stringham and Peter Templer, though not perhaps of his greatest creation, the abominable Kenneth Widmerpool. Just as Henry James disparaged the names that he found in Trollope, so Powell disparaged names that he found in Henry James. 'His proper names are . . . dreadful,' he wrote in his journal, having just finished *The Spoils of Poynton.* 'Why should a perfectly ordinary girl be called Fleda Vetch, or a country house Waterbath, names that would be perfectly acceptable in P. G. Wodehouse, not in a James type of novel?'

Powell in turn riled Philip Larkin, who found the *Music of Time* intolerably superior and pompous, full of 'Comic Mandarin, a descendant of Polysyllabic Facetiousness', and even worse, 'ultimately superficial'. 'A small example is Mr Powell's habit of calling people by place-names – Isbister, Widmerpool, and now Ada Leintwardine: an accepted practice, but hostile to suspended disbelief if one knows the places, or even of them.' Larkin himself is not faultless in his choosing of names: in his second and, sadly, his final novel, *A Girl in Winter*, he suddenly introduces into a world of Fennels and Linds and Brookeses and Greens a character in a dark crimson sports car called Jack Stormalong. His complaint against this practice of Powell's seems in any case odd, especially since a vast number of British surnames come originally from place names, and since Isbister – defined in the gazetteer as a seat and loch in mainland Orkney or a hamlet and loch in Whalsay, Shetland – is a place that most readers would never have heard of; and Widmerpool, probably, too.

Kenneth only bore the name Widmerpool, the narrator tells us, because his grandfather had married a woman bearing this name who was his social superior. Had that not been so, Powell's emblematic creation would have been Geddes. That surely would not have caught on as Widmerpool has. I once went to Widmerpool, Nottinghamshire, to see whether it deserved the obloquy which this choice of name has attached to it, but I subsequently read that Powell had denied that it had anything to do with this harmless community. *A Dance to the Music of Time* is certainly full of people whose surnames are place names, but many of these come from their being aristocrats, like the Earl of Bridgnorth (his family name, though, is Stepney), Lord Aberavon (a Gwatkin) and the Earl of Warminster (though his family name is Erridge, which differs by only one letter from a place in Kent).

Some of the surnames here are distinctly nudgy: Murtlock suggesting murder, as duly occurs; a Gossage is unprepossessing; a Bagshaw wears ill-fitting corduroy trousers; a Le Bas is on his way down. One can frequently guess the characters' social origins from the names that Powell has give them. Take, for instance, Ablett, Billson, Brandreth, Cheeseman, Conyers, Cutts, Fettiplace-Jones, Hagbourne-Johnson, Jeavons, Perkins, Tokenhouse, Tolland, Umfraville, Walpole-Wilson: if asked to distinguish upper-class people from lower-class, most people I think would be right on more than half of them. Perkins is a peer, which may sound counter-intuitive – but he is a *Labour* peer. This writer's choice of names, as members of the Anthony Powell Society point out, is illuminated by his passion for genealogy and his studies of the diarist Aubrey, while he also here and there borrows names already employed by other writers: Umfraville, for example, occurs in a book by Charlotte M. Yonge, of whom Powell's wife wrote a biography.

The name Perkins also occurs in a fascinating Wikipedia list of fictional prime ministers chosen by a variety of writers from Arthur Conan Doyle and Agatha Christie to Trollope, John Buchan, Robert Harris and the scriptwriters of *The Thick of It*. Perkins is Chris Mullin's PM in *A Very British Coup*. Trollope's collection includes Lord Drummond, Lord Brock, Lord de Terrier, Mr Gresham, Mr Daubeny, William Mildmay and Plantagenet Palliser, Duke of Omnium. Others installed in fictional Number 10s include Sir Thomas Doodle (*Bleak House*), Lord Bellinger in the Sherlock Holmes story 'The Adventure of the Second Stain', Lord Alloway (Agatha Christie: she also has a Hammett and a Hunberley), Edward Clare (rhymes with Tony Blair: probably not a coincidence) in Sue Townsend's *Number Ten*, Andrew Lang (who also calls Blair to mind) in Robert Harris's *Ghost*, Mark D'Arby in Michael Dobbs's *The Edge of Madness*, Raymond Gould in Jeffrey Archer's *First Among Equals*, and way over the top to suit the proceedings, Walter Outrage in Evelyn Waugh's *Vile Bodies*. The party to which they belong is not always stated, but look at the name and you may be able to guess.

There are countless other examples – most readers of fiction will have their own – of the kinds of names that writers choose for their characters, the ones that work and the ones that do not. Some seem to succeed almost by accident: Ian Fleming, who liked watching birds, lifted the name James Bond off a book by an ornithologist. Some have a flair for invention; some do not. The teacher and literary critic John Mullan greatly admires Martin Amis's naming: he wrote of Amis's *Money* that players at a tennis club were so well named you could almost feel their muscles. There was some consternation when it emerged that the central character in a novel Amis published in 2012 was called Lionel Asbo, but the book explains that Asbo had adopted this name at the age of eighteen, to mark his pride in having been given one.

Amis has always had a taste for offbeat surnames: 'Dickens couldn't resist a name that carries meaning', one critic wrote, 'and Amis can't either.' Keith Talent, Nicola Six and Guy Clinch inhabit *London Fields*, Keith Nearing and a model called Threnody, *The Pregnant Widow. Money* has not just a narrator called Self but a character called Martin Amis. Another name that crops up in this context is Cosmo Rodewald, which sounds like an Amis character, but is in fact the name of a Manchester concert hall where the writer has lectured, thus demonstrating, not for the first time, that real names can often match fictional ones for sheer unexpectedness.

Writers sometimes find themselves arraigned at literary festivals for choosing names which, in the view of their readers, point in the wrong direction or in no direction at all. The American novelist Paul Auster was one such target in a session at the Queen Elizabeth Hall in London, on which Stuart Evers reported for the *Guardian*. The audience, he said, 'perked up' – in the way that audiences do when someone asks a question everyone wanted to ask – when Auster was requested to say how and where he found characters' names.

Auster, Evers explained, favours names that are often strange, almost surreal: Jack Pozzi, Augustus Brill, Owen Brick, Marco Stanley Fogg. The writer 'became animated' as he explained the process – or lack of one. Apparently, his characters arrive in his head already equipped with names. In other words, he's the purest kind of inspirationalist, to whom *le nom juste* comes out of the blue.

Evers found this oddly insouciant: 'Names that work, names that do really make an impression on the reader, have a definite sense of poetry to them,' he wrote. 'Dickens's names are criticised, but they have a definite fizz. Twentieth-century novels are mostly more restrained, more moored to reality.' It seems that Evers's personal hate-list features Hardy, for giving Angel Clare the name Angel – though even that is topped by one of his favourite writers, Don DeLillo, calling a character Bucky Wunderlick.

I have left to the last in this incomplete tour of a very broad horizon one of the purest and most perfect emanations of popular British culture in the second half of the twentieth century: the television series *Dad's Army*. The choices made by its writers Jimmy Perry, who thought it up, and David Crofts, his co-writer and producer (who died in 2012), and Michael Mills, the head of comedy at the BBC who took charge of the project and worked through their scripts with them, are targeted with a wonderful precision.

The Home Guard of Walmington-on-Sea (Mills changed it from Brightsea-on-Sea to Walmington, which, like Mainwaring, isn't pronounced as it is spelled) are commanded by Captain Mainwaring, a bank manager, played by Arthur Lowe with such faithfulness that you can hardly believe that he and Mainwaring are different people. His languid, world-weary sergeant (John Le Mesurier, another surname that isn't pronounced as it is spelled) is called Wilson. (Le Mesurier, as it happens, was not this actor's real name. He began his career with his father's surname, Halliley, but switched to his mother's, Le Mesurier, part-way through a season with Croydon Rep.) Originally Le Mesurier was to have been the captain and Mainwaring/Lowe the sergeant, but in a moment of inspiration they switched them around.

The name Mainwaring is one of those quite often met with in higher-class families where the spelling traps those not in the know into mispronouncing it, as Cholmondeley is 'Chumley' among those who know, and Marjoribanks is 'Marshbanks'. Mainwaring of course is 'Mannering'. Wilson is as prosaic and unpretentious a name as they come; but it's Wilson, Mainwaring's subordinate both in uniform and day by day in the bank, who's the social superior. When Mainwaring graciously gives Wilson the chance to accompany him to a posh evening, the superior people with whom Mainwaring hopes to ingratiate himself sweep straight past him and fall upon Wilson whom they know from their public school days.

The third essential ingredient in *Dad's Army* is the local butcher, Jack Jones (Clive Dunn, made up to look many years older than he was: he died in 2012, at ninety-two), a veteran, as he rarely fails to recall, of campaigns under Kitchener. His, too, is a name judged to perfection: had Jones been awarded a name more glamorous or more memorable, the character would have curdled. 'Jones the butcher,' he says when he answers the phone, even on Home Guard duty. 'J. Jones Family Butcher' is boldly inscribed on the side of his van. The other name which could hardly have been bettered is that of the junior member of the platoon, whom we're always led to suspect is the son of the sergeant whom he calls Uncle, so mollycoddled by his mother that he has to wear a scarf even on parade. They called him Pike, a name that hauntingly echoes the question asked by Pistol of Henry V when the king is masquerading as a common soldier: 'Trail'st thou the puissant pike?' The pike was heavier than the musket; it took muscle to trail it. Few soldiers in the whole of British military history could have been less puissant than Private Pike.

Yet another inspired act of naming was that chosen for the bossy, blustering commander of a neighbouring Home Guard unit with a fiercely aggressive moustache, whom they dubbed

Captain Square, a surname that intriguingly also occurs in Fielding's novel *Tom Jones,* where Square is one of two men, the other being called Thwackum, who try to indoctrinate Tom in their opposed ways of thinking (Square is later disturbed in bed with one of Tom's mistresses). The Square in *Dad's Army* is square by nature: square in appearance, square in the certainty with which he stands four-square for his own opinions and in his bristling conviction that he is always right and everyone else – but particularly Mainwaring, whom he always addresses as Mainwaring – is wrong. 'Square' also in the sense that the word increasingly acquired in the second half of the twentieth century of being behind the times, and being proudly committed in every bone of his body to staying that way.

The whole sense of *Dad's Army* – it's really Great-Grandad's Army, by now – set in the 1940s when invasion threatened and people lived in fear of coming under Hitler's suzerainty, is of traditions and modes of behaviour rooted in the England that used to be; and to a surprising extent still detectably was, in the new, sometimes Veneeringly new, and more turbulent age of the 1960s and 1970s. Mainwaring, Wilson, Jones, Pike – these names, in a series endlessly revived on television, serve perhaps for older people in a new world of Khans and Zhangs and Blaszczykowskis as a sustenance, and a reassurance.

7

Transformations

New Names for Old

'I've been thinking a lot recently about names. What were you
before you were Bahama LeStarr?'
'Before I was Bahama LeStarr I was Apricot del Rio.'
Michael Frayn, *Skios*

The onomastic swap shop: upstairs

There's another Broughton, just west of Banbury in Oxfordshire.
It is not a substantial place, but it has a substantial history. You
can see it in the great house – it is called Broughton Castle, but
it's really a manor house: 'the English house at its first apogee
in the late 16th century,' Simon Jenkins says in *England's Thousand
Best Houses*, 'a place of great chambers and cosy parlours, attics
and knot gardens'. You can see it right alongside in the church
– also one of Jenkins's Thousand Best – most of all in the family
tombs and effigies.

You can see it too in the pub which, though it doesn't
vulgarise the connection, also commemorates the family who
for centuries have dominated the place, not least in its name.
It is now the Saye and Sele Arms. It used to be the Twisleton
Arms, but in time it changed the name, just as the family had
as it interwove Wykehams, Twisletons and Fienneses. A portrait
hangs in the pub dining room which seems certain to be a
Fiennes, and sure enough the barmaid says very promptly that

it's the 13th Baron Saye and Sele, Thomas Twisleton (though I later overhear her confiding to a customer that she'd only learned that this morning).

On the wall of one of the castle's galleries there is an intricate, beautifully decorated family tree, to help you disentangle the various strains of Twisleton, Eardley, Wykeham and Fiennes which went to make up the intertwined history of the Eardley-Twisleton-Fienneses and later, Twisleton-Wykeham-Fienneses, represented – until the ranks of hereditary peers were culled in 1999 – in the House of Lords by the 21st Baron, born in 1920 and still very much alive when I visited the place in the summer of 2012.

Geoffrey de Say was a baron of Magna Carta. His daughter Joan married William Fiennes, whose forebears came from Artois, a province of northern France between Picardy and Flanders. William of Wykeham, bishop of Winchester, a kind of proto-prime minister under Edward III and Richard II, bought Broughton in 1377. When he died in 1404, his sister's son, who fought at Agincourt and was Wykeham's heir, took his benefactor's name. But again the line ran out, and the Wykeham inheritance passed to Sir William Fiennes, who had married Margaret Wykeham. He died in the battle of Barnet in 1471.

The whole story of this convoluted dynasty is too long and intricate to disentangle here. But essentially, the seventeenth century brings the Twisletons into the story. James, eldest son of William Fiennes, the 9th Lord Saye and Sele, and his wife Frances Cecil had a daughter, Elizabeth, who married a Yorkshireman, Sir John Twisleton; their daughter Cecil was declared, in one of the rare exceptions to an all-male peerage, *de jure* Baroness of Saye and Sele. She married George Twisleton, also from Yorkshire, so the family in the great house were now Twisletons. Thereafter, though a series of tactical name changes, they progressed through Eardley-Twisleton-Fiennes to Twisleton-Wykeham-Fiennes, until in 1965 the 21st Lord Saye and Sele dispensed with Twisleton and Wykeham and settled for Fiennes

alone – pronounced, of course, as those who know the writings
of William Fiennes, a son of the house, or the acting of Ralph
and Joseph Fiennes, or the high adventures of Sir Ranulph will
be aware, as 'Fines': these things are rarely simple in aristocratic
families. Not all the family followed Lord Saye and Sele into this
modernisation. Some remain Twisleton-Wykeham-Fienneses.

There are portraits all over the house from the family's various
surname threads, including an Eardley or two (Eardley was part
of the name for a time) and further relatives and associates
whose connection is not always clear. Here is the Earl of Lincoln
(1517–84), part of another aristocratic line which kept running
out and having to be renewed with various cognate name
changes: he qualifies through a Twisleton connection. Sir Philip
Twisleton, knight, is pictured in 1640 with Lady T. comfortably
beside him. Then we have the Hon. Colonel Nathaniel Fiennes,
Speaker of Cromwell's upper house – for the family, rather to
my surprise, were Commonwealth men, fighting against the king.
Then William, 8th Lord and 1st Viscount, and Frederick Benjamin
Twisleton, who became Archdeacon of Hereford, of whom the
diarist Francis Kilvert records, having heard him in church, that
though he delivered a bumbling sermon it wasn't as bad as the
bishop's. Climbing the stairs, you may offer a friendly nod to
Henry IV of France, Sir Andrew and Lady Douglas, and HMS *Rivoli*
at rest in Minorca Harbour, together with a jolly nautical fellow
identified as Captain Collins RN, with a suitable lady beside him.

Pressing indefatigably on, we encounter the Rt Hon. Thomas,
13th Baron (the one who also hangs in the pub); and the Hon.
John Twisleton Fiennes, a dandy, with top hat, gloves and
buttonhole. Bit of a masher, this one, I thought, and sure enough,
'He's one of the bad ones,' a house guide confides – unlike the
good Archdeacon. An endearing collection of local people called
Leigh interrupt the family sequence, one described as 'Mr Leigh
of Adlestrop', a place name you rarely hear outside the most
famous poem by Edward Thomas. The Leighs were connections

by marriage; they were also kin to Jane Austen's family. Elsewhere, an Eardley, looking sated, and a Sampson, 1st Earl Eardley, by Romney, and Thomas James Twisleton dressed as a scout. Now and then, there are pictures of horses. On the final stairs there are portraits of Oliver Cromwell and a Prince of Orange.

Move on to the church and it's much the same story. The church is dedicated to the glory of God, but not far behind, one feels, to the glory of Twisletons, Wykehams and Fienneses. There are more of them in the church than outside in the graveyard, where a powerful chest commemorating the Honourable Edward Twisleton finds him among the old family names of the village: Claridge, Ellis, Hitchcox and Page. Inside there are monuments to all sorts of Twisletons and Fienneses, notably one to the Honourable Ellen Twisleton, the American wife of Edward, youngest brother of the 17th Lord Saye and Sele, whose tomb is in the churchyard. She died in 1862 at the age of forty-three; the inscription falls not far short of saying: 'she was a stunner'.

The tribute to the 13th Baron, Thomas Twisleton, an army general, for whom the barony had been called out of abeyance, is just as admiring, though in a more formal way: 'descended from a long line of illustrious ancestors, whose names are enrolled among the barons of Runnimede, the crusaders in Palestine, and the defenders of Freedom in our unfortunate civil war, after serving in the memorable campaign in Flanders, he took his hereditary seat in the British senate and during the stormy period of the French Revolution, when the timid wavered and even the bold were alarmed, he ever remained consistent, unchanged and incorruptible.' The sort of tribute, this, which seems to demand a standing ovation; but unhappily it overshadows inscriptions below for others who did not live to share all this family glory: Richard Fiennes lived a mere two days in 1658; James lived two months in 1666. Perhaps the most memorable monument, though, does not belong to this family: it's the tomb of Sir John de Broughton (died 1315), who built this church, restored to its raucous medieval colours – closely matched by the effigies of Sir Thomas Wykeham and an unexplained lady, a relative but apparently not his wife.

The symphony of names that you find at this place, and may have to spend hours thereafter trying to disentangle, reflects, as do the noble names I earlier picked out for their euphony, the adventurous nomenclature of aristocratic England. Your name was a very important part of the image you had of yourself, and so, the longer and grander the better. There's a character in Captain Marryat's nautical novel *Peter Simple* who avers that he seldom bows to anyone with a name of less than three syllables. Ideally in high social circles an imposing surname, hinting if possible at a distinguished ancestry going back at least to the Conquest, would be prefaced by the gorgeous forenames your parents had picked for you, in a sequence designed for their suitability when you became a great figure. And if when you became a great figure you did not have an appropriately fine and sonorous name, you could always make one up for yourself.

*

In the middle classes, it is more often the case that a name is simply sanitised: a Glasscock becomes a Glasscoe; possessors of names like Sidebottom, Rowbottom and Winterbottom demurely change the ending from -tom to -ham or abandon them altogether. While waiting for a bus in Broughton in Furness, I fell into conversation with a Canadian visitor who told me his name was Wynters. The family name had been Winterbottom, but one generation had changed it to Winters – they'd claimed to have wanted 'something simpler', he said – and another had further amended it by supplanting the 'I' with a 'Y'. Classier, I suppose.

Gradually over the years a mass adoption of terminal Es converted former Browns into Brownes, Clarks into Clarkes and Pains into Paines or Paynes and so on. The Revd Patrick Brontë, father of Charlotte, Emily and Anne, was born a Brunty, but upgraded his name, as he thought, not only by making it Bronte but by adding a diaeresis over the final letter to ensure that people pronounced it as two syllables rather than one. Many such changes were casual, informal tinkerings. Their social superiors, however, were engaged in more serious business. The incentive there, in a great many cases, might not entirely unfairly be described in one of two words – and sometimes by both: prestige and loot.

Some people took on new names as a way of avoiding their old ones. Richard Cromwell, who, against much wise advice, was chosen by his father Oliver to succeed him, having very soon been eased out of the job, reinvented himself as a humble villager called John Clarke in the Hertfordshire village of Cheshunt. (The name Cromwell was hardly authentic either: Oliver's great-grandfather, wishing to honour the memory of his kinsman Thomas Cromwell, had changed it from Williams.) Lord George Sackville, who everyone knew had been disgraced, declared unfit to hold any military rank whatsoever, and removed from the Privy Council because of his alleged cowardice at the battle of Minden in 1759, was relieved of this much-maligned name through an inheritance. He became Lord George Germain from 1770, and was thereafter remembered as the incompetent aristocrat who more than any others involved lost us the American colonies.

Yet taking the whole broad spectrum of the aristocracy and gentry, the picture was often this. If you wanted the house, the stables, the parkland, the deer and the peacocks, and possibly the heiress too, it might be an unavoidable step to sacrifice your name to qualify for the inheritance, even though those quiet evenings in your palatial library might be disturbed by the sound of forefathers turning in their unquiet graves.

The essential precondition of such events in the testator's mind was usually this: no male heirs have been born. The name has come down to an heiress. Unless resolute action is taken to impose it on a beneficiary, a hallowed name will die out. Again, you can find examples from places called Broughton alone. That was how in earlier times Twisletons had morphed into Fienneses at Broughton, Oxfordshire; how the name Sawrey was kept alive in Broughton, Furness; how Andersons became Pelhams in Lincolnshire – and how Fiskes were transformed into Wilkeses in Elmdon.

But the place to which you must turn to see this onomastic swap shop in action in its Victorian heyday is the ultra-formal mouthpiece of official decisions, the *London Gazette*. It is often supposed that though forenames can be changed at will, a change of surname requires an official procedure, usually by deed poll. But this is not so. If you want to alter your surname from Slummock to Worthington-Cadbury-St John-ffoulkes you may do so tomorrow. Unless you have done it for fraudulent purposes no bar can be raised against you.

But those with a higher place in the social hierarchy often required something more solemn and stately – often, not always. Some, like a man called Twaddle who upgraded himself to Tweeddale, were content with a line or two announcing a change in *The Times*, or even a more local organ. In 1906 an authority on these matters called Phillimore (whose father had changed the family name from Stiff in 1873), with a collaborator called Fry, published a bulky summary of every name change he had uncovered, harvested from a multiplicity of sources, though without in most cases any further explanation of why the change had been made.

The *London Gazette*, however, was lavish with explanations. The procedure was this. Following a stipulated formula, you approached the monarch for his or her assent, stating the old and new names and appropriate details and often – not always – providing some explanation for what you wanted to do. Your reward would be a notice in the *Gazette* announcing that the king or queen (it was always the queen for most of the nineteenth century) had been graciously pleased to accept your submission. The outcome, in a case in 1884 which involved an outcrop of the Broughton dynasty, was this:

> The Queen has been pleased to grant unto Harriet Elizabeth Robinson, of the Rectory, in the parish of Wootton, in the county of Oxford, Widow, and relict of Arthur Edward Robinson, Clerk, late Rector of Wootton aforesaid, and formerly wife of Fiennes Cornwallis (then Wykeham-Martin), late of Chacombe Priory, in the parish of Chacombe, in the county of Northampton, and of Leeds Castle, in the county of Kent, Esquire, sometime Major in the Fourth Regiment of Light Dragoons, second son of Charles Wykeham-Martin, of Leeds Castle aforesaid, Esquire, by Jemima Isabella, his wife (commonly called Lady Jemima Wykeham-Martin), daughter of James Mann, fifth and last Earl Cornwallis, all deceased, the mother and guardian of Fiennes Stanley Wykeham Cornwallis, her eldest son by the said Fiennes Cornwallis, a minor of the age of twenty years and upwards, Her Royal licence and authority, that he, the said Fiennes Stanley Wykeham Cornwallis, may, in compliance with a clause in the last will and testament of the said James Mann, Earl Cornwallis, deceased, assume and use the surname of Mann, in lieu of that of Cornwallis, and that he may bear the arms of Mann quarterly with his own; such arms being first duly exemplified according to the laws of arms, and recorded in the College of Arms, otherwise the said Royal licence and permission to be void and of none effect:
>
> And to command that the said Royal concession and declaration be recorded in Her Majesty's said College of Arms.

Sometimes the motive for making the change enshrined in this rigmarole is said to be some kind of respect (grateful, affectionate or whatever) for a dead relative, though one notices that those who expressed their respect for their newly dead relatives are frequently already occupying the mansion (no doubt complete with parklands, stables etc.) of the deceased. Respect in other words appears to owe something to previous gain. On many occasions, however, the change of name is specifically required. 'Where there's a will,' testators must have said to themselves, 'there's a way of preventing my hallowed surname from drifting into extinction.' In response to which, legatees must have said to themselves: there's plenty in this for me, even if it means changing, as one recipient had to do, from Belmont to Sly.

The outcome is frequently rather odd. A man whose second Christian name is his mother's surname is now required to adopt that surname in place of his own. So when Victor Hansard Yockney of Port Talbot changes his surname to Hansard, though he isn't required to do so, he procures himself a more cherishable surname at the cost of becoming Victor Hansard Hansard. Similar changes make Cathcart Boycott Wight into Cathcart Boycott Wight-Boycott, as required by a clause in the will of Thomas Boycott. They convert Quintin Dick Hume, who wishes to qualify for his inheritance from a maternal great-uncle, into Quintin Dick Dick. He thus loses the name of a great philosopher and makes himself sound like a very small East African antelope. There is also a Shirt who changes to Hirst, not as you might suspect to upgrade to a suitable anagram, but because it will open the way to a legacy. A succession of men called Newdigate, eager to qualify for inheritances from dead kinsmen, turn themselves into Newdigate-Newdegates, which some might consider imposing, but others ungainly.

Sometimes a will merely 'desires', 'requests' or even expresses an 'anxious hope' that the change be made. In the earlier years of the century the change is often 'demanded' or 'directed', in language that verges on bullying. Gradually, though, the proportion of legacies demanding a total name-change declines and the number that let the legatee off with nothing more than a tack-on increases. There are two kinds of tack-on. In one, Mr Crosby becomes Mr Crosby-Clark; in others, Mr Clark-Crosby, which means perhaps that the world is likely to go on thinking of him as a Crosby rather than as a Clark.

The chief engineers of change, as you leaf through the *London Gazette*, seem to be maternal uncles, augmented by the occasional maternal aunt and maternal grandparent. These are the people who feel the names in which they have taken such pride throughout life are threatened. They may themselves be doomed to extinction but they're damned if they'll let the name go down too.

Demands for less than total change, however, lead to the spread of double barrels, triple barrels, even quadruple barrels. One can see here the genesis of names familiar in our own day, such as Trevor-Roper, and Heathcoat-Amory (a Conservative Chancellor of the Exchequer) and Apsley Cherry-Garrard, the explorer, and Manningham-Buller, the name of a former Conservative MP and Lord Chancellor who was nicknamed Bullying Manner; also that of the woman who lately ran MI5. The name Rees-Mogg resulted when a Rees married a – probably socially superior – woman called Mogg. And a family called Schilizzi, despite achieving only a second barrel, soared into octosyllabity by becoming Vafiadacchi-Schilizzi in accordance with the will of Giovanni Vafiadacchi, merchant of what the British called Leghorn.

Yet such surnames seem mere baubles compared with some of those in the grandest families. Upgrading from one surname, or two, to three is routine. The Caves become Cave-Brownes and then Cave-Brown-Caves. John Lloyd Egginton adds an Ernlé; within a few months he's back, wanting an Erle as well. But even that fell short of the achievement of a Plunkett who in 1916 upgraded to Plunkett-Ernlé-Erle-Drax. (One of this family is a present-day Conservative MP, but you won't see the full panoply of his names on his posters. There he is simply Drax.) The Finch-Hattons tack on a Besly;

Guildford James Hillier Ellerker-Onslow becomes Guildford James Hillier Mainwaring-Ellerker-Onslow; the Heathcote-Drummonds add a concluding Willoughby; and the Marquess of Londonderry promotes himself from Vane-Tempest to Vane-Tempest-Stewart.

But four names are undoubtedly grander than three, a conclusion happily reached by Charles Henry Rolle Trefusis and his wife Wilhelmina, only daughter and heir of Sir John Hepburn Stuart-Forbes of Pitsligo and Fettercairn, as, in compliance with a deed of entail, they rename themselves Hepburn-Stuart-Forbes-Trefusis; by Sidney Carr Hobart-Hampden, Earl of Buckinghamshire, as he and his wife comply with the will of George Mercer-Henderson, under which he's required to restyle himself Sidney Carr Hobart-Hampden-Mercer-Henderson, though she, from now on, remains merely double-barrelled, as Georgiana Wilhelmina Mercer-Henderson, Countess of Buckinghamshire; by John Hovell-Thurlow and his wife, a Cumming-Bruce, as they get the queen's gracious assent to style themselves Hovell-Thurlow-Cumming-Bruce; or as Edward Montagu Stuart Granville Stuart-Wortley-Mackenzie, Earl of Wharncliffe, prefaces his surname collection with an added-on Montagu, making him Edward Montagu Stuart Granville Montagu-Stuart-Wortley-Mackenzie, greedy fellow; while the St John-Mildmays enter a new century as Shaw-Lefevre-St John-Mildmays. Yet even these plenipotentiary names do not match that of the father of Mary, Baroness Kinloss, wife of the Marquess of Stowe, when this couple are changing their surname from Morgan to Morgan-Grenville. He is Sir Richard Plantagenet Campbell Temple-Nugent-Brydges-Chandos-Grenville, 3rd Duke of Buckingham and Chandos, a name so long he'd have needed a page-boy to carry it.

Other applicants to Her Majesty appear to be almost hobbyists. Conspicuous here are the family who begin in 1814 with a change from William George Daniel to William George Tyssen Tyssen-Amhurst. In 1867 there appears in the lists a William George Tyssen Tyssen-Amhurst, formerly William George Tyssen

Daniel-Tyssen, who, along with his brother Francis and sister Amelia, wants the monarch's assent to change to Tyssen-Daniel-Amhurst. But they're a restless lot, and four years later they're applying to ditch the Daniel. Perhaps the three of them sit around of an evening after dinner has been cleared away and the servants are off to bed and the logs crackle in the grate, debating how their names might be further improved. At any rate the trio are back in 1877 wanting the queen's permission again to change their name to an ancient orthography and become Tyssen-Amhersts.

Some changes are triggered by marriage. A Brown marries an Elliot-Greive; they merge into Brown-Greive. A Dillwyn-Llewellyn marries a Venables (an heiress) and makes a sandwich of her as they become Mr and Mrs Dillwyn-Venables-Llewellyn. When a Joseph marries an Uttermare, they take the name Uttermare, which is that of the bride's first husband; but then she is the lady of the manor of Hatch Beauchamp, Somerset. Where a social superior (female) marries a social inferior, the social inferior may have to abandon the normal rules and take his wife's name rather than keeping his. Others appear to be motivated purely by pride. Jonathan Swift, in 1711, mocks a man who has serially upgraded his name: 'I know a citizen who adds or alters a letter in his name with every plum he acquires; he now wants only the change of a vowel to be allied to a sovereign prince, and that perhaps he may contrive to be done by a mistake of the graver upon his tombstone.' This was Sir Henry Furniss, whose name at birth had been Furnace, since when he had gone up through the gears to be Furnice, Furnise, Furness and Furnese – one step away from Farnese. One also suspects mere ostentation in the case of a Shropshire man called Price who for no stated reason makes himself into Price-Davies; he has previously in a kind of progression given his sons the forenames Stafford Davies, Hugh Arthur Lewis, and Llewellyn Alberic Emilius, while his daughter will now become Gwendoline Choliter Mary Sceynton Price-Davies.

A man who comes by a baronetcy will feel he deserves a grander name to go with it. In some cases, they claim to be disinterring an original name which has somehow got lost. Ring out the old, cried Alfred Lord Tennyson, ring in the new. One branch of his family had already been doing just that. The poet's father had been disinherited – one source, it seems, of his disillusionment, resentment and frightening rages. His younger brother, chosen to supersede him, who became a Tory MP, upgraded himself, as he thought, to Tennyson d'Eyncourt. D'Eyncourt was a name he laid claim to, as Alfred's biographer Peter Levi says, 'in pursuit of a Norman connection with messy dog-legs through the female line and some degree of improbability'. In the same cause he built an exuberant, boastful house at Tealby to which – Norman pretensions again – he gave the name Bayons Manor. His poet-nephew in contrast famously proclaimed that kind hearts were more than coronets and simple faith than Norman blood; though Levi says Alfred did consider tacking a d'Eyncourt on to his name when he was given his peerage.

Some of the changes are sad for those who enjoy diversity. An Ashpinshaw changes to Staunton. A Hogsflesh becomes a Herbert by announcement in *The Times*; a Peppercorn takes the name Harris. Other cases in the *Gazette* remain a mystery. Why, for instance, should a man with the neat name of Budd have decided to change to the cumbersome Holtsapffel? One can only guess at the thoughts that went through the heads of some of those who were changing the name only because if they didn't the money, the house, the park and the rest would go elsewhere. How did Tredenham Hugh Carlyon, of Germansweek, Devon, feel on being required, in order to benefit from the will of his maternal great-uncle, to scale his name down to Spry? What did William Mosley Perfect of Giggleswick make of having to cease to be Mr Perfect and becoming a mere Mr Dawson?

Still, inconvenient as some of these requirements might seem, recipients could at least reflect that they might have been worse. A compendium of eccentric wills compiled in the 1870s by William Tegg chronicled the case of a testator called the Hon. Mrs Araminta Monck Ridley who ordered that her bequests would no longer be valid if any of her children should become a Roman Catholic, or marry one, or 'join any Ritualistic brotherhood or sisterhood'. A man called Budd required a similar forfeiture should either of his inheriting sons grow a moustache. As for Mr Sargeant of Leicester:

As my nephews are fond of indulging themselves in bed in the morning, and as I wish them to prove to the satisfaction of my executors that they have got out of bed in the morning, and either employed themselves in business or taken exercise in the open air, from five to eight o'clock every morning from the 5th of April to the 10th of October, being three hours each day, and from seven to nine o'clock in the morning from the 10th of October to the 5th of April, being two hours every morning; this is to be done for some years, during the first seven years to the satisfaction of my executors, who may excuse them in case of illness, but the task must be made up when they are well, and if they will not do this, they shall not receive any share of my property. Temperance makes the faculties clear, and exercise makes them vigorous. It is temperance and exercise that can alone ensure the fittest state for mental or bodily exertion.

But the motive is not always money. There are other reasons for changing one's name, from simple self-aggrandisement to attempts to disguise an inconvenient truth; a habit not exclusive to, but nonetheless not unknown amongst, Members of Parliament. Here, one conspicuous case was a ripe old rogue called Albert Grant, member for Kidderminster from 1865 to 1868

and again for a matter of months in 1874 before he was unseated
for bribery. Known as Baron Grant – the barony, unlike some of
his other accoutrements, was honestly gained; the Italian government had awarded the title to him – Grant, born Abraham
Gottheimer in Dublin, appeared to be fabulously rich and gave
Leicester Square to London. Disraeli was solemnly warned by
advisers that if his philanthropy continued unchecked he might
have to be given a peerage. But the collapse of a dubious mining
company ruined him. A palatial house he was building in
Kensington was abandoned and soon after demolished, and he
ended his life in the poverty from which he had come – though
as Grant, not as Gottheimer.

An even more extraordinary case was that of a man who
said that his name was Lincoln – Frederick Trebitsch Lincoln
– and who in January 1910 defeated one of the town's most
famous sons to become Liberal MP for Darlington. He was
born Ignácz Timotheus Trebitsch, in Hungary. He emigrated
to Canada, then came to Britain and had himself installed as an
Anglican curate in Kent. Having sat in the British Parliament
for a mere ten months, he would later enhance his CV by
becoming a German spy, a member of the German government,
a plotter and conspirator in Tibet and China, and the abbot of
a Buddhist monastery. His names in that time – they included
Trautwein and Patrick Keelan in Germany, Chao Kung in China
– are uncountable.

The Grants and Lincolns left no lasting mark on politics. But
far more eminent politicians, into our own days too, have borne
names altered either by themselves or by their progenitors. They
include several past prime ministers. Disraeli's father spelled
the surname D'Israeli. Gladstone's father was Gladstones until he
moved from Scotland to Liverpool. Campbell-Bannerman started
as Campbell, Lloyd George as plain George. Ramsay MacDonald,
the illegitimate child of Anne Ramsay and John McDonald, was
registered at birth as James McDonald Ramsay. James Callaghan's

father changed the family name from Garoghan. John Major's father was Major-Ball, a name his brother hung on to. Tony Blair was born Blair, but only because his father, who was adopted, took the name of his adoptive parents rather than keeping his father's, which was Parsons. There were adaptations too for others who never made prime minister. Anthony Wedgwood Benn altered his name to change his image. He threw off not only the peerage he inherited – succeeding to the title Lord Stansgate meant he could no longer sit in the Commons – but his Wedgwood as well; Tony Benn was a shorter, simpler, less ostentatious name for one who sought to be seen as a Man of the People.

The champion parliamentary name-swapper of the twentieth century, though, was motivated in the old-fashioned way, by inheritances. A Conservative originally called Hugh Warrand first changed his name in 1920 on inheriting under special provision a baronetcy whose previous occupant had lost three sons in the Great War. That made him when elected in 1924 Sir Hugh Vere Huntly Duff Lucas-Tooth, a name he expanded in 1965 to Munro-Lucas-Tooth. A more eminent practitioner, who came close to the top of the Conservative Party, began life as Philip Lloyd-Greame, a name that he owed to his grandfather, Yarburgh Gamaliel Lloyd, who had added the Greame to comply with the will of his maternal uncle Yarburgh Yarburgh. The owner of that very odd name had been born Yarburgh Greame but changed it when he inherited his mother's estates. Rising gracefully up the scale, Philip became Sir Philip, and subsequently the Right Honourable Sir Philip – and then abandoned all that to become the Rt Hon. Sir Philip Cunliffe-Lister, which transformation ensured that he and his wife would acquire a great house and estate in Yorkshire Swinton Park, which had belonged to her industrialist father. A later, less elevated Member of Parliament who, as we have seen, had begun life as Ján Ludvík Hyman Binyamin Hoch in what is now the Czech

Republic became first Captain Ian and then Captain Robert Maxwell.

*

Here and there changes of name hint at intriguing histories. In a very few cases a father's name is taken by his illegitimate child. George Merrikin Lowis, of Grainthorpe, Lincolnshire, 'reputed son' of a father called Merrikin, takes the surname of his reputed father. In April 1869, the queen permits Alfred Jackson, a minor, to take the name of his 'natural and reputed' father, the late Alderman William Hodge, former sheriff and mayor of Hull, a mill-owner rich and successful enough to have given a statue of Edward I, its founder, to the town, who made this adoption of his name a condition of a bequest to his illegitimate son.

Sometimes a change has a whiff of old scandal about it. In 1874 a woman called Frances Bullock, living in the fine house at Uppark, changed her name to Bullock-Fetherstonhaugh. The house had belonged to Sir Henry Fetherstonhaugh, who in his cheerfully dissolute youth had enlisted Emma Lyon – who would later become Emma Hamilton – as one of his mistresses. After years of much more settled and decorous life, he astonished his neighbours by marrying one of his dairymaids, Mary Anne Bullock, whom he had heard singing as she went about her work. He was seventy; she was eighteen. When he died in 1846, she inherited the house and she and her sister Frances lived there in comfort and style until their deaths. George, father of H. G. Wells, was one of the gardeners and Sarah, his wife, was a maid. Wells as a child met the Bullock sisters and wasn't impressed, describing them as 'immense'. The estate eventually passed to the Earl of Clanwilliam, who had to adopt the name Fetherstonhaugh.

*

In the twentieth century, the pattern of name changes darkens. There are still those in the *London Gazette* intent on complying with wills, but alongside those is the hope of escape from social ostracism or outright persecution. In the second decade, the *Gazette* is full of records of people abandoning German and to a lesser extent Jewish names. It was not until the war started (in the early months of 1914: few had expected it) that the trickle grew to a flood. Thereafter, the applications and petitions flowed in until the government ruled that no one could change their name from now on unless by special provisions or marriage. A similar ban was imposed in the Second World War.

In the autumn of 1914, however, a Schneider is successfully changed into a Belassis, a Blumenfeld to a Bloomfield, and a Brueggemeyer to a Bridges. Some changes are wonderfully simple: Schwarz to Black, Schloss to Castle, Krauss to Cross. Louis-Leopold Martial Baynard de Beaumont-Klein dumps his Klein. Jessie Charlotte von Wurtzburg Schade Baroness von Wurtzberg boils herself down to Jessie Charlotte Lowth. Others are much more ambitious. There seems to be a tendency to go for upmarket English, and perhaps even more for upmarket Scottish, names. Stanley, a classic English aristocratic surname, finds new adherents in people until now called Schildt, Schleicher and Stolzenberger, while a Schmidt takes on the name Grosvenor-Smyth. And Nathaniel Ludwig Bleibtreu, also known as Bleibtruye, settles for the old Scottish name, which we came across in bloodthirsty times in the Scottish Borders, of Tweedie. The notorious newspaper publisher Alfred Harmsworth, Lord Northcliffe, had an assistant called Hamilton whom he allegedly said he knew must be Jewish because he had such a fine Scottish name.

Elsewhere, a man called Carl Zwicker adopts the name Charles Wesley, which Methodists might consider a shade impertinent. Other choices are more elusive: Heimendahl to Guild, Ohlenshlaget to Jannings. A Schuster becomes a Clatworthy.

Such changes continued through the twentieth century. In 2012

Giles Fraser, who resigned as Canon Chancellor of St Paul's over the 'Occupy' protests and went off to take over a parish in south London, revealed that his father, though not his mother, was Jewish, and had changed the family name from Friedeburg to Fraser to escape anti-Semitism. Even more surprisingly, the newly chosen Archbishop of Canterbury, Justin Welby, turned out to be not only the first oil trader ever to grace this office, but the son of a Jewish father called Bernard Weiler.

Discovery of such changes can sometimes create uncertainty. In a largely tolerant age, belated revelations about the unexpected origins of an old friend will rarely mean any substantial re-appraisal. In any case, anyone's make-up derives from hundreds and thousands of forebears with thousands of names: indeed, if you traced it back far enough you might find that the two of you were related. Yet a surname is part of the story of someone you thought you knew well, and it's worrying, or certainly disappointing, not to have known before.

But what this evidence ought really to undermine is the traditional faith – well, some people's traditional faith – in the hallowed old social order. Those poignant peers who talk of the banishment of hereditary peers as some kind of repudiation of the nation's most precious history – 'Take but degree away,' they like to say, 'untune that string, And, hark, what discord follows!' – cloud the fact that many hereditary peerages are not ancient at all, and are often traceable back to the heyday of Victorian and Edwardian plutocracy and dependent even before then on all kinds of dirty deals. Anyone who has studied these things knows that the rich man in his castle may have got there by ruthless ambition, perhaps even laced with fraud. Those sonorous names reverently pronounced on a state occasion are rarely all that they seem to be.

That starts at the very top. The names of our monarchy are confections. Had they stuck to their original names, instead of amending them into something more British, trying at sensitive times to eliminate the Germanic, they would not now be called Windsor. That mighty monarch and empress Victoria was a Saxe-Coburg-Saalfeld married to a Saxe-Coburg Gotha. Gyles Brandreth's book *Philip and Elizabeth* describes the alarm in the British Cabinet when news filtered out that Prince Philip wanted his wife to take his surname, Mountbatten, on the grounds that a father should be allowed to pass his name on to a son. 'What the devil does that young fool Edinburgh think that the family name has got to do with him?', Queen Mary, Elizabeth's grandmother, whose husband George V had made Windsor the family name by proclamation in 1917, is said to have snapped. The Cabinet asked Churchill to convey its views to the queen, and Windsor prevailed. Yet even Mountbatten was a fairly recent adoption, taken when Philip was naturalised. Before that he was Schleswig-Holstein-Sonderburg-Glücksburg. Had the queen been destined for a tennis career rather than for the throne, she might have appeared at Wimbledon as Mrs Saxe-Coburg-Gotha-Schleswig-Holstein-Sonderburg-Glücksburg.

Sabine Baring-Gould (whose grandfather changed the family surname from Baring to Baring-Gould) is not always to be relied on, but there's something exhilarating about watching him scythe his way through the peerage, leaving so much aristocratic pretension in tatters on its brilliantly polished floors. These Wellesleys, Dukes of Wellington, he says – the great Duke of Wellington was only fifty years dead when he wrote, and still venerated – they aren't really Wellesleys at all. The great duke's grandfather was a Colley who changed that to Wesley (other parts of the family switched it to Cowley) and later expanded it to a grander, more polysyllabic, form. The mighty Cavendishes who furnish Dukes of Devonshire ought by right to be Smithsons. The Mainwaring family of Over Peover, Cheshire, have no right to be Mainwarings: they have not a drop of old Mainwaring blood in their veins. The Trevors, the family that breeds our Lord Dacres, ought to be Brands. Nor do the Saye and Sele family escape his sharp eye. They haven't really been Fienneses since 1781.

Bastardy, he gleefully adds, is liberally represented in the gilded chamber. As indeed it is, in two forms. One is the acknowledged kind, which although it denied him the right to take the throne, his claim to which cost him his life, allowed the illegitimate son of Charles II and Lucy Walter to become Duke of Monmouth and Duke of Buccleuch.

The illegitimate progeny of our monarchs, even excluding the dubious cases, make up a sturdy contingent. William I was himself a bastard: that was the nickname by which he was known. To compile an accurate scoreboard of the illegitimate children of kings from that time onwards would defeat the most assiduous of researchers even after a lifetime. Largely unfounded claims are made on behalf of some. The champion, it seems generally agreed, is Henry I, who is credited with at least twenty and possibly twenty-five such offspring. Some sources believe that James V of Scotland had as many as twenty, half-siblings for the daughter who became Mary, Queen of Scots. Charles II admitted to fourteen illegitimate children, though a case can be made that the true count was twenty. Sometimes the calculations depend on whether a king was genuinely married or not. That applies with particular force to Henry VIII. If, as was successfully claimed on the king's behalf, his first marriage to Catherine of Aragon was invalid, then the daughter who became Queen Mary was illegitimate; if, however, that marriage was valid, then Elizabeth was the bastard child.

In times when such matters were more reliably documented, William IV, as Duke of Clarence, had ten children with his mistress Mrs Jordan (who in truth was neither Mrs nor Jordan: the Mrs was a courtesy title and the Jordan an invention). They were given the surname FitzClarence, thus encouraging the unreliable notion that names beginning Fitz are a signal of illegitimacy. The second son of this long liaison (the eldest was drowned in the Indian Ocean) became the Earl of Munster. The last credible case was a child expected by a woman called Susan Vane-Tempest who was packed off to Ramsgate in 1871 because of the well-founded assumption that Victoria's wayward son, later Edward VII, was the father. There is, however, no record of what became of the child, which was possibly not even born.

On the whole, however, such events at the very top of society were largely taken for granted – in painful contrast to the obloquy which went with the birth of a bastard child lower down the social hierarchy, as parish records powerfully indicate, sometimes recording the birth of a 'natural child' but sometimes of a 'bastard'. One birth in the Scottish Borders in 1715 is listed as 'a child proceeded from a scandal of adultery between James Michel and Barbara Samson called Helen Wilson'.

The second kind of aristocratic and gentry bastardy is the birth that hardly anyone (apart from the mother) knew to be illegitimate. Many products of their mothers' extra-mural adventures remained officially known as the children of their nominal fathers, and their names were passed on to posterity on the basis of this illusion. So there alone, there's a wealth of false trails, waiting to be unpicked by research into DNA.

There's a further instance of a non-paternity event which can mean that straight lines traced back through the ages are not to be trusted. Without DNA tests it is easy to miss adoptions, where again the blood in the veins is not that of the titular family. Sometimes the facts of adoption are known, sometimes not. Adoption was not legal in England until 1926 and, as Deborah Cohen explains in *Family Secrets: Living with Shame from the Victorians to the Present Day*, for many years the advice to adoptive parents was not to reveal the fact of adoption. Michael Gove, mentioned as a possible future leader of the Conservative Party and potential prime minister, was adopted at four months old. The names of his natural parents are not common knowledge. His mother, who named him Graeme rather than Michael, was a young unmarried woman who felt she could not cope on her own. His adoptive parents could not have children. We know of at least one prime minister – Ramsay MacDonald – who was illegitimate, but no records exist to establish how many senior politicians have been adopted.

The onomastic swap shop: downstairs

Grand though they were, the aristocracy and gentry had no monopoly when it came to abandoning the names they were born with and adopting others. Even in the humblest regions of society, even in the drabbest, least privileged, cottages in the hamlet around Broughton Castle and church, where no one bowed to you and no family portraits graced your walls, name change was common. A great number, perhaps almost half the population, surrendered their names year by year for others; and still do. True, here and there, when a bridegroom's social status was lower than that of his bride, they were allowed to take precedence. But in all other cases, they were on the receiving end, the passive end of the deal. They are called women.

Over the centuries, though the practice may have developed more slowly in Scotland and Wales than elsewhere, this was what was expected – and more than expected, required – that a woman would ditch her own name and take on her husband's. There were always a few radical souls who resisted, but until the twentieth century, and only then in any great numbers outside the most sophisticated addresses in the cities, the practice continued unchallenged. This was how the world worked. The man was head of the household. His word prevailed. Until the reforms of 1870 and 1882, when a man acquired a wife, he also acquired her property. That was the natural order of things. No, more than that: it was what God had ordained. In the opening chapter of Genesis, God makes the grass and the trees and the flora and fauna and the beasts of the field and the fowls of the air and brings them to the man, and the man names them. It doesn't say how Adam was named, but it's stipulated that after the fall, Adam names Eve – who is, after all, the product of one of his ribs. He calls her, in the Hebrew, Havvah, that is, Living or Life, which she may have been pleased with.

The traditional surname practice in Britain, in line with all that, has always been deeply sexist. Elsewhere, in Spain and Iceland for example, the woman's name can be perpetuated along with, or instead of, the man's. But in Britain, the man's name trumps the woman's; it is rarely the other way around. True, in tightly clustered villages, the woman's original name would not be forgotten. If you were born Betty Offer in Broughton, Hampshire, you might always be Betty Offer to those who had watched you grow up, even though you had married a Rogers – or, in the timeless terminology of village gossip, you'd be 'Betty Offer as was'.

In higher society, a wife was required for some purposes to take on her husband's forename as well. If Althea Jones married Alastair Brown, her correspondence would come to her as Mrs Alastair Brown. In some especially well-bred households, it still does today. The novelist Mrs Humphry Ward (1851–1920) had been a rebellious child, but when she married an Oxford don she used his Christian name as well as his surname, in preference to her own (which was Mary Augusta). Maybe this was the name as statement of intention: it helped assert she was not a feminist, a circumstance confirmed when she became a leading campaigner against votes for women, a cause then espoused both by her son, a Tory MP with a gambling habit, and her daughter.

This subjection – often a happy subjection, gladly embraced – applied in death, as in life. If you look in an English churchyard you will almost always find that the surname in which a woman is buried is that of her husband – and if he has died before her, she'll be described as his relict, or sometimes, even relic, as if she were just one more of his goods and chattels. In Scotland, however, you frequently find that a woman has died in the name she was born with. In the churchyard at Broughton, Borders, Janet Smith has been the wife of Gavin Greenshields, Charlotte

Dickie the wife of David Dickson, Margaret Kerr Sharpe the wife of Harry Thomson, Helen Aitken the wife of Thomas Gibson.

The practice is not universal, but it is common. A poem by Philip Larkin muses on the loss of a maiden name, not just for the girl who parted from it, but also for her friends, to whom her original surname, now lying disused in old lists and programmes, would still be the one by which they remembered her.

*

Yet though more women than ever now decline to comply with traditional practice, others embrace it. The first great explorer of surnames, William Camden, thought they should: 'Women with us at their marriage do change their names and passes into their husbands' names, and justly for that then *non sunt duo, sed caro una* [they are not two, but one flesh].' But anxious as always to judge things fairly, he adds that higher-class women in France and the Netherlands perpetuate their names; a woman called Villevill, marrying a man called Vavin, will be known as Mary Vavin Villevill: 'but I feare husbands will not like this note, for that some of their dames may be ambitiously over-pert and too-too-forward to imitate it.' The turbulent (some might even say, ambitiously pert) chick-lit novelist and Tory MP Louise Bagshawe could hardly wait to ditch the name under which she had published so successfully when she married her second husband, the rock group manager Peter Mensch. 'I have strong feelings of hero worship towards him,' she confided to *GQ* magazine. 'I was longing to brand myself with his name for a very long time.' (One could ponder for quite a long time her use of the verb 'brand'.) It's just possible that her view was coloured by the fact that 'Mensch' is an American slang word, derived from the Yiddish, which means 'an honest, decent morally principled person'. Bagshawe, her maiden name, derives from a place in Derbyshire. Her previous married name, which she did not publicly brand herself with, was LoCicero.

Some names adopted at marriage, as Louise Bagshawe / LoCicero may have felt on becoming a Mensch, seem like an upgrading, though looking at parish records one sometimes wonders if the prospect of change brought qualms. To acquire a suitable husband, some women in Broughton, Hampshire, had also to acquire the prominent village surname, Lush, a word that implied a drunkard. Another that may have caused them some qualms was Hoore. A woman recorded in the 1861 census at Broughton, Lincolnshire, has married, possibly with some trepidation, a man whose surname is Hell. William Hell is an innkeeper. His daughter Maria will escape her ominous surname by wedding a man called Fox, but the rest of the household is stuck with it. As an innkeeper, William Hell has a servant who lives on the premises. Her surname is Church.

Changes of name on marriage also awoke a whole range of superstitions. Some were favourable. A woman who married a man with the same surname as her own, as one of the Offers in Broughton, Hampshire, did, was believed to have acquired the power to cure whooping cough, a potentially fatal ailment, by baking a plain currant cake which the child had to be persuaded to eat. If a man called Joseph married a woman called Mary – a conjunction of names whose significance hardly needs explanation – a child could be saved by eating bread cut by Joseph and buttered by Mary; but in this case surnames did not come into it. But to marry someone who had only the first initial of your own name, not the whole of it, was considered hazardous: 'to change the name, but not the letter', it was said, 'is to marry for worse, not for better.'

*

Where the rich man in his castle regarded his name as a gleaming ingredient of his image, the poor man at his gate contented himself with what fate had ordained for him. Among men outside the highest ranks of society, a change of name on marriage was rare and might have been thought quite pointless, yet names in villages changed by an often unconsidered process of evolution. The Mershes in early-nineteenth-century Broughton, Hampshire, were all Marshes at the end of it, and the Pragnells, Prangnells, Pragneles, Prangeles, Prangneles and Prangells all came to be united as Pragnells – though the Beacham who, as we've seen, transformed himself into a Beauchamp almost certainly did that deliberately.

I have left until last the saddest case, of those who had names imposed on them, perhaps because like slaves they were properties of masters, or perhaps because, as a result of the circumstances of their birth, they had no names at all. There were other, rarer cases of imposition. Monarchs might sometimes order a man in their service, even of quite high rank, to change his name simply because they disliked it. According to William Camden, Edward I was displeased by names beginning with Fitz- (though a good many of his successors found them useful for the naming of illegitimate children) and ordered Lord John Fitz-Robert to change his name to John of Clavering, the name of lands in his barony.

In Scotland, men requiring the protection of clans would switch their name en masse to that of the clan. The historian of Scottish surnames, George F. Black, says 'the Gordons were hardly settled in Strathbolgy when the whole country around was full of men calling themselves Gordon . . . the native people having themselves no surnames, readily adopted that of their new lords.' When these general adoptions took place, 'they kept up [the] theory of blood-relationship which in nine cases out of ten had no other foundation whatever'.

A whole surname might be ordered by government to discard

its names, as the MacGregors were in 1603 after they had slaughtered a large number – 140 at least, but possibly as many as 200 – of the forces gathered by their neighbours, the more prosperous Colquhouns, at the battle of Glen Fruin, close to Loch Lomond. King James, then avidly awaiting the death of Elizabeth I in England, whose throne he hoped to inherit, summoned his privy council and an edict was issued, demanding that this 'unhappie and detestable race be extirpat and ruttit out, and never suffered to have rest or remaining within this countrey hierafter'. The very use of the name MacGregor was 'altoggidder abolisheed' and death was ordained for anyone found using it. Those provisions were reversed by Charles II, whose restoration the MacGregors had supported, but re-imposed when the Stuarts were ousted in the revolution of 1688, and then continued until 1774.

Some, though not officially required to do so, discarded their names after the failure of the Jacobite revolt; one is recorded in the *London Gazette* as having done so 'for prudential reasons'. A good many old Scots names were quietly Anglicised after Culloden in 1746. Much the same happened in Wales where, after the Act of Union, families who hoped to advance themselves decided they were more likely to do so if their names sounded more English. For many, the only compulsion here was ambition. But some were coerced. In *The Isles: A History* (1999), Norman Davies writes:

As the English administration advanced into Celtic areas, Anglicised surnames were imposed, often with eccentric results. In Wales, for instance, a small number of male Christian names were transferred into Anglicised surnames, and widely adopted en masse by the Welsh-speaking population. As a result, thousands upon thousands of unrelated families ended up with the same simple surnames, usually Jones, Williams, Thomas, Edwards, Hughes, or Davies – sowing immense confusion.

It's often assumed that names ending in 's' must be Welsh – see the churchyard in Broughton, Flintshire, where such surnames dominate as they do in so many churchyards across the principality – but in fact that usage started in England, a possessive form of alternative to the suffix -son prevalent in the north of England.

Not all were so easily weaned from ancient names. The Grahams, ruthlessly powerful and feared through the English Borders, were punished by banishment. Large numbers were deported to Ireland, simply on account of their surnames. But soon they were seeping back, some re-establishing themselves under the less-than-mystifying alias Maharg. In the end it made little difference: the Grahams, it has been computed, remain the largest single contingent in the Carlisle phone book.

Yet nothing happened in Britain to match the repeated orders issued elsewhere in Europe at the end of the eighteenth century and in the first decades of the nineteenth for Jews to abandon such surnames as they possessed and take on new ones ordained by governments. That was done in Austria, Prussia, Napoleon's France and Russia, and in Poland where one of the officials charged with enforcing it was E. T. A. Hoffmann, better known as a romantic writer and composer, and celebrated in Offenbach's *Tales of Hoffmann*. Few who came before him had surnames. 'Mr Hoffmann', wrote a contemporary observer, whose account Norman Davies prints in *Heart of Europe: A Short History of Poland*:

> does not receive clients every day, since he is usually occupied with his writing, and when he does condescend to see them, he is in such a hurry that one is not allowed to ask him about anything. Before dinner, on an empty stomach, he issues serious or melancholy surnames, after dinner more amusing ones . . . He glares at the client in deathly silence, and then shouts out the first word that comes to mind . . . Once, when Hoffmann had been playing the organ in

church, he issued a string of surnames with a religious flavour, such as HELGOT, HIMMELBLAU, KADZIDLO (incense), PANIEBOZEDOPOMOZ (Help-Us-Good Lord), BOZAKROWKA (Ladybird, or literally, God's Cow) and so on . . . one night Mr Hoffmann went drinking with a Russian colonel. In the morning he ordered cold water to be poured over his head, arrived in the office in a fine humour, and started issuing military surnames such as FESTUNG, FOJER, PISTOLET, SZYSPULVER TROMMELO, TROMPETER, HARMATA. That's as far as he got, because the rest of his clients fled.

The largest and humblest category for whom names were peremptorily prescribed was servants and slaves. Ironically these names came when they were freed – until then a single name was thought to suffice for their servile state. Servants and slaves found themselves lumbered with names that above all reflected no more than a whim on the part of their powerful masters – Scipio, Caesar, Nero at one end of the scale; at the other, the names more usually given to pets – indicative, as the anthropologists say, of their incomplete personhood. The celebrated freed slave Olaudah Equiano was given the name 'Gustavus' after the King of Sweden.

In an otherwise coolly academic book called *An Anthropology of Names and Naming*, an American anthropologist, Susan Benson, tells the humiliating story of her own family, which catches a British colonial administrator in the not uncharacteristically ambivalent posture of treating slaves and servants as inherently inferior beings – childlike creatures, incapable of progress out of that state – while using them as their sexual partners. The man who fathered her father, whose name was Browne, announced that the boy's surname was Benson and suppressed all documentation of his own part in the proceedings. A generation of latter-day Americans threw off such subject names and adopted their own: Cassius Clay became Muhammad Ali, Malcolm Little became Malcolm X, and the fine South African jazz pianist and bandleader formerly known as Dollar Brand became Abdullah Ibrahim.

But at least they had names. A further swathe of humanity had no names at all.

8

Deprivations

Surnames Lost, Stolen, Strayed – or Denied

> Tell me the name by which you were known at home to your
> mother and father and your friends in the town and country
> around. No one after all, whether of high or low degree, goes
> nameless once he has come into the world.
> King Alcinous to the unrevealed Odysseus, Homer's *Odyssey*
> (translated by E. V. Rieu)

Where would you be without it?

In the spring of 1851 a census enumerator arrived at Down Farm
on the edge of Broughton, Hampshire, and knocked on the door
of one of its farm workers' cottages. What he found must have
surprised him. The tenants were a man called William Blacklock
– a north-country surname, rare in this part of the world, though
he'd been born in Broughton – his wife Phoebe, and six children:
their sons Charles, sixteen, and John, thirteen – like their father
both employed as farm labourers – and four-year-old George,
and their daughters, Mary, fourteen, Sarah, eleven, and Elizabeth,
eight. But there was one more name to add to the list whose
origins were mysterious: a four-year-old girl unrelated to all these
Blacklocks, whom he described in the bleak words, 'friendless
pauper'. But at least the girl had a name: Martha Rogers.

There she was much more fortunate than many another poor
friendless, relationless child who had no name at all. Some years

before this, a boy had been brought by a woman whose identity he would never remember – though he knew it was not his mother – to the workhouse at St Pancras, then on the edge of London, where he found himself installed with many other children as bereft of friends or relations as he was. This boy would later be famous: his sufferings at St Pancras, and even worse in the mills in Nottinghamshire and Derbyshire to which he was later despatched, were recorded in a magazine called *The Lion* by a Lancashire journalist, John Brown, who had learned of his story and traced him. He later published his findings in a book which he called *A Memoir of Robert Blincoe, an orphan boy: sent from the workhouse of St Pancras, London, at seven years of age, to endure the Horrors of a Cotton-Mill, through his infancy and youth, with a minute detail of his sufferings, being the first memoir of the kind published* (1832). As John Waller argued in a book called *The Real Oliver Twist: Robert Blincoe – A Life that Illuminates a Violent Age* (2005), Charles Dickens was greatly influenced by Blincoe's testimony and drew on it for his novel.

By the time he talked to Brown, Robert had a name. But he only acquired it long after he left St Pancras. There, he had no name at all. He believed that his father had been a clergyman, which was why before that he had been known as 'Parson'. When he first met Brown, he told him, 'with tears trickling down his pallid cheeks and his voice tremulous and faltering', 'I am worse off than a child reared in the Foundling Hospital. Those orphans have a name given them by the heads of that institution, at the time of baptism, to which they are entitled. But I have no name I can call my own.' He was angry, even now, with the officers of the workhouse who had failed to register the name that he had been born with; or worse, as he now suspected, had known but suppressed it. The best he could do was to take on a name that he half remembered as the possible name of his father – though research then and since has failed to turn up a Reverend Mr Blincoe who might have shared with Robert's mother the 'mutual frailties', as Brown puts it, that had brought him into this merciless world.

Unlike others who shared his predicament, who – some in the workhouse, far more outside it when sent as cheap labour to factory owners – died through neglect or preventable accident, Robert Blincoe survived. He survived with stunted growth and some deformity, yet was able in time to become a mill-owner himself and to father a son who would one day take on the name and designation that may or may not have been those of Robert's own father, the Reverend Mr Blincoe.

What became of Martha Rogers is rather less clear. But subsequent censuses show that she wasn't, as one might have suspected, a stray child found in a shed or outhouse on the farm where the Blacklocks worked, as were some of such people, young and old, who figure in census returns. The record rather suggests some kind of unofficial adoption: ten years later, the census of 1861 finds Martha still with the Blacklocks, in Farley, a village near Winchester, where William worked as a shepherd. Martha is at school, and now described as a boarder. One decade more, and Martha, at twenty-five, is in service at an opulent house in the village of Wrotham, Kent, a few doors away from John Blacklock and his new family; but no longer as Martha Rogers, she now calls herself Martha Blacklock. Where she goes after that I have not been able to trace: she might just be the girl from Hampshire (birthplace village unspecified) who has married a man called Owen and is living in Poplar, east London – but if so, she has not been entirely honest about her age.

And, if so, she is well in advance of others whom successive censuses log as having no surname at all. Here, in the space where the surname ought to appear, the entry says bleakly: 'unknown'. In Cubitt Town on the Isle of Dogs – named, as I said in looking at eponyms, after William Cubitt who developed it – and in a street running down to the river called Johnson's Road – named after the company that ran the riverside ironworks at the bottom

– the 1871 census discovered the Smiths: James, a plate-layer on the railways, and Ruth, his wife; both, like many around them, born well away from London – James in Northamptonshire, Ruth in a place that the census records as Grantham, Lancashire. With them there are two sons, John and William, and also two lodgers: James Unknown, who is thirty, and Edward Unknown, nineteen. Edward was born in Plymouth; even more of James's identity is missing, since he has no idea where he was born.

A little way north, in Elizabeth Place, just off the East India Dock Road, where today the mighty temples of HSBC and Barclay and J. P. Morgan at Canary Wharf loom over ancient dockland institutions like the Mission to Seamen Institute, the census discovered the widow Maria Dobson, her sons Arthur and Walter, and two surnameless two-year-old children, Ada and Charles. Had they been in the workhouse they might have had names, bestowed on them, as we shall see in a moment, by officials who took them in. This wasn't a problem just in London. A census taker in Taunton in 1881 found himself confronted with a boarding house full of people who did not have – or claimed not to have – any names. In some cases this may have been merely a language problem: the entries for six of the census taker's collection say they are nameless Italians. The other, home-grown children are simply 'nameless'; the adults are classed as 'tramps'.

Oliver Twist was a novel, yet some of the naming procedures in workhouses were scarcely less crude than those Dickens invented:

'And now about business,' said the beadle, taking out a leathern pocket-book. 'The child that was half baptised Oliver Twist, is nine year old to-day.'

'Bless him!' interposed Mrs Mann, inflaming her left eye with the corner of her apron.

'And notwithstanding a offered reward of ten pound, which was afterwards increased to twenty pound. Notwithstanding the most superlative, and, I may say, supernat'ral exertions on the part of this parish,' said Bumble, 'we have never been able to discover who is his father, or what was his mother's settlement, name or con-dition.'

Mrs Mann raised her hands in astonishment; but added, after a moment's reflection, 'How comes he to have any name at all, then?'

The beadle drew himself up with great pride, and said, 'I inwented it.'

'You, Mr Bumble!'

'I, Mrs Mann. We name our foundlings in alphabetical order. The last was a S—Swubble, I named him. This was a T—Twist, I named *him*. The next one as comes will be Unwin, and the next Vilkins. I have got names ready-made to the end of the alphabet, and all the way through it again, when we come to Z.'

'Why, you're quite a literary character, sir!' said Mrs Mann.

Even in far more honest, salubrious institutions than this one, enforced namings were necessary. Here, the governors and the staff often resorted to practices which might otherwise seem entirely inappropriate. They would give the children the names of statesmen, religious leaders or famous heroes, even though these might be so ostentatious as to be a later embarrassment. In some cases, they gave their own names to inmates, only to learn later on that these former inmates, while up to no good, were passing themselves off as the genuine sons and daughters of their benefactors.

No place had a higher reputation than Thomas Coram's Foundling Hospital, opened in Hatton Garden in 1740 but transferred to Bloomsbury. Here the parents of many children were known, and the record books in the London Metropolitan Archive note that some were reclaimed by their parents, though these were outnumbered by those against whose entry of admission a word has been added: 'died'. There are names on this list which suggest that their surnames may well not have come direct from their forebears: John Belgrave, Caroline Brunswick, Elizabeth Churchill, William Pepys, Octavius Caesar, Charles Plantagenet, Charles Townshend, George Washington, William Hogarth, Horatio Nelson, Emma Hamilton, Burlington Yeoman, Martha Blandford, Thomas Constable – and even Thomas Coram (a lad who, for his subsequent achievements, was regarded as one of their outstanding alumni). Several, whether through accident or design, bear the surname Hope; one has the surname Anguish. There are also in the early years two boys listed under the name George Bush, a name yet to appear in lists of the internationally eminent.

In 1849 a man called John Brownlow, who had been an assistant to the secretary of the hospital for thirty-five years, succeeded to the office after cholera had at last removed his superior. He had by now started work on the first systematic history of the institution, in the course of which he summarised the naming procedures it had used as new entrants were brought to baptism on arrival. Early on, he said – a century back from the time where he was writing – they had given their charges courtly names such as Abercorn, Bedford, Bentinck, Montague, Marlborough, Newcastle, Pomfret, Pembroke, Richmond and Vernon. Having exhausted their stock of these, 'the authorities stole those of eminent deceased personalities, their first attempt being on the church', leading to the use of such names as Wycliffe, Huss, Ridley, Latimer, Laud, Sancroft, Tillotson, Tennison and Sherlock.

Next came poets and philosophers, after which 'the governors were most warlike in their notions, and brought from their graves Philip Sidney, Francis Drake, Oliver Cromwell, John Hampden, Admiral Benbow and Cloudesley Shovell'. Next came artists – Rubens, Van Dyke, Michael Angelo and both William Hogarth, a benefactor, and his wife. Then characters from novels: Charles Allworthy, Tom Jones, Sophia Western, Clarissa Harlowe. When pressure for places built up, they resorted to 'creeping things and beasts of the earth', and names borrowed from various handicrafts or trades. They also for a time tried using the names of friends, 'but it was found to be an inconvenient and objectionable course, inasmuch as when they grew to man and womanhood, they were apt to lay claim to some affinity in blood with their nomenclators'. The foundling hospitals and workhouses sent their children out into the world very young (Twist is turned out at nine). To have to go through everyday life in the slums of London with a name like Octavius Caesar or Cloudesley Shovell cannot have made their lot any easier.

Being a foundling, lacking a name, lacking any identity, somehow sensing that somewhere out there is a name that ought be yours – or alternatively finding your name is not after all your own, leaving you lost, uprooted, no longer sure who you are – such crushing insecurities did not end with the workhouse. One of the cruellest practices in the Irish institutions where girls who had illegitimate children, or others simply considered wayward, were put to unpaid work by the nuns who were charged with their care, sometimes for the rest of their lives, was the obliteration of the names they arrived with; their first names were changed and their surnames extirpated.

The man now well known as the former SAS man turned writer, Andy McNab – not his real name: because of his military provenance he was required to adopt a pseudonym for his writing – was left in a carrier bag – a Harrods bag, as he likes to point out – on the steps of a London hospital. His real-life surname came from adoptive parents who told him when he turned sixteen that he was adopted. The most he was able to learn was that his father was probably a Greek immigrant who worked in London bars. Of his mother he still knows nothing.

The birth certificate of a woman now known as Sarah Chilcott gives her place of birth as 'found on a train at Willesden Junction station'; for what it is worth, the train had probably come from

Richmond. She was given the name Sarah Frances Leonard by a social worker who used the name of a friend's new baby, her own middle name, and the surname of her former sociology lecturer. She was taken in by the Chilcotts, who never hid the fact that she was adopted, but although she was happy with them, the mystery of her origins always nagged at her, and according to an interview she gave to the *Daily Mirror* in May 2012, still does today. 'I have a void to fill,' she said. 'Everyone should know where they came from.' Her predicament is all the more grievous because she believes the truth could have been established. She discovered the name of a woman who gave birth to a daughter at the West Middlesex Hospital in Isleworth on 17 May 1964, which seems to have been the day before she was found on the train. Like Robert Blincoe more than a century earlier, she feels that had a greater effort been made to trace this woman, the mystery of her origins might by now have been solved.

David Sharp, an Oxfordshire bricklayer, was more fortunate. He had grown up as the son of Percy and Rose Sharp, but in middle life began to ask questions about his origins and enlisted the help of the Salvation Army's family tracing service, which successfully established his true parentage. He was the son of Rose Wort, wife of a serving soldier called Ernest Wort, who in his absence became pregnant and, desperate that her husband should learn nothing of it, advertised in the *Reading Mercury* for someone to take on the child. The boy was handed over at Reading station. Ernest was killed in the war, leaving Rose free to marry the father of the son she had given away, a man named David McEwan. The couple had a further son, Ian. When all this was at last disentangled, David learned that he had a brother: the novelist Ian McEwan.

Where fiction illuminates fact

Were you to judge from official records alone, the adoption, replacement or loss of a surname might seem a purely practical matter. There is no way of gauging the emotions involved. For those, one must turn to fiction. In eighteenth- and nineteenth-century fiction, the psychic pull of a name – and, even more, the psychic disorder that comes from having no reliable name – are evoked with a passion that tells us that readers, too, must have known what all this implied.

From the earliest days of the English novel, the trauma of a name denied and the apprehension that the name you live under does not really belong to you, or even describes someone you are not, is pervasive. The helpless isolation of never being sure who you are lights up page after page. Magdalen Vanstone's search for a solid identity is the core of Wilkie Collins's *No Name* (1862). Dickens returns again and again to the links between name and identity.

In *Clarissa* by Samuel Richardson (1748), the heroine is ordered by her father to 'change your name to my liking' by marrying the distasteful Mr Solmes. This, it is explained, is part of his strategy for building up the name (the name as reputation, as so often in the history of the surname) of the family. Clarissa's fear, the author explains, is that giving up her name at his insistence would signify that she had become her father's absolute and dependent property – a fate to which so many daughters in the mid eighteenth century were dolefully resigned. Later, Clarissa declines to marry her suitor Lovelace, who longs to make her the mother of future Lovelaces; by denying him, she dooms his name to oblivion – a rejection, in effect, not just of Lovelace but of the whole patriarchal concept he represents.

A year later there was published the tale of one of the most celebrated foundlings in literature, *Tom Jones*. In Fielding's novel the newly born infant Tom is discovered one night in the bed of worthy Squire Allworthy. Who put him there? Suspicion falls on a woman called Jenny Jones, who admits having done exactly that. Kindly, decent Allworthy (no mystery here about why his creator chose that name for him) treats him almost as his own son. Tom does not seem to brood on his bastard birth and uncertain origins and is undisturbed when it's (wrongly) assumed he has fathered an illegitimate son of his own. Yet his bastard status forbids all prospect of marriage with Sophia, the cherished daughter of Squire Western, whose father in his thoughtlessly cheery way habitually refers to Tom when speaking to Allworthy as 'your bastard'. Yet in the end, Tom qualifies to marry Sophia: not because his birth has proved to be legitimate, but because he's in fact the son, not of humble Jenny, but of Squire Allworthy's respectable sister Bridget and her clandestine lover Summers, the son of a clergyman. Tom may not be legitimate but at least he is now genteel. That's enough to persuade Squire Western that he's fit to take the role of his son-in-law.

In Fanny Burney's *Evelina*, published anonymously in 1778, the heroine is denied the name she believes to be hers by right because her father has asserted that he and her mother were never legally married. The kindly priest who looks after her, Mr Villars, gives her the surname Anville – suggesting in Burney's invention not so much a kind of failed anagram but the iron block on which a smith's hammer is struck. Not only, as the story develops, does she have to face deprivation of the name that should have been hers; that injustice is likely to deny her the other name she aspires to. She fears, too, that her presumed bastardy makes her unfit to marry Lord Orville, whom she loves. She is, she tearfully tells him, 'a child of bounty – an orphan from infancy – dependent, even for subsistence dependent, upon the kindness of compassion! – Rejected by my natural friends – disowned forever by my nearest relation . . .', which means that he has to let her 'return to obscurity'. In the end, of course, she gets a father's full acknowledgement, the family name she has coveted, and Orville's, too, as he intended all along.

There are far too many such plots in late-eighteenth-century fiction hanging on the rights and wrongs of a leading character's name to be listed here, but a new spate begins in the mid nine-teenth century, complete with such familiar devices as the legacy that seemed to be lost but is safe after all, the marriage that wasn't, and the death that wasn't. But now the stories are darker, reflecting the insatiable Victorian delight in melodrama. They are heralded by a rambling, ramshackle novel by the naval officer turned novelist, Captain Marryat, later more famous for adventure stories for boys, in 1836. He called it *Japhet, in Search of a Father*. A more accurate title would have been 'Japhet, in Sporadic Search of a Father', since the hero seems at various points of the story to have largely forgotten his search. There's a strong sense here of a writer in a hurry, making up the tale as he goes along (this was one of three novels which Marryat published that year). There are several engaging characters with Dickensian names like Cophagus, but that does not suggest that the captain was copying; the first of Dickens's novels did not appear until that year.

Japhet, who is the narrator, tells us at the start that on a certain day, at a certain time, which understandably he cannot remember, 'I, an infant of a certain age—was suspended by somebody or somebodies—at the knocker of the Foundling Hospital.' A letter to the governors of the hospital, signed by one Abraham Newland, was attached to the parcel containing him, which read: 'This child was born in wedlock—he is to be named Japhet. When circumstances permit, he will be reclaimed.' Attached to that was a £50 note.

Japhet's bizarre adventures, along with a fellow inmate of the hospital, Timothy Oldmixon (this surname, Marryat explains, having been taken from a name on a pump close to which he was found – again, an invention that squares with established fact), who travels with him as his servant, bring him into contact with various ingenious maskers and masqueraders, and above all with a man who introduces himself at the outset as a travelling quack doctor. But is this curious individual, with his tendency to

slip a Latin tag into every sentence, who he says he is? Or is he
the Gypsy leader, Melchior, as whom he next emerges? Is he even
perhaps the father for whom Japhet sometimes remembers that
he is searching? Or is he merely the agent who will finally take
our hero to the man who will give him a sense of his true
identity? All will end well, of course. He may be an unreclaimed
foundling, but Japhet will, at the end, as Marryat's readers will
have hoped and probably guessed all along, find he belongs in a
privileged rank in society.

The truth about one's name, the rights and the wrongs
attached to it, becomes an even more compelling question for
the best-read novelists of the Victorian age. Dickens's Oliver Twist
– the novel began to appear in instalments only a year after
Marryat's *Japhet* – may be the best-known hero deprived of his
name, but he's far from being the only one, even in Dickens,
whose novels are packed with characters shielding their true
identity, or parading contrived identities quite different from their
true ones. Esther, in *Bleak House*, whose name may or may not
be Summerson, is 'friendless, nameless, and unknown'. Her true
father, whose identity is unknown to her for much of the book,
is called Hawdon, but he hides behind masks and in his final days
assumes the ultimate mask: his name becomes Nemo – Nobody.

And who, in *Great Expectations*, is the unexpected, unwanted
caller at Pip's London chambers:

> 'I do not even know,' said I, speaking low as he took his
> seat at the table, 'by what name to call you. I have said that
> you are my uncle.'
> 'That's it, dear boy! Call me uncle.'
> 'You assumed some name, I suppose, on board ship?'
> 'Yes, dear boy. I took the name of Provis.'
> 'Do you mean to keep that name?'
> 'Why, yes, dear boy, it's as good as another – unless you'd
> like another.'

'What is your real name?' I asked him in a whisper.

'Magwitch,' he answered, in the same tone, 'chrisen'd Abel.'

And who is the sinister housemaid, Molly, whom Pip discovers in the unhomely home of the solicitor Jaggers: 'a woman of about forty . . . I had been to see Macbeth at the theatre, a night or two before, and . . . her face looked to me as if it were all disturbed by fiery air, like the faces I had seen rise out of the Witches' cauldron.' And what, for that matter, is the true surname of Estella, whose very name is so precious to Pip that he cannot bear to hear his rival uttering it?

Plots that turn on the matter of names, disguised, discarded, assumed, or falsely laid claim to, crop up in too many of Dickens's books to be itemised here. Yet even more than Dickens, Collins is fascinated, even obsessed, by names and their psychic importance. That may partly reflect his own tangled experience. Collins, who grew up as William but switched to his second forename, Wilkie, in effect used two surnames himself. One of his two long-serving mistresses, Martha Rudd, bore him three children. This household used the name Dawson. His other long-term mistress, Martha's social and intellectual superior, was known as Caroline Graves. She claimed to be the daughter of John Courtenay, a gentleman of Cheltenham; in fact, her father was a Teddington carpenter called Compton. When Collins met her, she said her first name was Elizabeth, but he called her Caroline. Her daughter by her marriage to George Robert Graves was named Harriet: Collins called her Carrie. At one point Caroline left him and married a man called Clow, but two years later she returned to him. She and Collins are buried in the same grave.

Even more than murder and threats of murder, and legacies denied and reclaimed, names – their manipulation, their potentialities for good but particularly for evil, their use in mask and masquerade – are repeated themes for this writer. Uncertainty over identity is the core of one of his two most famous novels.

Who is the *Woman in White* who appears so miraculously late one night as he walks home from Hampstead? How do there come to be two Anne Catheticks? The same preoccupations dominate two less famous books: *Armadale* and one to which he gave the name *No Name*. The plot of *Armadale* is a strange and impossibly convoluted beast, difficult to paraphrase, but essentially the story revolves around the wholly unlikely circumstance of there being two men called Allan Armadale, one who had the name but lost it, and one who was born without it but gained it. Each was born to a father whose name was Allan Armadale, though one of these had been born a Wrentmore and changed his name for an inheritance, while the other had been denied his born name Armadale. In one generation, one Armadale sheds his name to become Fergus Ingleby; in the next, one sheds his name to become (suitably bleakly) Ozias Midwinter. As the story proceeds, we also encounter a woman called Lydia Gwilt – the most vivid character in the story and one of the great Victorian villainesses – whose real name, needless to say, isn't Gwilt; a woman called Mrs Oldershaw, who calls herself Mrs Mandeville; and a dubious doctor called Downward who soon transmutes into Dr Le Doux, a creepy quack psychiatrist.

As his biographer Catherine Peters says, Collins was always intrigued by questions of identity, substitution and doubling, and that is the pattern in *No Name* too. It begins with the father of its central character, Magdalen Vanstone, being killed in a railway accident. When Magdalen was born, her father was still legally married to his discarded real wife. Now, with her death, he is free to marry Magdalen's mother. But by doing so, he invalidates his will. It is while he is on his way to Bristol to make the necessary amendment that he is killed on the railway.

Magdalen and her sister are now perpetually reduced to the status of women born out of wedlock. Suddenly she has lost her home and all her prospects. Her expected legacies are now destined to go to their father's mean and malevolent disinherited brother,

Michael. In her quest to find security, and a name to go with it, the previously blameless Magdalen (a name that straightaway recalls the New Testament Mary Magdalene, who, like this one, is sometimes a creature of virtue and sometimes a creature of vice) pursues a pathetic creature called Noel Vanstone, who as son and heir of her late uncle Michael inherits what should have been hers. For this purpose, she masquerades as her former governess, Miss Garth. Her true identity is detected by a woman who calls herself Mrs Lecount, though her real name is Lecomte. In the end, Magdalen is rescued from her namelessness and the hopelessness that goes with it by Captain Kirke, master of the good ship *Deliverance*, who lives at Aaron's Buildings – a sequence of names that groans with its weight of nudging significance.

Collins, in novels and plays, was the acknowledged master of melodrama, and all this, of course, is pure melodrama, untouched by the cramping hand of reality. Yet melodrama only works if there is something within it that chimes with something an audience may not necessarily think but assuredly feels. Collins, said Henry James, 'introduced into fiction those most mysterious of mysteries, the mysteries that are at our own doors'. He plays on a deeply significant aspect of mid-Victorian Britain, a world away from the one so often portrayed in which an ultra-decorous middle class is unwilling to allow the exposure even of unclothed legs on a piano. (The Victorians did indeed cover up piano legs but only to protect them from damage.) He seems to have detected a sense of insecurity about name and identity in the well-to-do and middle-class Victorian Britain now so often, and wrongly, portrayed as uniformly smug and comfortable – and to have traded on it.

The theme of duality – good and bad conjoined in the same person and heavily swathed in mask and masquerade – boils up again in Mary Elizabeth Braddon's sensational, and sensationally successful, *Lady Audley's Secret*, published in 1862. The overwhelmingly perfect Lucy Graham, a blameless governess, with a local reputation as 'the sweetest girl who ever lived', who has married Sir Michael Audley, is gradually unwrapped to reveal an almost Gwilt-like plotter and murderer whose true name is Helen Talboys – Talboys being the name of the husband whom she has murdered. Her scheming can begin when she is wrongly reported dead. Erroneous reports of deaths – faked or otherwise – are, like legacies, a staple feature of this genre.

It wasn't only sensational novels which fascinated respectable Victorian England with their glimpses of how others lived (and how, as they occasionally wondered with a curiosity spilling over into guilty envy, they might have lived themselves if freed from convention). They were closeted in respectability, but they sometimes felt a desire to dip into the tempting waters of unrespectability: another name, another identity, another life. 'It was always apparent when the Divorce Court was in session,' writes Deborah Cohen in *Family Secrets: Living with Shame from the Victorians to the Present Day* of what followed the divorce reform law of 1857 – until then, divorce had been largely the prerogative of rich men – and the opening of the doors of the court to all who wished to come:

> Outside the Gothic buildings of the Royal Courts of Justice was a throng clamouring for admittance. Loafers, so-called 'law students' and smartly attired ladies lined up two-deep to witness the proceedings. As soon as the doors opened, they crowded the passage-ways, swarming into boxes reserved for jurors and witnesses. It was the only court in Britain where wooden barriers were required to regulate spectators . . . For those lucky enough to gain front-row seats, opera glasses allowed scrutinising of the witnesses' countenances.

Much of that would have been motivated by prurience. Yet in an era when sensibility and empathy were increasingly considered essential ingredients of the manner in which intelligent people ought to conduct their lives, they could allow themselves some hint of sympathy for the predicaments which had overtaken fictional people like those they found in Collins and Braddon; could understand, at the end of the century, why Hardy, in publishing *Tess*, had, at the cost of incurring vitriolic criticism, used the full title: *Tess of the D'Urbervilles: A Pure Woman* – the supreme case of a book where life, and eventually death, hang on a surname. It all begins with the intervention of an amateur onomastician.

On an evening in the latter part of May a middle-aged man was walking homeward from Shaston to the village of Marlott, in the adjoining Vale of Blakemore, or Blackmoor. The pair of legs that carried him were rickety, and there was a bias in his gait which inclined him somewhat to the left of a straight line. He occasionally gave a smart nod, as if in confirmation of some opinion, though he was not thinking of anything in particular. An empty egg-basket was slung upon his arm, the nap of his hat was ruffled, a patch being quite worn away at its brim where his thumb came in taking it off. Presently he was met by an elderly parson astride on a gray mare, who, as he rode, hummed a wandering tune.

'Good night t'ee,' said the man with the basket.

'Good night, Sir John,' said the parson.

The pedestrian, after another pace or two, halted, and turned round.

'Now, sir, begging your pardon; we met last market-day on this road about this time, and I zaid "Good night," and you made reply "Good night, Sir John", as now.'

'I did,' said the parson.

'And once before that—near a month ago.'

'I may have.'

'Then what might your meaning be in calling me "Sir John" these different times, when I be plain Jack Durbeyfield, the haggler?'

The parson rode a step or two nearer.

'It was only my whim,' he said; and, after a moment's hesitation: 'It was on account of a discovery I made some little time ago, whilst I was hunting up pedigrees for the new county history. I am Parson Tringham, the antiquary, of Stagfoot Lane. Don't you really know, Durbeyfield, that you are the lineal representative of the ancient and knightly family of the d'Urbervilles, who derive their descent from Sir Pagan d'Urberville, that renowned knight who came from Normandy with William the Conqueror, as appears by Battle Abbey Roll?'

'Never heard it before, sir!'

'Well it's true. Throw up your chin a moment, so that I may catch the profile of your face better. Yes, that's the d'Urberville nose and chin—a little debased. Your ancestor was one of the twelve knights who assisted the Lord of Estremavilla in Normandy in his conquest of Glamorganshire. Branches of your family held manors over all this part of England; their names appear in the Pipe Rolls in the time of King Stephen. In the reign of King John one of them was rich enough to give a manor to the Knights Hospitallers; and in Edward the Second's time your forefather Brian was summoned to Westminster to attend the great Council there. You declined a little in Oliver Cromwell's time, but to no serious extent, and in Charles the Second's reign you were made Knights of the Royal Oak for your loyalty. Aye, there have been generations of Sir Johns among you, and if knighthood were hereditary, like a baronetcy, as it practically was in old times, when men were knighted from father to son, you would be Sir John now.'

The whole tragedy proceeds from this chance conversation. When Tess on their wedding night confesses the shame of her bastard son to Angel, he says bitterly: 'I think that parson who unearthed you and your pedigree would have done better if he had held his tongue.'

Ironically, as Parson Tringham declares, with all the scholarly, mocking enthusiasm of a Sabine Baring-Gould, the d'Urbervilles are no more truly d'Urberville than he is himself. Alec's father is a north-country merchant called Stoke, who, in a practice that Hardy would have taken from life, expands the name to Stoke d'Urberville before finally getting rid of the Stoke. He has changed his name in order to shed his former identity. The north-countryman, Hardy explains, 'felt the necessity of recommencing with a name that would not too readily identify him with the smart tradesman of the past and that would be less commonplace than the original bold stark words'. (Blend Hardy's 'bold' and 'stark' and you arrive at Stoke.)

Such exotic surnaming practices were unknown to people like the Durbeyfields, as to the real-life humble families who lived in this part of Wessex, 'who supposed that, though to be well-favoured might be the gift of fortune, a family name came by nature'. When Tess has her first meeting with Alec d'Urberville, son of the now-dead Stoke and therefore, says Hardy, 'the representative of the spurious house', she tells him: 'our names have been worn away to Durbeyfield, but we have several proofs that we are d'Urbervilles.'

Hardy, too, as ever drawing from real life, brings into the story a boy from that ultimate class that has no name at all. As the dairyman who employs her tells Tess, 'A boy came here t'other day asking for a job, and said his name was Matt, and when we asked him his surname he said he'd never heard that 'a had any surname, and when we asked why, he said he supposed his folks hadn't been 'stablished long enough.'

9

Prognostications

Will Surnames Survive?

He would answer to 'Hi!' or to any loud cry,
Such as 'Fry-me!', or 'Fritter my wig!'
Lewis Carroll, *The Hunting of the Snark*

There are still Gales in Broughton, Hampshire, some of whom as they pass the church gate may see Tom's tombstone and recognise some kind of relative, and Coopers and Blakes and Pragnells and Marshes, though no sign in the electoral registers now of such staple names of the past as Judd, Offer and Rogers. There's still a sturdy contingent of Tysons alongside Atkinsons and Butterfields and Hadwins – who like the Davises and Lansleys in Hampshire had begun to proliferate at the end of the nineteenth century – in Broughton in Furness, though no trace now of the once numerically dominant Dawsons or the socially dominant Sawreys and Cooksons, while the Whinerays (or Whinnerays or Whinnerrahs) who disappeared and then rose again are once more on this evidence gone from the territory.

Almost everywhere, the day of the village graveyard cluster is all but gone, reflecting the pattern of life in the modern village. The evidence is patchier now than for the nineteenth century, since census material remains locked away for a hundred years. But it's clear that the old tight localness, already eroding by the end of Victoria's reign, has disintegrated much further. That doesn't mean that the sense among some villagers of being part of the core village has gone. 'We're newcomers here,' a man in Broughton, Cambridgeshire, said to me. 'We've only been here about fifty years.'

Few now can imagine what it must have been like to leave a village that had until that point been your world. But here is Pip, in *Great Expectations*:

> But the village was very peaceful and quiet, and the light mists were solemnly rising, as if to show me the world, and I had been so innocent and little there, and all beyond was so unknown and great, that in a moment with a strong heave and sob I broke into tears. It was by the finger-post at the end of the village, and I laid my hand upon it, and said, 'Good bye, O my dear, dear friend'.

Except where public transport has gone and car ownership is limited, people can move about freely on a day-by-day basis to get to their work or their shopping, or on a longer-term basis in search of new homes, new occupations, new lives. Historians like David Hey have taught us that though Victorians moved more frequently than was once assumed, they rarely moved far, with the nearest market town as the limit of their aspirations. Only London for much of the nineteenth century was truly cosmopolitan. But now all sorts of places are cosmopolitan, with names from Africa, the Indian sub-continent, South America and Scandinavia cropping up in quite small villages, these Broughtons included.

Patel is now number 40 in the chart of most common surnames in Britain, ahead of such standard names of the past as Adams, Campbell, Carter and Cook, and its climb isn't finished yet. Singh is not far behind, and Mohammed might be there too were it not spelled in different fashions. Where once to find a suitable spouse as far from Broughton, Hampshire, as Swindon, let alone from London or Bristol, or as far from Broughton in Furness as

Manchester, let alone from Glasgow or Edinburgh, suggested a sense of adventure, now the engagement columns are full of troths being plighted with future brides and bridegrooms from across the world. A wealth of new and hitherto unfamiliar accents and with them new and hitherto unfamiliar surnames are coming up to the altar; or at least to the register office.

Surnames are fracturing. More couples are keeping both names when they marry, or abandoning both and choosing a neutral one. The UK Deed Poll Service, which engineers many changes, says that 'meshing', as they call it, has become one of the main reasons for changing names. A Miss Harley and a Mr Gatts, the *Daily Telegraph* reported, had become Mr and Mrs Hatts; a Mr Pugh and a Miss Griffin had reinvented themselves as Puffins. But increasingly couples choose not to marry. The Office for National Statistics reported in 2013 that the number of married couples had fallen by nearly half a million over the past sixteen years to 12.1 million; the number of cohabiting couples had increased from 1.5 million to 2.9 million. The number of married families with children had dropped by more than 600,000 over the past sixteen years to 4.8 million, while the number of cohabiting couples with children had risen from 539,000 to 1.3 million. So while marriage is still the majority choice, there's no mistaking the trend. And with over four in every ten marriages now ending in divorce, there are far more households with a mix of surnames: the woman's previous maiden name or name from a previous marriage, her husband's or partner's, and the variegated surnames of children from previous marriages or previous relationships.

There has been a vast increase in the proportion of children born outside marriage, some taking their father's name and some their mother's, but there's now no embarrassment there. Outside the most austere of God-fearing households, the stigma of bastardy, which blighted, even ruined, the lives of women and children through the centuries – except of course when they were royal or otherwise well-born – is now, thank goodness, buried. No child now would ever be listed for life like the one in the Scottish Borders (Chapter 7) as 'proceeding from a scandal of adultery'.

These changes in our society have also promoted the use of the double barrel in ordinary households – though 'meshing' is said to be catching up as an alternative solution. Miss White marries Mr Brown: their decision now is whether to present themselves to the world as Brown-Whites or White-Browns.

One place where such changes are hugely apparent is in the line-ups of football teams. That's not only in the Premiership either, though the shift occurring there would have seemed to earlier generations astonishing. There used to be three well-known double-barrelled practitioners: Ian Storey-Moore of Nottingham Forest, Forbes Phillipson-Masters of Southampton and Peter Rhodes-Brown of Chelsea. Their names were well known for their rarity. On the final Saturday of 2012, fifteen of the sixty-two teams in action in the three divisions below the Premiership had double-barrelled names on their team sheets.

At the highest level, the game has redefined the concept of cosmopolitan: some 60 per cent of Premiership players were born overseas. Here is the Arsenal team that took the field for the FA Cup final against Liverpool in 1971 (Arsenal won 2–1):

Wilson, Rice, McNab, Storey (substitute: Kelly), McLintock, Simpson, Armstrong, Graham, Radford, Kennedy, George.

A good mix of names with a couple of Mcs and Armstrong, Graham, Simpson and Wilson all names extremely familiar in places like Furness and the Borders.

And now, the Arsenal team that drew with Manchester United in 2005 (Arsenal won on penalties):

Lehmann, Lauren, Toure, Senderos, Cole, Fàbregas (substitute Van Persie), Gilberto, Vieira, Pires (substitute Edu), Reyes, Bergkamp (substitute Ljungberg).

By now, supporters had no more difficulty chanting the names of Fàbregas, Bergkamp and Ljungberg than they would have done thirty-four years before in acclaiming their Grahams and Georges. But it isn't only at the top of the game that such changes are visible. In 2013, Newcastle's ground at St James's Park, once home to such heroes as Jackie Milburn and Alan Shearer, cheered on new acquisitions whose names must have taxed the pronunciational skills of Tyneside: Mapou Yanga-Mbiwa, Yoan Gouffran, Moussa Sissoko and Massadio Haïdara. Even humbler clubs, too poor to ever aspire to buying a Bergkamp or a Fàbregas, fielded players whose names would once have baffled supporters. During the season 2012–13, Barking FC of the Essex Senior League sent out players called Jonathan Mogege, Ife Ogunbayo, Petrit Elbi, Theo Ola, Daniel Okah, Lance Lord George, and Dumebi GB-Dumaka. Nor are all the exotically named nowadays imports. Many such players were born and bred here. Yado Mambo of Charlton was born in Kilburn. Tendayi Darikwa of Chesterfield was born in Nottingham. Bondz N'Gala of Yeovil was born at Forest Gate, London. These are now British surnames.

The cast lists of soap operas reflect, though less so, the same change in society and the surnames that reflect that society: All but one of the characters in the first instalment of *Coronation Street*, broadcast on Valentine's Day 1960, are given names with the smack of roast beef about them. The exception is Linda Cheveski. By 2013, there's a regular contingent of Alahans, while *EastEnders* has found room for characters called Zainab Khan, Masood Ahmed, Tamwar Masood, A. J. Ahmed, Ayesha Rana, Rashid Kayani and Mrs Kayani.

The collapse of old certainties is everywhere changing the picture. In November 2012, nearly two decades after its first women priests were ordained, the Church of England synod voted – though not by a big enough margin to ensure that its will would prevail – in favour of women bishops. At almost the same moment the government committed itself to legislate to allow same-sex marriage. (How will surnames be determined then? Even more double barrels and 'neutral' names, no doubt.) And having attained the assent of Commonwealth countries, the government announced that the ancient tradition of men coming first in succession to the throne – vividly symbolised every Remembrance Sunday by the Princess Royal having to wait until after her brothers (male and therefore superior) to be allowed to deposit her wreath – was to be scrapped. If the Duchess of Cambridge produced a daughter before a son, then the daughter would accede to the throne; though given the royal family's longevity that might not be for quite some time. Newspapers soon reported that the daughters of peers had begun to demand parity in this respect with princesses.

Results from the 2011 census released at the end of 2012 reveal some radical changes, quite apart from the figures on immigration. That the rate of divorce has fallen over the decade partly reflects the fact that only the married can seek a divorce, and the proportion of people who are married has fallen from 50.9 to 46.6 per cent. But this, and much else like it, had clear implications for the future employment of surnames.

*

With so many sacred cows plodding their weary way towards the slaughterhouse, it seemed inevitable that the days of the wholly sexist convention that said a wife's surname, and those of the children, should succumb to that of her husband would be numbered also.

Some believe the decline and possibly fall of male domination will go further than that. Before long, some futurologists say, new medical techniques could eliminate any need for men in the conception of children. According to other prognosticators, men are doomed anyway. Professor Sykes, the DNA guru, cheerfully forecasts that the Y-chromosome, which is what makes men into men rather than women, is heading for extinction. 'One by one,' he wrote in the *Guardian*, 'Y-chromosomes will disappear, eliminated by the relentless onslaught of irreparable mutation, until only one is left. When that chromosome finally succumbs, men will become extinct.' Still, as he reassuringly adds, that change will take some time to occur – he would expect a fall below the 1 per cent level to occur in about 125,000 years.

Meanwhile, we may also observe the sidelining of the surname in many kinds of transaction. Companies which write to customers now usually use a forename rather than a surname. While an outfit anxious to help me to double-glaze would once have addressed me as 'Dear Mr McKie', now it's 'Dear David'. Next year, perhaps, it will be 'Dear Dave'. Such transitions have happened before. There was a time when a man felt gratified if his business or academic superior moved from saying 'Mr McKie' to 'McKie'. The surname alone was a kind of promotion, perhaps even a modest echo of the moment when a French relationship shifts from *vous* to *tu*. One could not imagine Sherlock Holmes, as he carefully points out to Dr Watson the wealth of wholly obvious information he's overlooked in assessing a case, addressing his friend as 'John'. It is always a dignified surname. 'The one firm point in a changing age', Holmes (not 'Sherlock') calls Watson (not 'John').

The burgeoning habit of giving a first name without a surname as an identification achieves friendliness at the cost of confusion. When I last worked in an office, telephone callers would ask: 'Can I speak to Sam?' If, to differentiate between the Sams in the office, you asked them to give Sam's surname, it would often transpire that none had been offered. 'I just got this message, call Sam,' the caller would say. This difficulty was compounded because Sam, short for Samantha as well as for Samuel, has joined the ranks of names that are now bisexual, along with others, such as Pat, which have caused confusion for many years now, and others, like Kim, that have steadily grown in popularity.

But here is another trend that seems certain to grow. If you don't like a surname, or, even, don't want a surname at all, why not ditch it and get a new one? In today's shop-around open society, why not? Want a new and more app-ridden phone? Go out and buy one. Want a new nose, or a thrustier bust? Same applies. There are plenty of qualified surgeons just bursting to give you one . . . Want a new surname? Easier still. You won't even have to fetch out your credit card. Whatever the deed poll companies tell you, they're free. Why continue to bear a name like Smellie or Higginbottom when you have the chance to rename yourself Beckham or Cowell, or (one word alone) Rihanna? And certainly the *Daily Mail* claimed, without citing its source, that changes of name in 2011 had soared to an unprecedented level.

In 1983, a young man called David Ashworth, then working for the think tank Demos, changed his name to Perri 6. Thirty years later he's Professor of Social Policy at Nottingham Trent University, working, his website says, on a study examining a neo-Durkheimian institutional theory of political judgement and of the origins of unanticipated and unintended consequences of policy in three fields of policy in British government between 1959 and 1974. He didn't exactly start a trend. No great national outbreak of 7s and 9s or 42s (which after all are the secret of life, the universe and everything) ensued; though I note that the Archbishop of Paris is named as Cardinal Vingt-Trois. But the man who runs the annual Isle of Wight music festival is called Rob da Bank. And in December 2012, the actress Kate Winslet married, as her third husband, the head of Marketing Promotion and Astronaut Experience at Virgin Galactic, Ned Rockn'Roll. So the example is there for all who may care to shake off their fetters and follow it.

Despite all that, the surname is not dead yet, and won't be dead unless differentiation becomes unnecessary. And though clusters have loosened, regional patterns remain. The Yorkshire and Lancashire Pennines still have a solid, if somewhat diminished, representation of Greenwoods and Hargreaveses and Tetleys and Ibbetsons. In *Surnames, DNA and Family History* by George Redmonds, Turi King and David Hey, there's a picture taken at a presentation at the Huddersfield and District Bowling Veterans Association in 2008. The presentation was made by an Armitage, accompanied by the association's president, a Lockwood. The recipients were called Bray, Crowther, Firth, Haigh, Hoyle, Pogson, Sheard and Sykes. All ten names occur in parish registers from 1538; the origins of nine (the exception is Sheard) are traceable back to the thirteenth and fourteenth centuries. These nine, says the book, all have their roots in places within a nine-mile radius of Huddersfield.

Tre, Pol and Pen still flourish in Cornwall. And though names like Gale, Blake and Cooper have thinned in Broughton, Hampshire, and others like Rogers and Judd seem to have gone altogether, you will still find them on Public Profile flourishing in the 1990s in the counties where they were prolific in the final decades of the nineteenth century. People will continue to browse in churchyards and muse on the lives of the people whose names can be found there. Indeed, that experience may, it is said, now be enhanced. A Dorset company called Chester Pearce, it was reported in September 2012, will for up to £300 etch a quick-response barcode on to a gravestone, bench, plaque or tree, serving up details of the life of whoever may lie there. ('Alas, poor Yorick, I didn't know him that well, Horatio, but fortunately there's a handy CV.') The managing director, Stephen Nimmo, said he got the idea after visiting the Kremlin Wall necropolis in Moscow. 'People often wander around cemeteries and look at gravestones and wonder who that person was,' he said. 'By using the QR codes they can find out all they need to know.' (Presumably customers will be required to wear headphones.) Perhaps that may enhance the sense of the place's localness, a sense that people still cherish, that answers their need to belong and identify with the community in which they live.

The localness of accent is modifying as standard pronunciation dominates radio and TV. It hasn't been lost altogether: in the street in Broughton, Cambridgeshire, on a sunny December morning, I overheard an exchange of village news in a bright, warm local accent you couldn't have heard in any other of my six Broughtons. But none of the speakers was young. The localness of the high street fades year by year as old family names disappear to be replaced by names such as the Co-op or, often in villages, no name at all since the shop has gone and people get their groceries from outfits with deracinated names such as Tesco. But the localness of a village churchyard survives.

Many years ago, in the Regal cinema, Crossgates, Leeds, then an exciting modern building, long since demolished to make way for flats, I saw a now forgotten film called *Don't Take It to Heart* (1944), written and directed by Jeffrey Dell and starring Richard Greene (later more famous as Robin Hood). In the inspired opening sequence, a coach is hurtling down a narrow winding country lane, insouciantly propelled, one-handed, by a man with a Gallic moustache wearing a Gallic beret, chewing and gazing about him Gallically as he goes. Walkers scatter as he approaches, oncoming cars swerve into ditches, he ploughs through a ford as if unaware that it's there – and all the while his passengers bounce up and down, now and then putting a desperate hand on the wheel to avert disaster.

At last the bus comes to rest in the village of Chaunduyt. Pronounced 'Cundit', a local explains to the stranger. In the village street every shop-front carries the same surname: Bucket. Everyone in the village, the stranger is told, is called Bucket, though the people who live in the manor house pronounce it 'Bouquet'. One shop is different. There has been a certain amount of intermarriage in Chaunduyt, it's explained. The name on this one is Pail.

It's the sort of England embedded in Ealing comedies, a fantasy built on a land which year by year is less like that, and in truth never really was. It's a parody; but such parodies only work if they've grown out of something recognisable. What is recognisable here is the localness, amounting to uniqueness, of village communities, and their ancient but still observable tendency to generate trademark surnames. There's a sense that goes beyond mere nostalgia that as old local references disappear, something valuable has been lost.

Most of the people who saw the movie in the Regal, Crossgates, that night must now be dead, and we've moved into a life they could not have imagined; where your standard conversation is no longer confined to the local street or the local church or the local pub, where people across the world can commune in seconds, face to face, thanks to the magic of Skype, and promote their opinions to hundreds they do not know through the magic of Twitter. But I hope it's not too sentimental to say (and even if it is, I shall say it) that the world of the Buckets and Bouquets and Pails of Chaunduyt is the world of the Broughtons and thousands of places like them, the world of the Hampshire Judds and Gales and Rogerses and the Furness Tysons, Dawsons and Whinerays, and thousands like them too. Romanticised, exaggerated, but based on an essential element in our history: something treasurable. Something to be taken to heart.

Appendix 1: National Names

This list contains the fifty most common surnames in Britain on the 2007 Electoral Register, as compiled by Dr Muhammad Adnan and Alistair Leak of University College London. Their likely meanings are based on the findings from several sources: the *Oxford Dictionary of English Surnames*, by P. H. Reaney and R. M. Wilson (eds) (R & W); the *Oxford Names Companion* section on surnames by Patrick Hanks and Flavia Hodges (eds) (H & H), the *Penguin Dictionary of British Surnames* by John Titford (ed.) (JT), and *The Surnames of Scotland* by G. F. Black (GB).

Were names that are clearly linked (e.g. Clark and Clarke and Davis and Davies) to be amalgamated, the rank order would be different. But then other names are closely linked too, e.g. Jones, Evans and Johnson.

1 Smith	occupational	worker in metal, blacksmith, farrier
2 Jones	patronymic	son of John – from Hebrew name meaning 'favoured by God'; outnumbers Smith in Wales (JT)
3 Williams	patronymic	son of William (from Norman Guillaume, 'one wearing a helmet')
4 Brown	nickname	describing hair, complexion or clothing or could derive from a personal forename, e.g. Brun

5 Taylor	occupational	a tailor. Black records thirty different spellings of this name in Scotland between 1296 and 1720
6 Davies	patronymic	son of David – from Hebrew name meaning 'beloved'
7 Wilson	patronymic	son of William or Will (see also Williams) though could come from places called Wilson
8 Evans	patronymic	son of Evan, a Welsh form of John (see also Jones)
9 Thomas	personal	from Aramaic name meaning a twin, by way of France
10 Johnson	patronymic	son of John (see also Jones and Evans)
11 Roberts	patronymic	son of Robert: from German name meaning 'famous', 'renowned'
12 Walker	occupational	a fuller, thickener of woollen cloth; or from Northumberland place name
13 Wright	occupational	carpenter, joiner, worker in wood where a smith worked in metal
14 Robinson	patronymic	son of Robin (or Robert)
15 Thompson	patronymic	son of Thomas (or Tom). Thomson frequent in Scotland
16 White	nickname	fair or white hair or complexion. Also dweller by curve in a river; one manning a lookout post (R & W). Black lists several Scottish variants, ten of which begin with a Q

17 Hughes	patronymic	from French name invoking 'heart', 'mind' or 'spirit'. Scots version is McKay (H & H)
18 Edwards	patronymic	son of Edward, from Middle English name meaning 'guardian of prosperity'
19 Green	locational	resident near a green (R & W)
	nickname	wore green clothes (H & H, JT); possibly played Green Man in May Day celebration (JT)
20 Hall	occupational	worker at the hall
	locational	dweller in or near a large house
21 Wood	locational	one who lives near a wood
	occupational	worker in a wood, or with wood
	nickname	old usage meaning 'violent', 'disturbed'
22 Harris	patronymic	son of Harry (or Henry, frequently pronounced Harry)
23 Lewis	patronymic	derived from Old French version of Ludwig, indicating a lord of war. In Wales, a replacement for Llewellyn (R & W)
	locational	from Hebridean island (though this is not suggested for neighbouring Harris)
24 Martin	personal	from Martinus, deriving from Mars, god of war
	locational	from place name in several counties

25 Jackson	patronymic	from Jack, John, James or Jacques. Never widespread in Scotland (GB)
26 Clarke	occupational	cleric, member of minor religious order; able to read and write when this was rare
27 Clark	occupational	as above. Other varieties, Clerk and Clerke
28 Turner	occupational	fashioner of wood. Possibly, organiser of a tournament (H & H)
	nickname	fast runner
29 Hill	locational	dweller on or near hill
	personal	derived from name such as Hilary, Hildebrand
30 Scott	nickname	person from Scotland. Within Scotland, one of Gaelic origin
31 Cooper	occupational	maker of wooden tubs, casks or baskets. In Scotland, could be person from Cupar (GB)
32 Morris	nickname	Moorish-looking, swarthy (or from personal name Maurice, which has the same meaning)
33 Ward	occupational	watchman, guard; possibly may also mean a dweller in Marshland (R & W)
34 Moore	locational	one who lives on moorland
	nickname	Moorish (see also Morris)
35 King	nickname	one who behaves or looks like a king; one who played a king in a pageant
	occupational	a member of a royal household
36 Watson	patronymic	son of Walter or Wat (from Germanic name indicating ruler of an army)

37 Baker	occupational	a baker (Baxter indicates a female baker)
38 Harrison	patronymic	son of Harry/Henry (see also Harris)
39 Morgan	personal	ancient Celtic name: sea bright, or great defender
40 Patel	occupational	omitted from all these reference books; a landowner or village chief
41 Young	nickname	young person; more often differentiating a younger family member from an older one (as junior)
42 Allen	personal	Alan, name of Welsh or Breton saint
	nickname	someone from Germany (see also French name for Germany, Allemagne)
43 Mitchell	personal	version of Michael
44 James	personal	derived from Jacob
45 Anderson	patronymic	son of Andrew
46 Phillips	patronymic	son of Philip, a name implying love of horses
47 Lee	locational	one who lives near a meadow; or comes from one of many places called Lee, Leigh, Lye etc. This surname also occurs as Lea and Leigh
48 Bell	nickname	one who is handsome; one who lives near a bell or an inn called the Bell
	occupational	maker or ringer of bells
	metronymic	descendant from Isabel

| 49 Parker | occupational | one who has charge of a park; one who works in a park |
| 50 Davis | patronymic | son of David (see also Davies above). |

A comparison of surnames *in England and Wales only* between 1853 and 2001 shows a general stability, but with a few notable exceptions – especially the rise of Patel. The earlier figures, which are those in brackets, were compiled by the office of the Registrar General: they are to be found in David Hey, *Family Names and Family History*, p. 189. The later figures have been derived from returns from the Office for National Statistics (to be found at Taliesin-arlein.net/names/search/_2.php).

(Where the symbol – appears in brackets, this means that this surname was not in the top 50 in 1853.)

1 (1) Smith		16 (22) White	
2 (2) Jones		17 (20) Edwards	
3 (3) Williams		18 (17) Hughes	
4 (4) Taylor		19 (18) Green	
5 (6) Brown		20 (15) Hall	
6 (5) Davies		21 (19) Lewis	
7 (8) Evans		22 (26) Harris	
8 (7) Thomas		23 (39) Clarke	
9 (12) Wilson		24 (–) Patel	
10 (10) Johnson		25 (23) Jackson	
11 (9) Roberts		26 (14) Wood	
12 (11) Robinson		27 (24) Turner	
13 (21) Thompson		28 (33) Martin	
14 (13) Wright		29 (28) Cooper	
15 (16) Walker		30 (25) Hill	

31 (34) Morris

32 (31) Ward

33 (41) Moore

34 (27) Clark

35 (32) Baker

36 (29) Harrison

37 (37) King

38 (36) Morgan

39 (47) Lee

40 (38) Allen

41 (35) James

42 (44) Phillips

43 (–) Scott

44 (45) Watson

45 (30) Davis

46 (42) Parker

47 (48) Bennett

48 (43) Price

49 (50) Griffiths

50 (–) Young

IN: Patel (24), Scott (43), Young (50)
OUT: Cook (40), Shaw (46), Carter (49)

Appendix 2: Broughton Names

These tables are designed to indicate the ebb and flow of surnames in selected places called Broughton. The results shown here are not definitive. Apart from errors I may have made myself in transcribing them, there are also problems with occasional errors made by the census takers, quite apart from those in the indexes provided by Ancestry, the source that I chiefly used. Such lists would be better made by people with a thorough knowledge of local history and geography, and advanced detective skills in deciphering handwriting.

(The sign = in these tables denotes that a surname has an equal score with that above or below it.)

Broughton, Hampshire	1841	1861	1881	1901	1911
1	Gale 44	Judd 35	Cooper 33	Carter 24	Davis 23
2	Cooper 37	Morgan 28	Pragnell etc. 23	Judd 23	Lansley 22
3	= Judd 31	Gale 26	Rogers 22	Lansley 22	Rogers 20
4	= Rogers 31	Woods 24	Stone 21	Stone 21	Stone 18
5	Morgan 30	= Tubb 23	Judd 19	= Marsh 20	Hinwood 17
6	Woodford 28	Woodford 22	Morgan 18	= Rogers 20	Blake 14
7	Tubb 20	= Cooper 21	Woods 17	Henwood/ Hinwood 18	Russell 13
8	Galton 19	= Noyce 21	Marsh 16	Brown 17	= Giles 12
9	Carter 17	Rogers 20	Sims 15	Bailey 16	= Judd 12
10	Pragnell etc. 16	Blake 19	Carter 14 Robinson 14 Woodford 14	Robinson 14	= Carter 11 = Marsh 11 = Robinson 11
Total inhabitants	971	955	901	820	840
TOP FIVE %	17.3	14.2	13.1	13.4	11.9
TOP TEN %	27.9	25.1	22.0	23.8	19.3

Broughton in Furness was not a separate parish in 1851. It was covered in two enumeration districts in the parish of Kirkby Ireleth. By 1861 it was a self-contained parish covering a wider area. The 1841 and 1861 results are therefore not comparable, and so 1841 is shown in italics.

Broughton in Furness	1841	1861	1881	1901	1911
1	*Dixon 33*	Tyson 54	Tyson 58	Dixon 54	Atkinson 48
2	*Tyson 25*	Dixon 45	= Dawson 31	Atkinson 31	Dixon 47
3	*Holme(s) 34*	= Dawson 33	= Dixon 31	Jackson 30	Tyson 37
4	*= Atkinson 23*	= Holme(s) 33	Shepherd 28	Dawson 29	Barker 27
5	*= Casson 23*	Park (e) 29	Barker 25	Tyson 25	Whineray 24
6	*Postlethwaite 20*	Jackson 25	Barrow 22	Barker 24	= Barrow 20
7	*= Dawson 18*	= Atkinson 24	= Clark 21	Simpson 23	= Jackson 20
8	*= Simpson 18*	= Newby 24	= Simpson 21	Thackeray 22	= Butterfield 19
9	*= Bellman 17*	Singleton 23	= Nicholson 20	= Butterfield 21	= Dawson 19
10	*= Nelson 17*	Simpson 22	= Todd 20	= Douglas 21	= Singleton 19
Total inhabitants	*568*	1,184	1,194	1,117	1,098
TOP FIVE (%)	*22.5*	16.4	14.5	15.1	16.7
TOP TEN (%)	*38.3*	26.4	23.2	25.1	25.5

Broughton, Cambridgeshire

1841		1861		1881*		1911	
Male/Maile	24	Wright	24	Munns	16	Clark/Clarke	15
Pain	19	Maile	22	Payne	15	Wright	14
Hitchcock	17	Cross	15	Colbert	14	Cross	13
Hubbard	14	Hawks	14	Wright	13	Munns	12
West	14	Newman	14	Cross	13	Colbert	11
Hempstead	11	Pain/Payne	14	Shelton	13	Fordham	10
How	11	Munns	12	Dean	10	Ayres	9
Muns	11	Hitchcock	11	Hitchcock	9	Hitchcock	8
Beard	10	Phillips	11	Fordham	9	Sawyer	8
Bulling/Cross	9	Hempstead	11	Ilett	9	SEVERAL	7
TOP FIVE (%)	24.2		22.4		24.2		25
TOP TEN (%)	38.6		37.4		41.3		41.2

* one page missing from 1881 census

Broughton, Northamptonshire

1841		1861		1881		1911	
Lenton	31	Lenton	38	Lenton	48	Lenton	29
Hight	29	Sail	31	Jacques*	41	Chapman	27
Garratt	23	Hight	25	Thompson	28	Essam	24
Lilley*	23	Lilley*	24	Sail/Sale	27	Riches	24
Lilleman*	21	Essam	21	Essam	24	Thompson	21
Sail	18	Lea/Lee	21	Taylor	21	James	20
Neal	17	Jacques*	21	Read/Read	20	Moore	20
Hills	16	Lilleman*	20	Morriss	16	Toseland	19
Wood	16	Dilley	15	SEVERAL	14	Sharp/ Sharpe	17
Eaton/Johnson	14	Bird	15			SEVERAL	16
TOP FIVE (%)	21.5		18.8		19.1		11.6
TOP TEN (%)	35.1		31.3		28.8		20.1

Broughton, Lincolnshire

1841		1861		1881		1911	
Hare	39	Hare/Hair	35	Clark(e)	52	Graves	40
Neal	18	Clark(e)	27	Thompson	34	Stothard	33
Foster	14	Neal	27	Green	31	Clark(e)	31
Barley	12	Foster	26	Parish	27	Wells	29
Hart	12	Green	25	Wright	26	Bowers	28
Parish	12	Parish	22	Metcalf(e)	23	Robinson	25
Hobson	12	Bowers	21	Foster	22	Ayre	19
Stark	12	Thompson	21	Sergeant	22	Barley	19
Hocknell	11	Barley	20	Dent	21	Parish/Parrish	19
Day/Johnson	10	Wright	19	Bowers/White	20	Nixon	18
TOP FIVE (%)	18.5		15.9		14.6		11.6
TOP TEN (%)	29.5		28		24.6		18.8

* inc. variants

Broughton, North Wales

1841		1861		1881		1911	
Davies	39	Crofts	36	Crofts	43	Crofts	49
Sheen/Shone	28	Jones	34	Williams	34	Davies	33
Piercey	27	Davies	29	Davies/Davis	31	Evans	24
Jones	25	Price	25	Price	27	Jones	21
Crofts	24	Sheen/Shone	23	Jones	20	Williams	19
Edwards	18	Thomas	23	Thomas	19	Price	18
Williams	18	Evans	18	Connah	18	Connah	12
Owen/Owens	18	Williams	16	Evans	18	Roberts	11
Roberts	17	Edwards	12	Hough	14	Lloyd	10
Thomas	16	Connah	11	Edwards	13	Griffiths	10
7/8 end in S		7 end in S		6 end in S		7 end in S	
TOP FIVE (%)	35.4		37.8		37.3		29.9
TOP TEN (%)	56.9		58.4		58.1		43.2

Broughton, Borders

1841	1851**		1881		1911	
	Lawson	22	Bryden	18	Anderson	15
	Anderson	21	Henderson	18	Melrose	15
	Wilson	21	Newbigging	17	Dickson	14
	Newbigging	19	Graham	15	Murray	13
	Hope	18	Smith	15	Kitchen	12
	Robb	18	Watson	15	Noble	12
	Somerville	18	Brown	14	Lawson	11
	Alexander	16	Clark	14	McDonald	11
	Dickson	16	Grieve	13	Newbigging	11
	Watson	16	Sandilands etc.	11	Robinson	11
TOP FIVE (%)		11.5		12.5		10.4
TOP TEN (%)		21.1		22.7		18.8

** No separate information available for 1841

The pattern of names in the remote Orkney settlement of Broughton (for which no separate records are available before 1871) indicates a high level both of oscillation and of distinctive surnames: names such as Berstane, Drever, Foulis, Garrioch, Groat, Harcus and Seatter are not found in other Broughtons examined in this book. Across Orkney as a whole, the pattern of surnames, as a second table shows, is far more stable, with Sinclair way ahead of the rest in every census.

Broughton, Orkney

1871		1881		1891	
Allan	18	Garrioch	6	Rendall	5
Garrioch	6	Sinclair	6	Pottinger	4
Macdonald	5	Drever	5	Drever	3
Reid	5	Reid	5	Garrioch	3
Drever	3	Allan	4	Foulis	2
Stevenson	3	Stevenson	4	Balfour	1
		McDonald	3	Peterson	1
		Pottinger	3	Smith	1
		Rendall	2	Stevenson	1
		Balfour	1		
1901		1911			
Bews	9	Seatter	6		
Stout	8	Harcus	5		
Pottinger	6	Pottinger	3		
Swanney	6	Rendall	3		
Drever	5	Drever	2		
Rendall	5	Garrioch	2		
Berstane	3	Groat	1		
Gray	3	Smith	1		
Garrioch	2				
Logie	2				
Seatter	2				
Pottinger	1				
Smith	1				

All-Orkney Top Ten

1841		1881		1891	
Sinclair	906	Sinclair	967	Sinclair	1,002
Flett	759	Flett	650	Thomson	568
Spence	633	Spence	616	Spence	552
Muir	479	Muir	569	Johnston	543
Rendall	473	Thomson	540	Muir	543
Johnston	468	Rendall	519	Flett	527
Miller	468	Scott	509	Scott	524
Scott	462	Johnston	508	Rendall	523
Thomson	459	Miller	475	Drever	502
Smith	438	Smith	465	Tulloch	491
1901		**1911**			
Sinclair	922	Sinclair	838		
Spence	491	Rendall	491		
Johnston	489	Johnston	466		
Rendall	479	Flett	445		
Muir	465	Thomson	416		
Flett	443	Tulloch	412		
Thomson	442	Sutherland	411		
Tulloch	439	Spence	399		
Sutherland	424	Muir	396		
Drever	419	Drever	371		

All figures by courtesy of the Orkney Family History Society.

Appendix 3: Dickens's 'Available' List

This list is included in John Forster's life of Dickens. Some names appear in the novels. Many more don't. A few appear twice.

Towndling. Mood. Guff. Treble. Chilby. Spessifer. Wodder. Whelpford. Fennerck. Gannerson. Chinkerble. Bintrey. Fledson. Hirll. Brayle. Mullinder. Treslingham. Brankle. Sittern. Dostone. Cay-lon. Slyant. Queedy. Besselthur. Musty. Grout. Tertius Jobber. Amon Headston. Strayshott. Higden. Morfit. Goldstraw. Barrel. Inge. Jump. Jiggins. Bones. Coy. Dawn. Tatkin. Drowvey. Pudsey. Pedsey. Duncalf. Tricklebank. Sapsea. Readyhuff. Dufty. Foggy. Twinn. Brownsword. Peartree. Sudds. Silverman. Kimber. Laughley. Lessock. Tippins. Minnitt. Radlowe. Pratchet. Mawdett. Wozenham. Snowell. Lottrum. Lammle. Froser. Holblack. Mulley. Redworth. Redfoot. Tarbox. Tinkling. Duddle. Jebus. Powderhill. Grimmer. Skuse. Titcoombe. Crabble. Swannock. Tuzzen. Twemlow. Squab. Jackman. Sugg. Bremmidge. Silas Blodget. Melvin Beal. Buttrick. Edson. Sandlorn. Lightword. Titbull. Bangham. Kyle/Nyle. Pemble. Maxey. Rokesmith. Chivery. Wabbler. Peex/Speex. Gannaway. Mrs Flinks. Flinx. Jee. Harden. Merdle. Murden. Topwash. Pordage. Dorret/Dorrit. Carton. Minifie. Slingo. Joad. Kinch. Magg. Chelyson. Blennam. Bardock. Snigsworth. Swenton. Casby-Peach. Lowleigh/Lowely. Pigrin. Yerbury. Plornish. Maroon. Bandy/Nandy. Stonebury. Magwitch. Meagles. Pancks. Haggage. Provis. Stiltington. Stiltwalk. Stiltingstalk. Stiltstalking. Ravender. Podsnap. Clarriker.

Compery. Striver/Stryver. Pumblechook. Wangler. Boffin. Bantinck. Dibton. Wilfer. Glibbery. Mulvey. Horlick. Doolge. Gannery. Gargery. Willshard. Riderhood. Pratterstone. Chinkible. Wopsell. Wopsle. Whelpington. Whelpford. Gayvery. Wegg. Hubble. Urry. Kibble. Skiffins. Wodder. Etser. Akershem.

Sources and Bibliography

General books on surnames

Bardsley, Charles, *Our English Surnames* (London, 1873)
— *Curiosities of Puritan Nomenclature* (London, 1880)
— *A Dictionary of English and Welsh Surnames* (London, 1901)
Baring-Gould, Sabine, *Family Names and Their Story* (London, 1910)
Black, George F., *The Surnames of Scotland: Their Origin, Meaning and History* (New York, 1946)
Camden, William, *Remains Concerning Britain*, edited by R. D. Dunn (Toronto, 1984)
Guppy, Henry B., *The Homes of Family Names in Great Britain* (London, 1890)
Hanks, Patrick and Flavia Hodges, with special consultant for Jewish names, David L. Gold, *A Dictionary of Surnames* (Oxford, 1988)
Hanks, Patrick, Flavia Hodges, A. D. Mills and Adrian Room, *The Oxford Names Companion* (Oxford, 2002)
Hey, David (ed.), *The Oxford Companion to Local and Family History* (Oxford, 1996)
— *Family Names and Family History* (Hambledon, 2000)
— *How Our Ancestors Lived: a history of life a hundred years ago* (Richmond, Surrey, 2002)
Lower, Mark Antony, *Patronymica Britannica* (London, 1860)
Matthews, C. M., *English Surnames* (London, 1966)
McKinley, Richard, *A History of British Surnames* (London, 1990)
Reaney, P. H., *The Origin of English Surnames* (Oxford, 2005)
Reaney, P. H. and R. M. Wilson, *Oxford Dictionary of English Surnames* (Oxford, 2005)

Redmonds, George, *Surnames and Genealogy, a new approach* (Bury, 2002)

Redmonds, George, Turi King and David Hey, *Surnames, DNA, & Family History* (Oxford, 2011)

Titford, John (ed.), *Penguin Dictionary of British Surnames* (London, 2009)

Weekley, Ernest, *The Romance of Names* (London, 1914)

— *Surnames* (London, 1916)

Sources for researchers

Several commercial organisations offer services for surname researchers. In England and Wales, Ancestry is the official partner of the National Archives. In Scotland, ScotlandsPeople is a partnership between Brightsolid and the Scottish National Archives. The Church of Jesus Christ of Latter-Day Saints (the Mormons) record names for the purpose of posthumous baptisms, a practice from which, in cases where objections were made, especially by Jewish organisations, they have desisted. Their coverage is free. It is complete for the 1881 census but not for others. See also the practical guidance in David Hey, *Family Names and Family History*, listed above.

Ancestry: www.ancestryeurope.lu/about-ancestry;www.ancestry.co.uk

British Surnames and Surname Profiles: www.britishsurnames.co.uk

Church of Jesus Christ of Latter-Day Saints: https://familysearch.org

Genes Reunited: www.genesreunited.co.uk

GENUKI: www.genuki.org.uk

Scotlands People: www.scotlandspeople.gov.uk

Society of Genealogists: www.societyofgenealogists.com. Also www.findmypast.co.uk

The Genealogist: www.thegenealogist.co.uk

Public Profiler, directed from University College London by

Professor Paul Longley, Alex Singleton, Richard Webber, UCL Visiting Professor, and Dr Daryl Lloyd, logs most names, though not all, from the 1881 census and provides names found in the electoral registers of 1998 for comparison: gbnames. publicprofiler.org.

Great Britain Names maps of most common surnames in Britain, compiled by Dr Muhammad Adnan and Alistair Leak of UCL using 2007 electoral registers: www.uncertaintyofidentity.com/ GB_Names/Mapping.aspx.

Steve Archer's Surname Atlas logs all names from the 1881 census. It is available on CD from him at www.archersoftware.co.uk or through the Guild of One-Name Studies: www.one-name.org.

Surveys: Leicester University's forty-surname study analysing Y-chromosomes of 1,478 men carrying forty British surnames at www.le.ac.uk/ge/maj4/40Surnames.html

People of the British Isles: a project funded by the Wellcome Trust to investigate the genetic make-up of the rural population of the British Isles, both to help medical research and to illuminate patterns of migration: www.peopleofthebritishisles. org. See also Robin McKie, *Face of Britain* (listed below).

Sources by chapter

2 *Constellations*

Barker, Paul, *Hebden Bridge: A Sense of Belonging* (London, 2012)

Coleman, Neil, Ros Gingell, Simon Napper, Martin Rose and Tony Walker (eds), *Worton & Marston Domesday Book 2000: a year in the life of two Wiltshire villages* (Worton, Wilts, 2000)

Greenhalgh, W., *Broughton-in-Furness and the Duddon Valley: A Guide and History* (Broughton, 1989)

— *A Broughton Miscellany: pages from the history of Broughton-in-Furness* (Broughton, 1992)

— *A Second Broughton Miscellany: more pages from the history of Broughton-in-Furness* (Broughton, 1996)

Parr, Dr Robert, *The Hampshire Broughton: A Social History of a West Hampshire Village* (Broughton, 2002)

Parr, Dr Robert and Baron Sewter, *Broughton in Hampshire* (Broughton, 1990)

Richards, Audrey and Jean Robin, *Some Elmdon Families* (Elmdon, 1975)

Robin, Jean, *Elmdon: Continuity and Change in a North-West Essex Village, 1861–1964* (Cambridge, 1980)

Strathern, Marilyn, *Kinship at the Core: An anthropology of Elmdon, a village in North-west Essex in the nineteen sixties* (Cambridge, 1981)

3 *Translocations*

Bragg, Melvyn, *The Adventure of English: The Biography of a Language* (London, 2003)

Gwynn, Robin, 'England's "First Refugees"', *History Today*, issue 5 (1985)

Roth, Cecil, *A History of the Jews in England* (Oxford, 1964)

Shaikh, Thair, 'Surrey town plays host to Korean World Cup Fever', *Daily Telegraph*, 23 June 2002

Zangwill, Israel, *Children of the Ghetto: a study of a peculiar people* (London, 1892)

4 *Excavations*

Daily Telegraph, 'Bungay vs Bungay – all 22 football players share the same name', 8 May 2012

Ferguson, Robert, *Surnames as a Science* (London, 1883)

Frazer, Sir James George, *The Golden Bough: A Study in Magic and Religion* (London, 1922)

Galton, Francis, *Hereditary Genius: An Inquiry into Its Laws and Consequences* (London 1869)

— *Inquiries into Human Faculty and its Development* (London, 1883)

McKie, Robin, *Face of Britain: How Our Genes Reveal the History of Britain* (London, 2006)

Sykes, Bryan, *Blood of the Isles: Exploring the Genetic Roots of our Tribal History* (London, 2006)

5 *Confrontations*

Buchan, James Walter (ed.), *A History of Peeblesshire* (Glasgow, 1925)

Cochrane, James, *Stipple, Wink & Gusset: Men and Women Who Gave Their Names to History* (London, 1992)

Fraser, George MacDonald, *The Steel Bonnets: The Story of the Anglo-Scottish Border Reivers* (London, 1971)

Manser, Martin, *Dictionary of Eponyms* (London, 1998)

McWilliam, Rohan, *The Tichborne Claimant: A Victorian Sensation* (London, 2006)

Scott, Sir Walter, *Tales of a Grandfather* (Edinburgh, 1878)

Tweedie, Michael, *The History of the Tweedie, or Tweedy, family: A Record of Scottish Lowland Life and Character* (London, 1902)

Veitch, John, *The History and Poetry of the Scottish Border – their main features and relations* (Edinburgh, 1893)

6 *Manipulations*

Arnold, Matthew, *The Function of Criticism at the Present Time* in *Essays in Criticism* (London, 1864)

Brennen, Tim, 'On the Meaning of Personal Names for Identity: a view from cognitive psychology', *Names*, 48.2 (June 2000)

Chamary, J. V., 'The Name Game: How Names Spell Success in Life and Love', *BBC Focus magazine*, January 2010

Christenfeld, Nicholas and Britta Larsen, 'The Name Game', *The Psychologist*, March 2008

Einav, Liran and Leeat Yariv, 'What's in a Surname? The Effect of Surname Initials on Academic Success', *Journal of Economic Perspectives*, 20 (1) (2006)

Engers, Maxim, Joshua Gans, Simon Grant and Stephen P. King, 'First Author Conditions', *Journal of Political Economy*, 107 (1999)

Evers, Stuart, 'Which character has the worst name in fiction?'; www.guardian.co.uk/books/booksblog+paulauster

Forster, John, *The Life of Charles Dickens* (London, 1872–4)

Fowler, Alastair, *Literary Names: Personal Names in English Literature* (Oxford, 2012)

Holloway, Richard, *Leaving Alexandria: A Memoir of Faith and Doubt* (Edinburgh, 2012)

Hoyland, John, 'Feedback', *New Scientist*, 5 November 1994

Izbicki, John, *Life Between the Lines: A Memoir* (London, 2012)

Jung, Carl Gustav, *Synchronicity: An Acausal Connecting Principle* (London, 1985)

Lake, David, 'Who's On First? Listing Authors by Relative Contributions Trumps the Alphabet', *Political Science & Politics*, vol. 43, issue 01 (January 2010);
dss.ucsd.edu/~dlake/documents/LakePSessay.PDF

Lodge, David, *The Art of Fiction: Illustrated from Classic and Modern Texts* (London, 1992)

MacInnes, Colin, *Absolute Beginners* (London, 1959)

Merton, Robert K., *The Sociology of Science: Theoretical and Empirical Investigations* (Chicago, 1973)

Mullan, John, *Anonymity: A Secret History of English Literature* (London, 2007)

Anthony Powell Society is at www.anthonypowell.org

Pritchett, V. S., *A Cab at the Door;* and *Midnight Oil* (London, 1979)

Room, Adrian, *Dictionary of Pseudonyms* (London, 1998)

Sitwell, Edith, *The English Eccentrics* (London, 1933)

Sutherland, John, 'What's in a name?', *Guardian*, 17 November 2006

Turner, E. S., *Boys Will Be Boys* (London, 1948)

Valentine, Tim, Tim Brennen and Serge Brédart, *The Cognitive Psychology of Proper Names, or, The Importance of Being Ernest* (London, 1996)

Wiseman, Richard, 'Is your name to blame for your unhappiness?', *Daily Telegraph*, 22 May 2007

Yglesias, Matthew, *Alphabetism*;
Thinkprogress.org/yglesias/2010/02/27/196312/alphabetism

7 *Transformations*

Brandreth, Gyles, *Philip and Elizabeth: Portrait of a Marriage* (London, 2004)

Cohen, Deborah, *Family Secrets: Living with Shame from the Victorians to the Present Day* (London, 2013)

Davies, Norman, *The Isles: A History* (London, 1999)

— *Heart of Europe: A Short History of Poland* (Oxford, 1984)

Jenkins, Simon, *England's Thousand Best Churches* (London, 1999)

— *England's Thousand Best Houses* (London, 2003)

London Gazette; www.london-gazette.co.uk

Phillimore, W. P. W. and E. A. Fry, *An Index to Changes of Name . . . 1760–1901* (London, 1905)

Tegg, William, *Wills of Their Own, Curious, Eccentric and Benevolent* (London, 1879)

Vom Bruck, Gabriele and Barbara Bodenhorn (eds), *The Anthropology of Names and Naming* (Cambridge, 2006)

Wasserstein, Bernard, *The Secret Lives of Trebitsch Lincoln* (New Haven, CT, 1998)

8 *Deprivations*

Brown, John, *A Memoir of Robert Blincoe etc.* (London, 1832)

Carless, Angela, '"I'm desperate to find the mum who left me on a train": Woman's hunt for answers after being abandoned as a newborn', *Daily Mirror*, 7 May 2012

Peters, Catherine, Introduction to *Armadale* by Wilkie Collins (Oxford, 1989)

— *The King of Inventors: A Life of Wilkie Collins* (London, 1991)

Acknowledgements

My thanks are above all due to Nigel Wilcockson, publishing director at Random House, who suggested this book, and came up during its progress with a torrent of sharp and constructive ideas for it; also to his colleagues at Random House, Najma Finlay, Amy Mitchell, Imogen Lowe and, especially, Natascha Spargo, who designed the book's wonderfully ingenious cover. Then to my ever-helpful agent Jonathan Pegg, and to Jane Robertson – as always, the most vigilant of copy-editors. At an early stage, three professionals on this territory, David Hey, Turi King and Kevin Schürer, provided useful advice. I also acknowledge with gratitude the help I received from the Bunting Society, especially Mary Rix, its chairman and record-keeper, and Jerry Green, its webmaster, who arranged my visit to its annual get-together; from Kirsty Gray, then chairman of the Guild of One-Name Studies, since appointed Director of English Studies at the Canadian National Institute of Genealogical Studies; from Mary Thomson of the Borders Family History Society, and George Gray of the Orkney Family History Society; and from the Anthony Powell Society and its secretary, Dr Keith Marshall. And, as ever, my thanks to my wife Beryl, who compiled the index, as well as extirpating some of the imperfections in the original text.

Index

Of the nearly 2000 surnames mentioned in the course of the book, only those that are discussed at some length or that are among the fifty most common surnames in Britain (see Appendix 1), are included in the index.